OXFORD ISLAMIC LEGAL STUDIES

Series Editors:
Anver M. Emon, Clark Lombardi, and Lynn Welchman

THE LEGAL THOUGHT OF JALĀL AL-DĪN AL-SUYŪṬĪ

OXFORD ISLAMIC LEGAL STUDIES

Series Editors:
Anver M. Emon, Clark Lombardi, and Lynn Welchman

Satisfying the growing interest in Islam and Islamic law, the Oxford Islamic Legal Studies series speaks to both specialists and those interested in the study of a legal tradition that shapes lives and societies across the globe. Islamic law operates at several levels. It shapes private decision making, binds communities, and it is also imposed by states as domestic positive law. The series features innovative and interdisciplinary studies that explore Islamic law as it operates at each of these levels. The series also sheds new light on the history and jurisprudence of Islamic law and provides for a richer understanding of the state of Islamic law in the contemporary Muslim world, including parts of the world where Muslims are minorities.

ALSO AVAILABLE IN THE SERIES

Coercion and Responsibility in Islam
A Study in Ethics and Law
Mairaj U. Syed

Islamic Legal Revival
Reception of European Law and Transformations in Islamic Legal Thought in Egypt, 1875–1952
Leonard Wood

Shari'a and Muslim Minorities
The Wasati and Salafi Approaches to Fiqh al-Aqalliyyat al-Muslima
Uriya Shavit

Domestic Violence and the Islamic Tradition
Ayesha S. Chaudhry

Shari'a and Social Engineering
The Implementation of Islamic Law in Contemporary Aceh, Indonesia
R. Michael Feener

Religious Pluralism and Islamic Law
Dhimmis and Others in the Empire Law
Anver M. Emon

Narratives of Islamic Legal Theory
Rumee Ahmed

The Legal Thought of Jalāl al-Dīn al-Suyūṭī

Authority and Legacy

REBECCA SKRESLET HERNANDEZ

OXFORD
UNIVERSITY PRESS

OXFORD
UNIVERSITY PRESS

Great Clarendon Street, Oxford, OX2 6DP,
United Kingdom

Oxford University Press is a department of the University of Oxford.
It furthers the University's objective of excellence in research, scholarship,
and education by publishing worldwide. Oxford is a registered trade mark of
Oxford University Press in the UK and in certain other countries

First Edition published in 2017

Impression: 1

Published in the United States of America by Oxford University Press
198 Madison Avenue, New York, NY 10016, United States of America

British Library Cataloguing in Publication Data
Data available

Library of Congress Control Number: 2017943885

ISBN 978–0–19–880593–9

Printed and bound by
CPI Group (UK) Ltd, Croydon, CR0 4YY

Series Editors' Preface

Rebecca Skreslet Hernandez offers in this book an interdisciplinary intellectual biography of acclaimed jurist Jalāl al-Dīn al-Suyūṭī, who lived in what is now modern-day Egypt. A self-proclaimed juristic light, al-Suyūṭī authored treatises that were both important and provocative in his own day and continue to inform Islamic education around the world today. Hernandez's intellectual biography is an important contribution to the study of Islamic law generally. There are few biographies of premodern Muslim jurists, and most of those that have been written reflect a mid-twentieth-century historical positivism in their narrative framework and methodological approach, despite developments in intellectual history in the fields of, for instance, political theory. In this book, Hernandez draws upon discourse analysis, literary criticism, and socio-legal studies to situate al-Suyūṭī and his texts in context, to reflect on audience reception, and to ascertain the stakes implicit in his literary production. Hernandez produces a highly nuanced image of al-Suyūṭī through a complex and creative set of reading practices. She charts new ground in the field of Islamic law and legal studies generally—new ground that will certainly prompt future scholars to follow suit.

Anver M. Emon
Clark Lombardi
Lynn Welchman

Acknowledgments

This research would not have been possible without the support of so many wonderful colleagues, family, and friends. This book grew out of a dissertation completed at Georgetown University's Department of Arabic and Islamic Studies. I would like to thank members of my committee who generously devoted time to this project, including Felicitas Opwis, John Voll, and Reem Bassiouney. Dr. Opwis exemplifies what a great advisor can be. She encouraged me when I needed encouragement and challenged me when I needed to be challenged, all the while managing to be both professional and caring. Whenever I need to place a figure or intellectual trend within its historical context, I know that I can rely on the insights of Dr. Voll. In addition to my committee, other colleagues offered valuable insights and advice, including Jonathan A.C. Brown. I also thank my wonderful students at Georgetown and at the College of William & Mary for pushing me to be the best that I could be.

I was lucky enough to meet Elizabeth Sartain in Cairo and to benefit from her incredible knowledge of al-Suyūṭī's work during the early stages of the research. I would also like to thank in particular Shaykh ʿAmr al-Wardānī of Egypt's Dār al-Iftāʾ who helped to make al-Suyūṭī's legacy come alive and who carved out many hours of his busy schedule to discuss the texts with me. This work also continues the legacy of the outstanding academic mentors who helped to guide my scholarly career, especially Tamara Sonn, Barbara Stowasser, and Michele Dunne.

This research benefited from a number of grants and funding opportunities. I would like to thank Georgetown University's Graduate School of Arts and Sciences for their financial support of my graduate studies over the last several years. A Foreign Language and Area Studies (FLAS) fellowship sponsored by the U.S. Department of Education allowed me to pursue language study and dissertation research in Cairo. Also, a Prince Alwaleed Bin Talal Fellowship helped to support my research during the summer of 2010.

I appreciate very much the support and expert guidance of Anver Emon and the editors of the Oxford Islamic Legal Studies Series. Elinor Shields and

Jamie Berezin have helped in the publication process and two anonymous reviewers contributed valuable insights and improvements to the manuscript. An earlier version of Chapter 1 appeared in the journal *Islamic Law and Society* published by Brill. Many thanks to David S. Powers and to the anonymous reviewers for their helpful advice on a draft of the article. I am also grateful to the Aga Khan University's Institute for the Study of Muslim Civilisations for the opportunity to present ideas from Chapter 5 at a conference in 2016.

I am truly fortunate to have such an excellent group of mentors. Any remaining errors in the text are purely my own.

Last but not least, I am grateful for the support of my family, especially my parents, who patiently read through drafts of this work and who have been constant in their support of me. I consider them to be my role models, both intellectually and spiritually, and it is to them that this book is dedicated. This research would not have been completed in a timely manner without the help of my in-laws, particularly my marvelous mother-in-law, Roxanne Hernandez. My husband Nelson deserves special acknowledgment for his unfailing kindness and loving care. Finally, I wish to express boundless affection for our sweet Helen and charming Hector who grew along with this project.

Table of Contents

Introduction

A CONTESTED LIFE

The great fifteenth-century polymath, Jalāl al-Dīn al-Suyūṭī (d. 911/1505), is a figure who requires interpretation. Al-Suyūṭī's life and work is intriguing not only due to the controversies that the author stirred up during his own time period, but as a result of the competing narratives and ironies surrounding this eminent scholar even today. The areas of irony or mistaken understanding regarding al-Suyūṭī seem to fall along two main lines. The first is a disconnect between how the author saw himself and how this projected identity was perceived by many of his colleagues and contemporaries in late Mamluk Egypt. The second is the further disconnect between the enormous popularity that al-Suyūṭī's works continue to enjoy among scholars and students in the Muslim world and the relative lack of attention that he has received in western academia.

Jalāl al-Dīn al-Suyūṭī claimed nothing less than to be the best scholar of his time. Al-Suyūṭī dared to claim the level of unrestricted legal reasoning (*ijtihād*) in the three disciplines of religious law (*al-aḥkām al-sharʿiyya*), Prophetic traditions (*al-ḥadīth al-nabawī*) and the Arabic language (*al-ʿarabiyya*)—a feat that he claims was not achieved by anyone since the great Taqī al-Dīn al-Subkī (d. 756/1355).[1] Al-Suyūṭī defines the role of the *mujtahid* according to the expectations of jurists of his own time, a period well beyond the formation and subsequent consolidation and systematization of the four

[1] Al-Suyūṭī, *al-Taḥadduth bi-niʿmat Allāh*, edited by E.M. Sartain, 2 vols. (Cambridge, U.K.: Cambridge University Press, 1975), 2:205. As this study will show, the fields of knowledge that al-Suyūṭī considers indispensable to the aspiring *mujtahid* (including those of *ḥadīth*, jurisprudence, and the Arabic language) also happen to be the very fields in which he excels.

The Legal Thought of Jalāl al-Dīn al-Suyūṭī: Authority and Legacy. Rebecca Skreslet Hernandez.

major Sunni schools of law. Therefore, he is careful to distinguish between the independent *mujtahid* (*mujtahid mustaqill*) and the *mujtahid* who is unrestricted in the sense that he can derive rulings from the primary sources of the Qurʾān and Sunna and yet is also affiliated with a particular school of legal thought (*madhhab*).[2] The latter type, the *mujtahid muṭlaq muntasib*, is the rank that al-Suyūṭī claims for himself. It would be a mistake, he says, to equate the independent *mujtahid* (which applies only to the eponyms of the legal schools) and the unrestricted *mujtahid*, as al-Suyūṭī's contemporaries did, just as it would be wrong to relegate al-Suyūṭī to the lesser rank of *mujtahid muqayyad* who, due to a deficiency in his knowledge of *ḥadīth* or Arabic language, is not qualified to interpret the sources directly but must simply follow the opinion of other scholars within the school.[3]

As E.M. Sartain has observed, it was not the audacity of the status claims themselves on the part of al-Suyūṭī that so rankled his colleagues, but the tone in which these claims were delivered. Al-Suyūṭī's portrayal of himself as a *mujtahid* is grounded both in his belief in his own superior talents as well as in his disdain for the low level of learning of most of his contemporaries. Indeed, in a legal opinion (fatwa) on the subject of the apocalypse and the need for a renewer of the faith, al-Suyūṭī makes the vivid assertion: "whoever puffs himself up and claims to rival me and to deny my claims to *ijtihād* and peerless scholarship at the turn of this century and asserts that he opposes me and mobilizes others against me is one that, if he and they were to be assembled on a single plateau and I blew on them one breath, they would become like scattered dust."[4] Al-Suyūṭī's intractability, Sartain suggests,

[2] In his classification of *mujtahids*, al-Suyūṭī follows a typology similar to that of an earlier Shāfiʿī jurist, al-Nawawī (d. 676/1277). See Norman Calder, "Al-Nawawī's Typology of *Muftīs* and its Significance for a General Theory of Islamic Law," *Islamic Law and Society* 3: 2 (1996): 137–64. Devin J. Stewart discusses scholarly ranking and juridical hierarchies, including parallel typologies of *mujtahids* in both Sunni and Shiʿi traditions and covering a range of regions and historical periods, in his "Islamic Juridical Hierarchies and the Office of *marjiʿ al-taqlīd*," *Shīʿite Heritage: Essays on Classical and Modern Traditions*, edited by L. Clarke (Binghamton, N.Y.: Global Publications, 2001), 137–57.

[3] Al-Suyūṭī, *al-Radd ʿalā man akhlad ilā al-arḍ wa-jahil ann al-ijtihād fī kull ʿaṣr farḍ* (Alexandria: Muʾassasat Shabāb al-Jāmiʿa, 1985), 98.

[4] Al-Suyūṭī, *al-Kashf ʿan mujāwazat hādhihi al-umma al-alf* in *al-Ḥāwī li-l-fatāwī*, 2 vols. (Beirut: Dār al-Kutub al-ʿIlmiyya, 2000), 2:81. Translations from al-Suyūṭī's fatwas are mine unless otherwise indicated.

> was due largely to his conviction that he alone, in an age of increasing ignorance, was a true scholar, and it must have been this conviction which led him, first to claim the right to exercise *ijtihād*, and secondly to express his hope that he might be recognized as the *mujaddid*, or restorer, believed to appear at the turn of every century to bring about a religious revival.[5]

Were al-Suyūṭī's attempts to frame himself as a *mujtahid* and *mujaddid* successful in the eyes of his contemporaries? The short answer is no. Although he did find some supporters, especially amongst his own students, rivals like al-Sakhāwī (d. 902/1497) were quick to attack al-Suyūṭī's qualifications as a *mujtahid*. In his scathing biographical entry on al-Suyūṭī, al-Sakhāwī points to his lack of accomplishments in logic and arithmetic and accuses him of having exaggerated his number of works and even of stealing outright the works of other scholars and attributing them to himself.[6] Another enemy, Ibn al-Karakī (d. 922/1516), criticized al-Suyūṭī's claims to be a *mujaddid*, decrying al-Suyūṭī's arrogance and pride in the superiority of his scholarship.[7]

It is undeniable that al-Ṣuyūṭī stirred up disputes at several times in his life that became so rancorous that the ruler was compelled to intervene. The situation came to a head in 903/1498 when the Sufi residents of the Baybarsiyya *khānqāh* rebelled against al-Suyūṭī's leadership as their shaykh and supervisor of the endowment that provided their monthly stipends.[8] Tensions became so great that al-Suyūṭī was forced to go into hiding at one point in fear for his life. After his dismissal from the Baybarsiyya in 906/1501, al-Suyūṭī went from partial to full retirement, resigning from his remaining academic posts and retreating to his house on Rawḍa until his death in 911/1505. Sartain characterizes al-Suyūṭī's withdrawal from public life in part as a result of his disillusionment about the declining state of scholarship, but especially due to "the bitterness and disappointment he

[5] E.M. Sartain, *Jalāl al-Dīn al-Suyūṭī: Biography and Background*, 2 vols. (Cambridge, U.K.: Cambridge University Press, 1975), 1:61.

[6] See Muḥammad b. ʿAbd al-Raḥmān al-Sakhāwī, *al-Ḍawʾ al-lāmiʿ li-ahl al-qarn al-tāsiʿ*, 12 vols. (Cairo: Maktabat al-Qudsī, 1934–1936), 4:65–70.

[7] Sartain, *Jalāl al-Dīn al-Suyūṭī*, 78. Ibn al-Karakī, as Sartain points out, was a favorite of Sultan Qāytbāy and tried to turn the ruler's opinion against al-Suyūṭī. Many sought Ibn al-Karakī's worldly influence, but not his knowledge. Al-Suyūṭī responds by likening him to a privy, "to which one repairs to satisfy a need" (Sartain, *Jalāl al-Dīn al-Suyūṭī*, 80).

[8] I discuss this incident in detail in Chapter 1.

felt when his colleagues refused to acknowledge him as the outstanding scholar he believed himself to be."[9]

Although al-Suyūṭī's framing effort may have been a failure during his lifetime, the irony is that he succeeded as a *mujtahid* almost in spite of his own efforts. Al-Suyūṭī's lasting legacy and reputation can be attributed to the enduring popularity and value of his works. This popularity stems not only from the sheer quantity of works that the author produced (estimated at close to 500 titles) but also from their quality.[10] It is no surprise that al-Suyūṭī's most influential works are in the fields he considered to be the most noble and worthy of study: the Qurʾānic sciences, *ḥadīth*, and the Arabic language. Al-Suyūṭī's succinct and practical completion of Jalāl al-Dīn al-Maḥallī's exegesis of the Qurʾān, *Tafsīr al-Jalālayn*, is still popular and his *Itqān fī ʿulūm al-Qurʾān* "remains a work of reference wherever Ḳurʾānic sciences are taken up."[11] Of al-Suyūṭī's many important titles in *ḥadīth* collection, criticism, and terminology, his *Jāmiʿ al-jawāmiʿ* (and its abridgement, *al-Jāmiʿ al-ṣaghīr*) and his *Tadrīb al-rāwī fī Taqrīb al-Nawāwī* are worthy of special mention as works that are in regular use. In the subject of the Arabic language, al-Suyūṭī's major work is *al-Muzhir fī ʿulūm al-lugha*.

As far as al-Suyūṭī's legal thought is concerned, his fatwas and treatises are still read and his work on legal precepts, *al-Ashbāh wa-l-naẓāʾir fī l-qawāʿid al-fiqhiyya*, is still taught as a key text of Shāfiʿī *fiqh*. Al-Suyūṭī's fatwas have been compiled in a two-volume set, *al-Ḥāwī li-l-fatāwī*, which continues to come out in new editions. Even during the author's lifetime, al-Suyūṭī says proudly that his works have traveled as far as Syria, the Ḥijāz, Yemen, India, the Maghrib, and Takrūr (in West Africa).[12] Although al-Suyūṭī was able to travel quite extensively within Egypt and went on pilgrimage to Mecca, his fame abroad was due largely to the spread of his works and his response to questions from both near and far.[13]

[9] Sartain, *Jalāl al-Dīn al-Suyūṭī*, 84.

[10] The Sufi biographer, Yūsuf b. Ismāʿīl Nabhānī (d. 1932), writes that the greatest of al-Suyūṭī's miracles was the number of his books. See Nabhānī, *Kitāb Jāmiʿ karāmāt al-awliyāʾ*, 2 vols. (Beirut: Dār al-Kutub al-ʿIlmiyya, 1996), 2:132. I am grateful to Jonathan A.C. Brown for alerting me to this reference.

[11] E. Geoffrey, "al-Suyūṭī," *Encyclopaedia of Islam*, Second Edition (Brill Online, 2011).

[12] Sartain, *Jalāl al-Dīn al-Suyūṭī*, 41.

[13] Al-Suyūṭī's *al-Ḥāwī li-l-fatāwī* contains a section in which he answers questions directed to him from the people of Takrūr. It seems that al-Suyūṭī carried on a correspondence with

Indeed, al-Suyūṭī's opinions as a jurist may have been received with more acclaim and admiration abroad than they were in his own scholarly circles at home in Cairo. Marlis Saleh observes, not without irony, that "al-Suyūṭī seems to have been appreciated best at a distance," citing positive biographical entries by ʿAbd al-Wahhāb al-Shaʿrānī (d. 973/1565), Ibn Iyās (d.c. 930/1524), Najm al-Dīn al-Ghazzī (d. 1061/1651), and Ibn al-ʿImād (d. 1089/1679).[14] Saleh also notes "what might be termed a revival of interest in al-Suyūṭī and his work," including two international conferences on al-Suyūṭī in 1976 and again in 1993.[15] If it is possible, as Saleh suggests, to "attempt to judge the value placed on a given work by succeeding generations by seeing whether or not that work was copied and has left surviving manuscripts" and whether or not, in modern times, the work has been published, then al-Suyūṭī's repertoire is impressive indeed.[16] Saleh counts 392 works by al-Suyūṭī "that have been published at least once, not counting additional editions of the same title," and one effort to locate extant manuscripts yielded as many as 724 works.[17]

Five centuries after his death, al-Suyūṭī's works still occupy a place of honor as core texts in the curriculum of many leading institutions of higher learning across the Islamic world. In a recent video, the former state Mufti of Egypt asserts that al-Suyūṭī's treatise on legal precepts is taught to post-graduate students at al-Azhar and is considered the best work of its kind.[18] As al-Suyūṭī might have predicted, his works have endured long after the words of his enemies have scattered like dust. Even so, there remains a disconnect between the respect accorded the medieval jurist in the modern Muslim world and the attention he has received in western academia.

scholars in Takrūr and received representatives from West Africa who would stop in Cairo on their way back from pilgrimage. These scholars would then bring copies of al-Suyūṭī's works back with them. On al-Suyūṭī's influence in Takrūr see E.M. Sartain, "Jalāl al-Dīn al-Suyūṭī's Relations with the People of Takrūr," *Journal of Semitic Studies* 16 (1971): 193–8; and J.O. Hunwick, "Notes on a Late Fifteenth-Century Document Concerning 'al-Takrūr,'" in *African Perspectives*, edited by Christopher Allen and R.W. Johnson (Cambridge, U.K.: Cambridge University Press, 1970), 7–33.

[14] Marlis J. Saleh, "Al-Suyūṭī and His Works: Their Place in Islamic Scholarship from Mamluk Times to the Present," *Mamlūk Studies Review* 5 (2001): 80.

[15] Ibid., 81–2. [16] Ibid., 88. [17] Ibid., 88–9.

[18] ʿAlī Gumʿa, "Imām Galāl al-Dīn al-Suyūṭī," accessed July 2, 2014, https://www.youtube.com/watch?v=zyYmhKlJScc.

APPROACH OF THE STUDY

Published in 1975, E.M Sartain's *Jalāl al-Dīn al-Suyūṭī: Biography and Background* remains the only full-length critical study in English of al-Suyūṭī's life and work. Sartain gives the reader a detailed overview of al-Suyūṭī's place in late Mamluk Egypt but explains that since her work is "primarily a historical and not a literary study, no attempt has been made to evaluate al-Suyūṭī's works. The proper assessment of al-Suyūṭī's contribution as a scholar is a task which must be left to specialists in each of the fields in which al-Suyūṭī worked."[19] While it is commendable that so much of al-Suyūṭī's work has been published, scholars have yet to subject the majority of this corpus to detailed analysis and scholarly criticism. Some helpful efforts have been made to address al-Suyūṭī's contributions in such fields as the Qur'ānic sciences,[20] history,[21] grammar,[22] and literature.[23] As far as al-Suyūṭī's legal thought is concerned, some work has been done on al-Suyūṭī's role in the debates surrounding the existence of the *mujtahid* in late medieval Islam,[24] and an article[25] by Mufti Ali looks at al-Suyūṭī's opposition to Greek logic based on three treatises and a fatwa, which I will discuss in detail in Chapter 2. I have not, however, seen any attempts to

[19] Sartain, *Jalāl al-Dīn al-Suyūṭī*, vii.

[20] For example: ʿAbd al-Ḥalīm Hāshim Sharīf, *al-Suyūṭī wa-juhūduhu fī ʿulūm al-Qur'ān* (Cairo: Al-Ṣadr li-Khidamāt al-Ṭibāʿa, 1991).

[21] For example, there are two English translations of al-Suyūṭī's *Ta'rīkh al-Khulafā': History of the Caliphs*, translated by H.S. Jarrett (Karachi: Karimsons, 1977) and *The History of the Caliphs Who Took the Right Way: Being a Translation of the Chapters on al-Khulafā' al-Rāshidūn from Ta'rīkh al-Khulafā' of Jalāl al-Dīn al-Suyūṭī*, translated by ʿAbdassamad Clarke (London: Ta-Ha Publishers, 1995).

[22] For example: Muṣṭafā Shakʿa, *Jalāl al-Dīn al-Suyūṭī: masīratuhu al-ʿilmiyya wa-mabāḥithuhu al-lughawiyya* (Egypt: Sharikat Maktaba wa-Maṭbaʿat Muṣṭafā al-Bābī al-Ḥalabī, 1981).

[23] There has been some excellent literary criticism done on al-Suyūṭī's *maqāmāt*. For example: ʿAwaḍ Al-Ghubārī, *Maqāmāt al-Suyūṭī: dirāsa fī fann al-maqāma al-miṣriyya* (Cairo: Dār al-Thaqāfa al-ʿArabiyya, 2005) and Samīr Maḥmūd Durūbī, *Sharḥ maqāmāt Jalāl al-Dīn al-Suyūṭī*, 2 vols. (Beirut: Mu'assasat al-Risāla, 1989).

[24] I will examine in detail two articles dealing with this subject: Ignaz Goldziher, "Ignaz Goldziher on Al-Suyūṭī," edited and translated by J.O. Hunwick, *The Muslim World*, 58:2 (1978): 79–99, and Ella Landau-Tasseron, "The 'Cyclical Reform': A Study of the *Mujaddid* Tradition," *Studia Islamica* 70 (1989): 79–117.

[25] Mufti Ali, "A Statistical Portrait of the Resistance to Logic by Sunni Muslim Scholars Based on the Works of Jalāl al-Dīn al-Suyūṭī (849–909 [sic.]/1448–1505)," *Islamic Law and Society* 15:2 (2008): 250–67. This article is based on the author's dissertation: *Muslim Opposition to Logic and Theology in Light of the Works of Jalāl al-Dīn al-Suyūṭī (d. 911/1505)*, Ph.D. Diss. (Universiteit Leiden, 2008).

execute a comprehensive assessment of al-Suyūṭī's contribution to any of the fields in which he excelled.

This book offers a new theoretical interpretation of al-Suyūṭī's legal thought. The analysis differs from Sartain's excellent historical study in two major respects. First, this study goes beyond a "traditional" Islamic studies approach by drawing on tools and methodologies from a variety of disciplines, including discourse analysis, sociolinguistics, anthropology, history, religious studies, and literary criticism. These tools help to answer more than just the limited question of what al-Suyūṭī says in his legal writing, but also how he says it and to what end. The analysis approaches a set of selected texts with the assumption that the author seeks to frame his identity as a superior legal scholar and to assert his authority as a jurist relative to that of his opponents and to other competing sources of authority within his socio-political context (particularly those associated with the Mamluk political elite). The study provides a multi-disciplinary theoretical case study of al-Suyūṭī's legal writing that fills in part of a picture that Sartain has outlined.

Interdisciplinary methods facilitate a detailed analysis of the discursive strategies that the jurist uses to construct, negotiate, and transmit his authority within society and through his use of the written word. Sociolinguistic theories in particular provide a valuable tool in this endeavor because they remind us that the content, form, and context of discourse are inseparable; all three aspects contribute to the meaning of a given utterance. In other words, the 'what?' the 'how?' and the 'why?' of discourse inform each other, and if one focuses on one of these and neglects the others, one misses part of the story. The goal is to look beyond what the text says in order to determine what it might mean (with the assumption that meaning is shaped by context). Finally, theories like Wenger's "communities of practice" teach us that it is not enough to assert authority through words alone; identity must be negotiated both discursively (though text and talk) and socially through practice.[26] Thus, the contention is that the discursive identity of the jurist consists of what he says about himself, what others say about him, and what he does in practice.

[26] Etienne Wenger, *Communities of Practice: Learning, Meaning, and Identity* (New York: Cambridge University Press, 1998), 151.

The second way in which this study differs from Sartain's classic work is that it connects the legacy of the medieval jurist to modern debates. Al-Suyūṭī's legal work emerges at a key transitional moment in Islamic thought where the pre-modern and the early modern meet. As this analysis will show, al-Suyūṭī's formulation of the important concepts of independent legal reasoning (*ijtihād*) and religious renewal and revival (*tajdīd*) resonate with reformers seeking to counter the common assumption that such innovative thought was no longer possible in later centuries. Also, as already mentioned, al-Suyūṭī's seminal work on legal precepts, *al-Ashbāh wa-l-naẓāʾir*, continues to occupy a place of honor in the curriculum of institutions of higher learning and religious training, such as Egypt's al-Azhar. The legacy of Imam al-Suyūṭī as a master of Shāfiʿī jurisprudence seems to be at odds, therefore, with the image of the bitter and disappointed scholar shut away from the world in brooding isolation.

Most importantly, though, the question of who speaks with an authoritative voice in society is one that has only gained in relevance and urgency in modern times. In recent years, the political and social upheaval touched off by the "Arab Spring" revolutions has brought about an intense crisis of authority and leadership in several Middle Eastern and North African nations. Questions of legitimacy, legal interpretation, and constitutional government must be resolved with reference to modern political norms, but also to the deep and powerful legacy of Islamic law and its influence today. Al-Suyūṭī's concept of the role of the jurist in society is germane to this discussion, especially in his native land of Egypt. At a time when increasing numbers of people in the Arab world have raised their voices to demand democratic forms of government that nevertheless stay true to the principles of Sharīʿa, the issue of who has the ultimate authority to interpret the sources of law, to set legal norms, and to represent the "voice" of Sharīʿa principles in society is still in dispute. In resolving this issue, no less than the future of the new Egypt is at stake.

A Conversation about Religious Authority

This study joins a rich conversation in the field of Islamic Studies surrounding the construction and negotiation of religious authority in medieval and modern Islamic contexts. The first issue that arises is how to define authority within the context of religious traditions. Can authority and power be used interchangeably, for example, or must one be defined in contrast with the other?[27] In their introduction to *Speaking for Islam: Religious Authorities in Muslim Societies*, Gudrun Krämer and Sabine Schmidtke point out that, despite Weber's influential classification of authority as distinct from coercive power, it can be difficult to distinguish between the two.[28] Further complicating the definition is the sheer variety of forms and discourses through which aspects of religious authority may be articulated.

As Krämer and Schmidtke suggest, one of the key ways in which religious authority is expressed in monotheistic religious traditions based on revealed scriptures is by defining a canon of authoritative texts and setting the normative standards of interpretation of those texts. This process has the added effect of excluding alternate methodologies of interpretation, which come to be classified as deviant and heretical in light of the emerging norms.[29] In his study of Ḥanafī jurisprudence, Brannon Wheeler argues that the application of a canon (in this case, the authority of the Qurʾān as mediated by the Sunna) requires an interpreter and a tradition of interpretation in order to reach its full effect. The interpretive tradition that builds up over generations thus plays a key role in relating the canonical texts to changing circumstances.[30] The process through which an interpretive tradition is created and perpetuated pedagogically strongly favors the scholarly

[27] Khaled Abou El Fadl differentiates between coercive authority as "the ability to direct the conduct of another person through the use of inducements, threats, or punishments" and persuasive authority as the normative power to "direct the belief or conduct of a person because of trust." The difference is that of being "in authority" in contrast to being "an authority." One heeds an authority "in deference to the perceived special knowledge, wisdom or insight" of that person. See Abou El Fadl, *Speaking in God's Name: Islamic Law, Authority and Women* (Oxford, U.K.: Oneworld Publications, 2001), 18.

[28] Gudrun Krämer and Sabine Schmidtke, "Introduction: Religious Authority and Religious Authorities in Muslim Societies; A Critical Overview," in *Speaking for Islam: Religious Authorities in Muslim Societies* (Leiden: Brill, 2006), 1.

[29] Krämer and Schmidtke, *Speaking for Islam*, 1–2.

[30] See Brannon M. Wheeler, *Applying the Cannon in Islam: The Authorization and Maintenance of Interpretive Reasoning in Ḥanafī Scholarship* (Albany: State University of New York Press, 1996). Jonathan A.C. Brown also uses the notion of canon and canonization as starting points for his *The Canonization of al-Bukhārī and Muslim: The Formation and Function of the Sunnī Ḥadīth Canon* (Leiden: Brill, 2007).

class (*ʿulamāʾ*) in general and the jurists (*fuqahāʾ*) in particular as a subset of *ʿulamāʾ*.

The disproportionate emphasis placed on jurists in the secondary literature on religious authority in Islam may be partially the result of the jurists' own agency and efforts to position themselves as knowledgeable interpreters of authoritative sources with the ability to dictate acceptable norms of practice. It is the jurists rather than the caliph, for example, who set the theoretical boundaries of interpretation limiting the number of Sunni legal schools to four by the tenth century CE. Legal discourses of the tenth and eleventh century reflect a growing awareness of consensus (and violation of consensus) as a conceptual framework through which 'orthodoxy' and 'heresy' came to be defined. Devin Stewart shows in his detailed analysis of Shiʿi legal theory and institutions that, far from being cut off from their Sunni counterparts, Shiʿi jurists developed their own *madhhab*s and legal framework in conjunction with (and in response to) parallel developments in Sunni centers of learning. Despite theories of the absolute authority and guidance of the Imam in Shiʿi thought, it seems that Shiʿi jurists were unwilling to surrender their ability to shape the law, at times even identifying with Sunni *madhhab*s as a means of maintaining influence.[31]

A number of studies have noted the tendency on the part of pre-modern Muslim scholars to establish rankings and typologies of scholars as intellectual heirs of the Prophet's authority. As noted previously, the classification of different levels of *mujtahid*s and the designation of a centennial renewer (*mujaddid*) were popular devices for establishing hierarchies amongst jurists in particular. Biographical and autobiographical literary genres also act as a suitable forum for the discursive negotiation of rank and authority. Reflecting on the origins and development of *ṭabaqāt* as a form of biographical literature distinct from annalistic history, Michael Cooperson suggests that the genre arose out of a compelling interest on the part of pre-modern scholars to compile lists and genealogies of people with similar attributes and eventually to organize them into distinct professional groupings (*ṭāʾifa*s). The identity of the individual serves to reinforce the authority

[31] Devin J. Stewart, *Islamic Legal Orthodoxy: Twelver Shiite Responses to the Sunni Legal System* (Salt Lake City: University of Utah Press, 1998), 56–7.

of the group as it competed with rival groups for symbolic heirship to the Prophet.[32] Jurists made productive use of the *ṭabaqāt* genre to fulfill a number of pragmatic aims, including legitimizing the authority of the *madhhab*, preserving knowledge, defending the 'orthodoxy' of the doctrine and practice of the group, and asserting the authority of the author by situating him within the hierarchy associated with past generations.[33]

Finally, studies of the doctrines, discourses, and institutions associated with the mystical tradition in Islam have added a valuable dimension to discussions of religious authority in Islamic Studies. Of particular relevance to this study are works that pay attention to the sociology of Sufism (but without losing sight of theological and doctrinal aspects of Sufi thought as well). Vincent Cornell's influential study of Moroccan Sufism takes a multidisciplinary approach to the concept of sainthood, acknowledging that discourse plays a role in the process by which saints are recognized in society. Cornell is critical of simplistic "neo-Weberian" approaches to Sufism that equate charisma with *baraka* without taking into account the many other terms that the tradition itself uses to characterize the ethical/activist, doctrinal, social, juridical, generative, and religio-political aspects of saintly authority.[34] Nathan Hofer's social, religious, and political history of the popularization and institutionalization of Sufism in Ayyubid and Mamluk Egypt also provides helpful context for the power dynamics that shaped al-Suyūṭī's fifteenth-century intellectual milieu.[35]

[32] See Michael Cooperson, *Classical Arabic Biography: The Heirs of the Prophets in the Age of al-Maʾmūn* (Cambridge, U.K.: Cambridge University Press, 2008). In regards to the development and function of *ṭabaqāt* works, Makdisi writes: "The Traditionalists may or may not have created the *ṭabaqāt*; but there can be no doubt that they adopted it for a specific purpose. Their motivation was *to identify the scholars who had the legitimate authority to determine religious orthodoxy*" [emphasis in the original]. This impulse was not confined to *ḥadīth* scholars but included jurists and scholars of the Arabic language as well. See George Makdisi, "Ṭabaqāt-Biography: Law and Orthodoxy in Classical Islam," *Islamic Studies* 32:4 (1993): 373.

[33] For an excellent example of a study analyzing the rhetorical strategies used by a jurist of the late Mamluk era (Ibn Qāḍī Shuhbah) to negotiate authority in a legal *ṭabaqāt* work (*Ṭabaqāt al-fuqahāʾal-shāfiʿiyya*), see R. Kevin Jaques, *Authority, Conflict, and the Transmission of Diversity in Medieval Islamic Law* (Leiden: Brill, 2006). See also Felicitas Opwis, "The Role of the Biographer in Constructing Identity and Doctrine: Al-ʿAbbādī and his *Kitāb Ṭabaqāt al-Fuqahāʾ al-Shāfiʿiyya*," *Journal of Arabic and Islamic Studies* 11 (2011): 1–35.

[34] See Vincent J. Cornell, *Realm of the Saint: Power and Authority in Moroccan Sufism* (Austin: University of Texas Press, 1998), especially Chapter 3, "Knowledge, Power, and Authority in Monographic Biography," 63–92.

[35] Nathan Hofer, *The Popularisation of Sufism in Ayyubid and Mamluk Egypt, 1173–1325* (Edinburgh: Edinburgh University Press, 2015).

Framing the Jurist

Forty years after the publication of Sartain's study of al-Suyūṭī's life and work, a growing trend in contemporary scholarship seeks to re-envision the life and legacy of important pre-modern figures within the Islamic legal sphere. A few recent works that consider the multi-faceted identity of a particular pre-modern jurist and search for clues within the social context to counter misconceptions about that jurist will be noted here.[36] One uniting factor of such studies is that they reveal an inherent tension between the historian's efforts to locate the jurist within his local political and social context while also drawing conclusions about that jurist's legacy as reflected in the discourses of subsequent generations of scholars.

Bernard Haykel's study of the life and legacy of Muḥammad al-Shawkānī (1759–1839) is a good example of this tension. On the one hand, Haykel shies away from drawing generalizations about al-Shawkānī as a reformer by lumping him together with other eighteenth-century scholars "under one ideological rubric."[37] However, at the same time, the whole premise of Haykel's book is that al-Shawkānī's "Traditionist" approach carried an appeal beyond his immediate context that resonated with later *salafī*-minded reformers who then appropriated his views as ammunition in ideological battles that al-Shawkānī could not have anticipated during his own time.

A useful model for this project is Scott Kugle's study of the Moroccan jurist and Sufi saint, Aḥmad Zarrūq (d. 1493).[38] As a close contemporary of

[36] Other noteworthy studies that attempt to capture the life, methodology, and influence of individual jurists include: Bernard G. Weiss, *The Search for God's Law: Islamic Jurisprudence in the Writings of Sayf al-Dīn al-Āmidī* (Salt Lake City: University of Utah Press, 1992); R. Kevin Jaques, *Ibn Hajar* (New Delhi: Oxford University Press, 2009); George Makdisi, *Ibn ʿAqīl: Religion and Culture in Classical Islam* (Edinburgh: Edinburgh University Press, 1997); Kate Zebiri, *Maḥmūd Shaltūt and Islamic Modernism* (New York: Oxford University Press, 1993); Christopher Melchert, *Ahmad ibn Hanbal* (Oxford, U.K.: Oneworld Publications, 2006); Malcolm H. Kerr, *Islamic Reform: The Political and Legal Theories of Muhammad ʿAbduh and Rashid Rida* (Berkeley: University of California Press, 1966); Muhammad Khalid Masud, *Islamic Legal Philosophy: A Study of Abū Isḥāq al-Shāṭibī's Life and Thought* (Islamabad: Islamic Research Institute, 1977); Sherman Jackson, *Islam and the State: The Constitutional Jurisprudence of Shihāb al-Dīn al-Qarāfī* (Leiden: Brill, 1996); and Stefan Reichmuth, *The World of Murtaḍā al-Zabīdī (1732–91): Life, Networks and Writings* (Cambridge, U.K.: Gibb Memorial Trust, 2009).

[37] Bernard Haykel, *Revival and Reform in Islam: The Legacy of Muhammad al-Shawkānī* (Cambridge, U.K.: Cambridge University Press, 2003), 13.

[38] I am grateful to John Voll for alerting me to this study. A complementary study to Kugle's book is Knut S. Vikør's *Sufi and Scholar on the Desert Edge: Muḥammad b. ʿAlī al-Sanūsī and his Brotherhood* (London: Hurst & Company, 1995). Vikør looks at the life and work of the North

al-Suyūṭī (d. 1505), Zarrūq lived through "the transitional period in Islamic society from the late medieval era to the early modern."[39] He exemplified both the spiritual identity of a Sufi saint as well as the scholarly authority of the jurist, thus proving that the two are far from being irreconcilable. Kugle's approach is interesting in the way that he links the present and the past. Rather than leaving Zarrūq's legacy till the end, Kugle's book opens in the United States post-September 11, 2001 before backtracking to medieval Fes. Kugle argues that even though Zarrūq's saintly authority was rejected by his contemporaries and his ambitions for reform never realized, the scholar's spiritual and intellectual legacy has acquired new currency in the struggle of modern Sufis (like Shaykh Ḥamza Yūsuf) against "fundamentalist" ideologies.[40]

Another instructive aspect of Kugle's work is the delicate balance that he achieves between issues of identity and authority on the one side and textual analysis on the other. Kugle surveys an impressive number of Zarrūq's works on a range of subjects, including prodigious archival material. Kugle brings across very clearly the sensitive and often perilous environment in which Zarrūq was operating and catalogues his efforts to construct the ideal identity of the "juridical saint" and the "conservative rebel" in opposition to the critique of most of his colleagues. Given this dangerous rhetorical environment, Kugle tends to place more emphasis on the "legal, theological, ethical, and sociological dimensions" of Zarrūq's arguments rather than focusing on the particular linguistic techniques that he employs through detailed textual analysis.[41]

Finally, in his *The First Islamic Reviver: Abu Hamid al-Ghazali and his* Revival of the Religious Sciences, Kenneth Garden builds on previous "revisionist" literature to construct a brilliant reassessment of al-Ghazālī's (d. 505/1111) major works, especially his masterpiece, *Iḥyāʾ ʿulūm al-dīn*. Garden looks for

African reformer al-Sanūsī (d. 1859) in light of three "conceptual polarities," namely: "the relationship between the political and scholarly, between the centre and periphery, and between the Sufi and the scholar," 265.

[39] Scott Kugle, *Rebel Between Spirit and Law: Ahmad Zarruq, Sainthood, and Authority in Islam* (Bloomington: Indiana University Press, 2006), 2.

[40] Ibid., 221.

[41] Ibid., 158. Some exceptions include Kugle's analysis of Zarrūq's use of the term '*bidʿa*' (166–70) and his use of the metaphor 'eating the flesh of carrion' to accuse his enemies of corruption (195–6).

clues in the controversies and political and scholarly disputes surrounding these works to find significance not just in what al-Ghazālī says but also in what he does not say. In the end, Garden is able to draft a new narrative and to uncover the 'real' al-Ghazālī, not as "a solitary and otherworldly seeker, but as an engaged scholar, rooted in his age, connected to some of its most powerful men, and using every tool at his disposal to promote a revivalist agenda."[42] Garden goes on to say that al-Ghazālī's counterparts are to be found "among the Muslim revivers of subsequent ages, many of whom were inspired by al-Ghazālī, and who have been particularly numerous in the modern era."[43] One such scholar who longed to follow in the footsteps of al-Ghazālī and to be recognized as the reviver of religion in his age was Jalāl al-Dīn al-Suyūṭī whose own contentious narrative is the subject of this study.

ORGANIZATION OF THE STUDY

As noted earlier, this research aims to answer three broad questions: What does al-Suyūṭī say about the authority and religious identity of the jurist in his legal writing? How does he say it using language? And why does he choose to say it in the way that he does? Finally, the analysis goes beyond the time of al-Suyūṭī to examine how these works are being appropriated by modern jurists in contemporary Egypt as they struggle to define who they are in turbulent times. This study seeks to show, therefore, how al-Suyūṭī's own crisis of identity and authority as one of a select group of trained experts vested with the moral responsibility of interpreting God's law has echoes in contemporary debates surrounding who can claim to speak authoritatively in modern Muslim societies.

As an interpreter of al-Suyūṭī and his world, I analyze in detail a few texts that speak particularly to the role of the jurist in al-Suyūṭī's personal frame of reference and within the larger context of late medieval Mamluk Cairo (and that carry significant implications for jurists today). The texts on which the study is focused are ones that the author produced in the midst

[42] Garden, *The First Islamic Reviver: Abu Hamid al-Ghazali and his* Revival of the Religious Sciences (New York: Oxford University Press, 2014), 9.
[43] Ibid.

of conflict and that stirred up further controversy in their own right. One assumes that it is in these moments of crisis that al-Suyūṭī feels most keenly the need to reinforce his own authority relative to that of his opponents.

The texts selected for this study are two fatwas (legal opinions) by al-Suyūṭī written in response to specific issues, various treatises, and a section from his autobiographical work concerning the concepts of *ijtihād* (independent legal reasoning) and *tajdīd* (religious renewal), plus al-Suyūṭī's full-length book on legal precepts (*qawāʿid fiqhiyya*). The strategy in approaching these texts is to look both for internal evidence in the text and external evidence in the context in order to gain access to the author and his world indirectly.[44] Each chapter is intended to illustrate a different aspect of al-Suyūṭī's legal persona and contains a balance between detailed textual analysis and "big picture" questions about the historical and social context within which the author operated. Taken as a whole, the individual aspects form a coherent framework within which the jurist situates himself and frames his own authority.

Just as the themes and case studies vary from chapter to chapter, the methodological focus also shifts depending on the type of data. The aim, therefore, in deciding which linguistic concepts to apply to which texts is to let the form and content of the text drive the methodology. In other words, I single out texts that contain some element of controversy, on the one hand, and that speak to the role of the jurist in al-Suyūṭī's context on the other. I then select an appropriate linguistic methodology that best allows us to understand how and why al-Suyūṭī frames his arguments in the texts in the way that he does. As suggested earlier, the task of choosing specific case studies from al-Suyūṭī's extensive array of legal works, as well as determining to which discourse strategies I should direct my attention, are themselves acts of interpretation. I do not seek to deny my own role as a modern interpreter of a late fifteenth-century figure. Rather, my aim is to augment our understanding of the role of the jurist, as framed by al-Suyūṭī, using insights from several different disciplines.

[44] Kristen Brustad discusses the potential benefits of such an approach in her article, "Imposing Order: Reading the Conventions of Representation in al-Suyūṭī's Autobiography," *Edebiyāt* 7:2 (1997): 327–44.

I approach the texts with the basic assumption that the discourse demonstrates the pragmatic goals of its users within its real and immediate social context. In each case I ask the question: what goals does the author hope to accomplish in the text and what sort of rhetorical or discursive techniques does he use to achieve those goals? Also, in what ways does the form of the text help to meet these objectives? It should be noted that I do not dictate what al-Suyūṭī's pragmatic goals should be, only how they are communicated. As Michele Dunne explains in her work on democracy in Egypt: "I determined that I could get further by examining *what* speakers did in public discourse and democracy and *how* they did it with language than by considering *whether* they should have done it or not."[45]

That being said, some discursive techniques are more effective than others in meeting the pragmatic goals of the speaker and this success is manifested in the power dynamics surrounding the text. To use Wenger's term, in an "economy of meaning"[46] there are winners and losers—those whose narratives shape public discourse and those whose words are lost in the fray. As the following discussion will show, the linguistic methodology employed in this study will allow me to evaluate to some degree the relative effectiveness of al-Suyūṭī's rhetorical techniques both during his lifetime and beyond. In this final section, I outline the content and argument of each chapter.

CHAPTER OVERVIEW

1. Authority by Persuasion: Power Relations in al-Suyūṭī's Legal Opinion on Scholarly Stipends

This chapter provides historical background and gives the reader a snapshot of the socio-political context of late Mamluk Egyptian society in which al-Suyūṭī competed for authority. In an age of economic, political, and intellectual deterioration, al-Suyūṭī insists in a controversial fatwa[47] that the

[45] Michele Durocher Dunne, *Democracy in Contemporary Egyptian Political Discourse* (Amsterdam: John Benjamins Publishing Company, 2003), 3.

[46] Wenger, *Communities of Practice*, 199.

[47] *Al-Inṣāf fī tamyīz al-awqāf* in *al-Ḥāwī li-l-fatāwī*, 2 vols. (Beirut: Dār al-Kutub al-ʿIlmiyya, 2000), 1:150–2.

"true" scholar appointed to a position in an endowed institution is entitled to funding by virtue of his learning regardless of whether or not he fulfills the duties stipulated in the endowment deed. Using Foucault's criteria for analyzing power relations,[48] I argue that al-Suyūṭī differentiates the rights of the scholar from those of the founder of the endowment (usually a member of the Mamluk ruling elite) and those of the Sufi students in the institution most of whom, he says, lack the qualifications necessary to deserve such an entitlement. Al-Suyūṭī tries to negotiate a delicate power dynamic in which the political regime depended on the religious scholars (*ʿulamāʾ*) to affirm its legitimacy, while, at the same time, the scholars had come to rely more and more on patronage by the state in the form of stipends and lucrative posts in endowed institutions. In opposition to the coercive authority of the state officials, al-Suyūṭī appeals to the moral authority of the scholar as a representative and interpreter of God's law.

The dispute over how endowment funds should be distributed culminated in a crisis in which al-Suyūṭī was dismissed from his position and even feared for his life. The events of al-Suyūṭī's dismissal as supervisor at the Baybarsiyya institution in 906/1501 and forced seclusion during the reign of Sultan al-ʿĀdil Ṭūmānbāy may represent a setback for al-Suyūṭī in the short term, but his efforts to assert persuasive moral authority in this matter were effective in the end. Al-Suyūṭī's own actions, both in refusing to accept monetary gifts from Sultan al-Ghawrī and his gradual withdrawal from public life to focus on his scholarship, demonstrate his ability to bring power into being (as Foucault would put it) and to negotiate his own identity as a scholar activist (*ʿālim ʿāmil*) through practice. It is in this light that biographers like ʿAbd al-Wahhāb al-Shaʿrānī (d. 973/1565) interpret al-Suyūṭī's quarrels with the sultan and the Sufis of the Baybarsiyya. The sultan received his punishment in the form of an early death, while al-Suyūṭī's authority as a saint and righteous scholar was assured.[49] Al-Suyūṭī manages to keep the moral high

[48] Foucault suggests that five factors must be considered in analyzing a given set of power relations: a system of differentiations, objectives pursued by each of the actors, a means of bringing power relations into being, a system of institutionalization, and degrees of rationalization. See Michel Foucault, "The Subject and Power" in Hubert L. Dreyfus and Paul Rabinow, *Michel Foucault: Beyond Structuralism and Hermeneutics* (Chicago: Chicago University Press, 1983), 221–4.

[49] Al-Shaʿrānī, *al-Ṭabaqāt al-ṣughrā* (Cairo: Maktabat al-Thaqāfa al-Dīniyya, 2005), 17–18.

ground in the wake of the Baybarsiyya incident and to overcome any short-term damage to his reputation. Sultans and students come and go, after all, but al-Suyūṭī's legal opinions have been preserved.

2. Authority by Association: Consensus vs. Ignorance in al-Suyūṭī's Legal Opinion on Logic

In another controversial fatwa,[50] al-Suyūṭī claims to represent a consensus of scholars opposed to the study of Greek logic on the grounds that it can lead to philosophical speculation of a heretical nature. While ostensibly a condemnation of logic, upon closer examination this fatwa serves to bolster al-Suyūṭī's own claim to have achieved the rank of *mujtahid* in spite of his own lack of expertise in the discipline of logic. Thus, al-Suyūṭī faces the rhetorical challenge of proving his own understanding of a discipline the study of which he has already prohibited.

Al-Suyūṭī tries to evade these problems by using the form of the fatwa itself to frame the issue as one of correct righteous opinion versus heretical ignorance. The question and answer format of the fatwa allows al-Suyūṭī to refute a collection of statements made by an opponent to whom he refers only as *al-jāhil*, or "the Ignoramus." In directing his wrath against this person, al-Suyūṭī avoids appearing critical of his respected Shāfiʿī exemplar and recognized fellow *mujaddid*, al-Ghazālī, whose controversial comments about logic in his *Mustaṣfā* underlie the whole debate. Al-Suyūṭī refutes the notion that knowledge of logic is a prerequisite for the *mujtahid* by attributing it to "the Ignoramus." He tries to position his own opinion as being in line with those of the great scholars of the past or, in other words, with his "community of practice."

In fact, no such consensus against the study of logic existed during al-Suyūṭī's time, thus making the 'logic' of al-Suyūṭī's logic fatwa even more tortured. I argue, therefore, that the strategies that al-Suyūṭī uses to assert authority by association in the logic fatwa are the least successful of those examined in this study. There are several possible reasons why this might be the case. First, by emphasizing the opposition to logic displayed by some scholars and omitting the views of those who disagree with him, al-Suyūṭī's

[50] *Al-Qawl al-mushriq fī taḥrīm al-ishtighāl bi-l-manṭiq* in *al-Ḥāwī li-l-fatāwī*, 1:244–6.

framing of the issue misrepresents the status of logic as a generally accepted part of the curriculum during his time period.[51] In a sense, by casting his lot with Ibn al-Ṣalāḥ, Ibn Taymiyya, and others who were forthright in their criticism of logic, al-Suyūṭī picks the losing side of the debate. Furthermore, the rigidity and lack of nuance of his views on the logic issue results in their marginalization (in contrast to those who took a more balanced approach). Finally, al-Suyūṭī was already fighting an uphill battle with most of his contemporaries on the matter of his status as a *mujtahid* and the logic debate did not serve to convince them of his claims.

3. Authority by Articulation: The Language of Religious Revival and Reform in al-Suyūṭī's *Tajdīd* Genre

Chapters 3 and 4 are intended as a bridge between what al-Suyūṭī has to say about himself as part of his efforts to project authority as the leading scholar of his time and what others say about him, including his modern legacy. Although al-Suyūṭī failed to convince many of his contemporaries of his status as a *mujtahid* and *mujaddid*, his articulation of the concepts of *ijtihād* and *tajdīd* have proven influential to later scholars seeking to connect their own projects of reform to the classical tradition.

For example, by following al-Ghazālī's lead and declaring his desire to be recognized as a *mujaddid*, al-Suyūṭī made it easier for would-be *mujaddid*s such as Shaykh Aḥmad Sirhindī (d. 1034/1624) and Usumanu Dan Fodio (d. 1232/1817) to do the same in later centuries. Secondly, al-Suyūṭī's insistence that at least one *mujtahid* must be present in every age, and that the community must renew its focus on the traditional sciences of Qurʾān and *ḥadīth* and stamp out un-Islamic encroachments threatening the integrity of the religion, proved inspirational to early modern and modernist thinkers of a *salafī* mindset such as Muḥammad al-Shawkānī (d. 1839) and Rashīd Riḍā (d. 1935).

Bakhtin's literary concept of genre and Wuthnow's discussion of the "problem of articulation" as it plays out in social history add valuable insights into the ultimate success of al-Suyūṭī's formulation of *tajdīd*.

[51] Nicholas Rescher argues that, by the 8th/13th century, *madrasa* students studied logic as a regular part of their theological training. See Rescher, *The Development of Arabic Logic* (Pittsburgh: University of Pittsburgh Press, 1964), 62.

Bakhtin describes in broad terms how an artist is able to unlock the resources of the genre (its semantic forms, themes, plots, and mythologies) to create a "great work" that transcends the barriers of its epoch and continues to gain in significance over time.[52] Wuthnow explains that in order to influence larger intellectual and social trends, a great work of art or literature must speak to the environment in which it was produced while, at the same time, disarticulating from it to acquire a "broader, even universal and timeless appeal."[53]

Al-Suyūṭī's contribution to the wider "*tajdīd* genre" in Islamic thought allowed his vision of *ijtihād* and *tajdīd* to break free of the narrow context of his squabbles with other scholars to help shape how others would view these concepts in the future in their own intellectual and social contexts. This discursive effort on the part of al-Suyūṭī to assert his authority as a jurist through articulation translates into practice as people continue to reap the benefit of his works. In spite of the controversies and ugly episodes that marred al-Suyūṭī's reputation (in some circles) during his lifetime, by both the sheer quantity and quality of his works, al-Suyūṭī's legacy is a testament to the notion that writing well is the best revenge.

4. Authority by Aggregation and Abstraction: The Pragmatics of Communication in al-Suyūṭī's Book on Legal Precepts

In addition to his views on *ijtihād* and *tajdīd*, al-Suyūṭī's lasting influence in Islamic legal thought lies in the area of legal precepts (pithy maxims or questions that sum up areas of the law). Al-Suyūṭī's *al-Ashbāh wa-l-naẓāʾir* stands as a core work in this genre of legal literature and is still a popular textbook for advanced students at Egypt's premier institution of religious learning, al-Azhar. The *qawāʿid* genre speaks to the need to define universal principles representing the essence of Islamic substantive law and gives the jurist a quick frame of reference with which to apply these principles to the formulation of new rulings.

[52] M.M. Bakhtin, "Response to a Question from the *Novy Mir* Editorial Staff," in *Speech Genres and Other Late Essays*, edited by Caryl Emerson and Michael Holquist, translated by Vern W. McGee (Austin: University of Texas Press, 1986), 4.

[53] Robert Wuthnow, *Communities of Discourse: Ideology and Social Structure in the Reformation, the Enlightenment, and European Socialism* (Cambridge, Massachusetts: Harvard University Press, 1989), 3.

Using as a starting point the pragmatic theory of H.P. Grice and others, I argue that legal precepts fulfill a number of key discursive functions for the jurist and that both form and context play a role in shaping their meaning. For example, in the chapter of *al-Ashbāh wa-l-naẓāʾir* dealing with the legal maxim, *al-ʿāda muḥakkama* ("custom should be made to serve as an arbiter"), al-Suyūṭī carefully selects cases and opinions that reflect not only the cumulative thinking of past authorities (particularly those within the Shāfiʿī legal school) but that speak also to the needs of the context in which he is operating. Al-Suyūṭī focuses on instances where a contradiction or discrepancy exists and employs a selective use of custom to resolve the issue. Pragmatic theory can help us to see where such discrepancies exist and how a jurist like al-Suyūṭī resolves the issue by bringing in contextual factors.[54]

It is with al-Suyūṭī's *Ashbāh* that he is most successful in asserting his authority as an aggregator, abstractor, and framer of the law. The power wielded by the aggregator is manifested in his ability to influence how others access information. In our contemporary society, search engines like Google act as filters through which we can target the information we seek and sift out extraneous data. No one will dispute that Google programmers (and the corporation they represent) have an extraordinary and sometimes uncomfortable level of control over how people access information. Al-Suyūṭī's authority as an aggregator and abstractor of the law rests on the power of framing, or "taking some aspects of our reality and making them more accessible than other aspects."[55]

Of course, the ultimate authority of the jurist lies in his ability to interpret God's law from its sources and to make this interpretation accessible to Muslims who wish to act in conformity with the Sharīʿa. In the post-formative era, it was assumed that the jurist would work within one of the established legal schools and that he would derive rulings in reference to the

[54] Other scholars have approached Islamic texts using pragmatic theories of communication as a frame of reference. For example, Marilyn Robinson Waldman looks at Persian historiography in light of speech act theory in *Toward a Theory of Historical Narrative: A Case Study in Perso-Islamicate Historiography* (Columbus: Ohio State University Press, 1980). Mohamed M. Yunis Ali examines Islamic legal discourse through the lens of Gricean pragmatics in *Medieval Islamic Pragmatics: Sunni Legal Theorists' Models of Textual Communication* (Richmond, Surrey: Curzon Press, 2000).

[55] Jim A. Kuypers, *Rhetorical Criticism: Perspectives in Action* (Lanham, MD: Lexington Books, 2009), 181.

textual sources as well as to the precedent put in place by earlier authorities within the school. The process by which a jurist gives preference to certain opinions within the school over others is known as *tarjīḥ*.[56] This concept is of paramount importance because it constitutes the primary method through which later jurists like al-Suyūṭī could still practice a form of *ijtihād*. In so doing, these later jurists manage to redefine what it means to do *ijtihād*. According to this framework, if one were to ask whether al-Suyūṭī realized his persona as a *mujtahid* successfully through practice, then the answer would have to be yes.

5. Authority by Allusion: The Legacy of al-Suyūṭī in Contemporary Egypt

The final chapter brings the discussion of al-Suyūṭī's legal persona squarely into the modern era. This section brings to light how contemporary jurists in Egypt use the legacy of the great fifteenth-century scholar in their efforts to frame their own identities and to assert authority as interpreters and spokesmen for the Sharīʿa in a political arena that is highly polarized and fraught with tension. In the midst of Mursī's embattled presidency, leading scholars at Egypt's state religious institutions rushed to news and social media outlets to affirm their status as representatives of "orthodoxy" and to distance themselves from more extreme *salafī* trends that threaten to change the way Islamic law is practiced in the modern Egyptian state. It is striking how closely the image of the moderate Sunni, Sufi-minded, theologically sound scholar grounded in the juristic tradition (according to the accepted legal schools) fits with the persona that al-Suyūṭī strove so tenaciously to construct.

This chapter looks at three contemporary commentaries on al-Suyūṭī's important book on legal precepts, *al-Ashbāh wa-l-naẓāʾir*. All three commentaries are by senior scholars at the state fatwa-issuing authority, Dār al-Iftāʾ, and all three were published on YouTube during the crucial period following the 2011 revolution that ousted Mubārak and the 2013 coup that

[56] For a detailed analysis of *tarjīḥ* and *taṣḥīḥ* (rendering an opinion as correct according to the leading authorities within the legal school) and other concepts making up the "operative terminology" of Islamic substantive law, see Wael B. Hallaq, "Can the Shariʿa Be Restored?" in *Islamic Law and Challenges of Modernity*, edited by Yvonne Yazbek Haddad and Barbara Freyer Stowasser (Oxford, U.K.: AltaMira Press, 2004), 21–53; see also Wael B. Hallaq, *Authority, Continuity, and Change in Islamic Law* (Cambridge, U.K.: Cambridge University Press, 2001), 239.

removed Mursī from the presidency. I argue that the three scholars, each in his own way, uses his commentary on al-Suyūṭī's fifteenth-century work of jurisprudence to make pragmatic allusion to the validity of the Azharī methodology (*manhaj*). In this context, the Azharī *manhaj* refers primarily to a methodological approach to textual and legal interpretation, but includes also a larger ideology that encompasses both Ashʿarī theology/doctrine and Sufi-oriented conduct. Positive assertions of what constitutes a mainstream Sunni identity are made, either explicitly or implicitly, in reference to a rival approach that is portrayed as extremist, corrupt, and ignorant.

Al-Suyūṭī's story, as I tell it in this book, is ultimately a story about authority. I agree with Bruce Lincoln's assertion that authority can be studied not as an abstract concept, but as an aspect of discourse or speech.[57] The dynamics of authority can be observed by looking at how a speaker uses language, which become most apparent in times of crisis or when the authority of the speaker is challenged. In highlighting five different discursive strategies in this study, I do not mean to suggest that these five are the only ones available to a given speaker or that each one is confined to the particular text featured in the separate chapters. Association and persuasion, for example, are two strategies that occur throughout al-Suyūṭī's legal writing. For each chapter, I emphasize one strategy that I think best speaks to the pragmatic goals of the jurist in producing the text. It is my aim that, when taken as a whole, the discursive strategies analyzed here will constitute a coherent framework with which to understand how a pre-modern jurist is able to speak authoritatively in society. Al-Suyūṭī's efforts did not end with his death but have echoes today in the discourse of modern jurists striving to respond to their own set of challenges.

[57] Bruce Lincoln, *Authority: Construction and Corrosion* (Chicago: University of Chicago Press, 1994), 2.

1

Authority by Persuasion: Power Relations in al-Suyūṭī's Legal Opinion on Scholarly Stipends[1]

INTRODUCTION

In 903/1498, the Sufis of the Baybarsiyya lodge became so enraged with their shaykh, Jalāl al-Dīn al-Suyūṭī, that they seized him and hurled him into a fountain. The same Sufis had so poisoned the atmosphere between al-Suyūṭī and the reigning sultan, al-ʿĀdil Ṭūmānbāy, that by 906/1501 the shaykh was forced to go into hiding for fear of his life.[2] These events mark the climax of a tense situation that had built up over several years, brought on by personal rivalries as well as political and economic factors outside of any direct control by the individuals involved. Indeed, although the Baybarsiyya incident may seem a trivial chapter in the saga of political upheaval and economic deterioration that marked the later Mamluk period, it is, as this chapter will argue, an instructive case study in power relations and authority at a precarious moment in Islamic history.[3]

[1] An earlier version of this chapter appeared as Rebecca Skreslet Hernandez, "Sultan, Scholar, and Sufi: Authority and Power Relations in al-Suyūṭī's *Fatwā* on *Waqf*," *Islamic Law and Society* 20:4 (2013): 333–70, and is used here with permission from Brill. I am grateful to David S. Powers and to the anonymous reviewers for their insightful comments on earlier drafts of the article. Any remaining errors in the text are purely my own.

[2] E.M. Sartain, *Jalāl al-Dīn al-Suyūṭī: Biography and Background*, 2 vols. (Cambridge, U.K.: Cambridge University Press, 1975), 1:97–9. These events are narrated by the historian Ibn Iyās in his *Kitāb Badāʾiʿ al-zuhūr fī waqāʾiʿ al-duhūr*, 5 vols. (Cairo: al-Hayʾa al-Miṣriyya al-ʿĀmma li-l-Kitāb, 1984), 3:388.

[3] For a helpful introductory essay on the concept of authority as it relates to Muslim societies, see Devin DeWeese, "Authority," in *Key Themes for the Study of Islam*, edited by Jamal J.

The Legal Thought of Jalāl al-Dīn al-Suyūṭī: Authority and Legacy. Rebecca Skreslet Hernandez.

Leonor Fernandes writes that when Baybars al-Jāshankīr (r. 708–709/1308–1309)[4] founded the Baybarsiyya, he "opened the way for the full integration of the khanqah institution into Mamluk society and ensured the historical importance of his foundation forever."[5] The *khānqāh* was a cross between a lodge or residence and a teaching facility for students training in the religious sciences and in *taṣawwuf* (Islamic mysticism). With a total of 400 Sufi affiliates, 100 of whom were in residence, the Baybarsiyya was indeed a major institution and its shaykh an important figure. The shaykh was responsible for making sure that the stipulations in the endowment deed were followed, including the distribution of funds for employee salaries, stipends for scholars and students, and general maintenance.[6] In addition to the *khānqāh* itself, the endowment also included a *ribāṭ* (hospice for impoverished residents) and a mausoleum (*qubba*), each with its own staff, as well as agricultural lands in Egypt and Syria. By the fourteenth and fifteenth centuries, the line between the *khānqāh* and *madrasa* had become blurred as more emphasis was put on teaching in the *khānqāh*.[7]

The quarrels that arose between al-Suyūṭī and the Sufi residents of the Baybarsiyya reveal a great deal about how power relations had become

Elias (Oxford, U.K.: Oneworld Publications, 2010), 26–52. Two other concise and cogent discussions that provide an overview of Islamic religious authority as it relates to issues of legitimacy, knowledge transmission, and power include Hilary Kalmbach, "Introduction: Islamic Authority and the Study of Female Religious Leaders," in *Women, Leadership and Mosques: Changes in Contemporary Islamic Authority*, edited by Masooda Bano and Hilary Kalmbach (Leiden: Brill, 2012), 1–30; and Gudrun Krämer and Sabine Schmidtke, "Introduction: Religious Authority and Religious Authorities in Muslim Societies; A Critical Overview," in *Speaking for Islam: Religious Authorities in Muslim Societies*, edited by Gudrun Krämer and Sabine Schmidtke (Leiden: Brill, 2006), 1–14.

[4] Not to be confused with al-Ẓāhir Baybars al-Bunduqdārī (r. 658–676/1259–1277).

[5] Leonor Fernandes, "The Foundation of Baybars al-Jashankir: Its Waqf, History, and Architecture," *Muqarnas* 4 (1987): 21.

[6] In addition to the *shaykh al-ṣūfiyya* and Sufi residents, the personnel of the Baybarsiyya *khānqāh* as stipulated in the endowment deed included a water attendant, a lamp lighter, a janitor, a doorkeeper, a cook, and those responsible for distributing bread and broth to the Sufis. See Fernandes, "The Foundation of Baybars," 25–6.

[7] In addition to the work of Fernandes, Nathan Hofer's study on Sufism in Ayyubid and Mamluk Egypt is revealing of the many functions played by Sufi-related institutions in society, including the ideological functions of these institutions. Hofer's work reflects the broader significance behind the institutionalization and popularization of Sufism during this period by focusing on three Sufi "collectivities" and their complex interactions with state authority: the Sufis of the state-sponsored *khānqāh* of Saʿīd al-Suʿadāʾ, the nascent Shādhiliyya brotherhood, and unaffiliated Sufi activists in Upper Egypt. See Nathan Hofer, *The Popularisation of Sufism in Ayyubid and Mamluk Egypt, 1173-1325* (Edinburgh: Edinburgh University Press, 2015).

institutionalized through the system of religious endowments (*awqāf*). Also, conflicts between the scholar and the sultan make evident the results of a breakdown in the *waqf* system during times of economic uncertainty and widespread corruption and abuse. The financial crisis led to a decline in revenues, including funds set aside for endowments and stipends for scholars. Treatises by al-Suyūṭī dealing with these endowments and how funds should be disbursed and employees appointed are indicative not only of al-Suyūṭī's position in regards to several different legal controversies surrounding the administration of *waqf* revenues, but also speak to a broader dynamic of how power was defined and distributed among state officials, the scholarly elite, and the common people in Mamluk society.

Al-Suyūṭī's role in the crisis over scholarly stipends in late Mamluk Egypt is of particular interest because it reveals a great deal about the jurist's conception of his own place in society relative to state authority and to the Sufi students under his supervision. In his writing on stipends, al-Suyūṭī creates a hierarchy in which scholars, by virtue of their learning, take precedence over the Mamluk *amīr* and Sufi students. To argue this point, al-Suyūṭī makes forceful use of the linguistic techniques at his disposal as a privileged scholar.

This chapter explains how al-Suyūṭī uses language to differentiate between the three levels of the state, the scholar, and the Sufis. As a jurist, al-Suyūṭī makes the case for his preferred group within the institutional framework of *iftāʾ* (issuing legal opinions) and using the modes of argumentation expected from a scholar of his rank. In contrast to the power wielded by a judge (*qāḍī*) in his capacity as an official appointed by the state, al-Suyūṭī deploys the moral authority of the jurist charged with interpreting God's law. Also, unlike the state authority, whose weapon is the sword, al-Suyūṭī promotes the interests of his group and discredits those of his opponents, using the persuasive power of the pen.

First, this chapter surveys the historical background by describing economic and political factors influencing Mamluk society in general and al-Suyūṭī's struggles with the administration of the Baybarsiyya lodge in particular. Second, it examines one of al-Suyūṭī's legal opinions concerning endowments, paying special attention to what the text suggests about the operation of power relations at the time. Taking a careful look at al-Suyūṭī's writing on the subject of state funding of scholarly activities through the lens of power relations helps to explain not only the personal objectives of the author, but also the significance of his views within the larger debates and issues that occupied the minds (and pocketbooks) of jurists in 9th/15th century Cairo.

HISTORICAL BACKGROUND

Evaluating the Sources

This analysis focuses on one of al-Suyūṭī's legal opinions, *al-Inṣāf fī tamyīz al-awqāf* ("Fairness in Distinguishing Endowments").[8] I have chosen to analyze this opinion because it summarizes the scholar's positions and offers numerous telling statements about how the author perceives his role relative to the state authority and to the Sufis whose stipends he is in charge of distributing. We are also fortunate to have access to a letter by al-Suyūṭī addressed to the Sufis of the Baybarsiyya that he intended to be read aloud to them.[9] The letter provides an interesting point of comparison with the author's legal treatises and, like the fatwa, contains significant information about how power relations functioned both in this particular instance and beyond. Evidence from historical and biographical literature and the work of other jurists rounds out the picture.

Historians have access to a wealth of historical material about the Mamluk era, including historical chronicles, biographical dictionaries, manuals of statecraft and legal documents, such as endowment deeds (*waqfiyyas*) and fatwas. Using these sources, historians have been able to construct an impressive history of military, political, economic, and social life under Mamluk rule in Egypt and Syria. However, these sources do have some drawbacks. For example, manuals of statecraft such as those of Ibn

[8] The Arabic text of the fatwa can be found in Jalāl al-Dīn al-Suyūṭī, *al-Ḥāwī li-l-fatāwī*, 2 vols. (Beirut: Dār al-Kutub al-ʿIlmiyya, 2000), 1:150–2.

[9] The Arabic text of the letter as well as a French translation can be found in Albert Arazi, "*Al-Risāla al-Baybarsiyya* d'al-Suyūṭī: Un Document sur les Problèmes d'un *Waqf* Sultanien sous les Derniers Mamlūks," *Israel Oriental Studies* 9 (1979): 329–54. Sartain paraphrases the main points of the letter in *Jalāl al-Dīn al-Suyūṭī*, 94–6.

Shahīn[10] and al-Qalqashandī[11] tend to give an idealized, "systematic, yet all too often static and—in al-Qalqashandī's case—even anachronistic view of the contemporary social and political order."[12] A similar difficulty applies to manuals for notaries on drawing up endowment deeds, since the provisions stipulated in the *waqfiyya* were at times breached in practice.[13] Fatwas, too, are not immune from such dangers, as conditions varied considerably from one institution to the next, thus limiting the relevance of the opinion. Also, as George Makdisi cautions: "One must avoid here the tendency to consider a fatwa as a statement of fact. It was merely a legal opinion; it may or may not have been put into execution."[14]

The Rise of the *Waqf* System Under the Mamluks

In spite of their pitfalls, our sources provide a pretty clear view of the process through which endowments became institutionalized as part of the Mamluk state and were transformed over time to accommodate changing conditions. Although private endowments had existed since the first centuries of Islam, it was not until the tenth and eleventh centuries that *waqf* was "first used by state officials as an instrument of policy, most notably in the case of the madrasas."[15] A turning point came during the Ayyubid period when Ṣalāḥ

[10] Khalīl b. Shāhīn al-Ẓāhirī, *Kitāb Zubdat kashf al-mamālik wa-bayān al-ṭuruq wa-l-masālik* (Cairo: Dār al-ʿArab li-l-Bustānī, 1988).

[11] Aḥmad b. ʿAlī al-Qalqashandī, *Ṣubḥ al-aʿshā fī ṣināʿat al-inshā*, 10 vols. (Cairo: al-Muʾassasa al-Miṣriyya al-ʿĀmma li-l-Taʾlīf wa-l-Tarjama wa-l-Ṭibāʿa wa-l-Nashr, 1964).

[12] Ulrich Haarmann, "Rather the Injustice of the Turks than the Righteousness of the Arabs: Changing *ʿUlamāʾ* Attitudes Towards Mamluk Rule in the Late Fifteenth Century," *Studia Islamica* 68 (1988): 63.

[13] Donald P. Little, "The Nature of *Khānqāhs*, *Ribāṭs* and *Zāwiyas* under the Mamlūks," in *Islamic Studies Presented to Charles J. Adams*, edited by Wael B. Hallaq and Donald P. Little (Leiden: Brill, 1991), 92–3. For an example of how such a document could be subverted, see also Little's "Notes on Mamluk Madrasahs," *Mamlūk Studies Review* 6 (2002): 9–20.

[14] George Makdisi, *The Rise of Colleges: Institutions of Higher Learning in Islam and the West* (Edinburgh: Edinburgh University Press, 1981), 37.

[15] Adam Sabra, *Poverty and Charity in Medieval Islam* (Cambridge, U.K.: Cambridge University Press, 2000), 70. For detailed information on the development and functions of the *madrasa* as an institution in Ayyubid and Mamluk Egypt, see Gary La Viere Leiser, *The Restoration of Sunnism in Egypt: Madrasas and Mudarrisūn, 495–647/1101–1249*, Ph.D. Diss. (University of Pennsylvania, 1976); and Robert Hunter Moore, *The Role of the* Madrasah *in The Structure of Islamic Legal Education in Mamluk Egypt (1250–1517)*, Ph.D. Diss. (Emory University, 2010).

al-Dīn endowed the first Sufi lodge (*khānqāh*) in Cairo in 569/1173.[16] Many historians suggest that Ṣalāḥ al-Dīn's interest in endowing Sunni educational institutions may have been linked with his desire to free Egypt from its Shiʿi Fatimid past and to promote Sunnism as the new state-sanctioned form of religion.[17] Even with the precedent set by the patronage of Ṣalāḥ al-Dīn and that of the Ayyubids in founding institutions like the *khānqāh*, it was "not until the Mamluks came to power that the institution underwent the full development that led to its complete acceptance by the religious class and its integration into Egyptian society."[18] Indeed, the Mamluk era (1250–1517) witnessed such a striking profusion of religious endowments that the historian al-Maqrīzī (d. 845/1441) devoted a large section of his *Khiṭaṭ* to an inventory of "several hundred" endowed institutions.[19]

Patronage of Scholars

With this proliferation of state-sponsored religious, social welfare, and educational institutions came a corresponding increase in what has been termed the 'institutionalization' or 'bureaucratization' of the *ʿulamāʾ* as a scholarly elite. Although the *ʿulamāʾ* had long valued their independence from the state authority, in the second half of the eleventh century, scholars started to lose some of their autonomy and became more closely involved in state institutions.[20] When this process of institutionalization increased in the twelfth and thirteenth centuries, the new patronage came to yield tangible benefits for those who agreed to participate: "permanent provision of special places of instruction, residence, and employment for a majority

[16] Fernandes, "The Foundation of Baybars," 22. See also part one in Hofer, *The Popularisation of Sufism in Ayyubid and Mamluk Egypt*, 35–102.

[17] Muḥammad Muḥammad Amīn, *al-Awqāf wa-l-ḥayāt al-ijtimāʿiyya fī Miṣr* (Cairo: Dār al-Nahḍa al-ʿArabiyya, 1980), 66. Eerik Dickinson also suggests that the Ayyubids, as non-Arabs, sought religious legitimacy through their numerous endowments and generous support of scholars like Ibn al-Ṣalāḥ. See his "Ibn al-Ṣalāḥ al-Shahrazūrī and the *Isnād*," *Journal of the American Oriental Society* 122:3 (2002): 481–505.

[18] Fernandes, "The Foundation of Baybars," 21.

[19] Carl Petry, "A Paradox of Patronage During the Later Mamluk Period," *The Muslim World* 73 (1983): 190. See Aḥmad b. ʿAlī al-Maqrīzī, *al-Mawāʿiẓ wa-l-iʿtibār fī dhikr al-khiṭaṭ wa-l-āthār*, 2 vols. (Cairo: Dār al-Ṭibāʿa al-Miṣriyya, 1853–54), 2:244–452.

[20] Michael Winter, "ʿUlamāʾ Between the State and Society in Pre-modern Sunni Islam," in *Guardians of the Faith in Modern Times: ʿUlamāʾ in the Middle East*, edited by Meir Hatina (Leiden: Brill, 2009), 25.

of scholars and lasting endowments to pay the salaries of the personnel and building costs."[21]

By the beginning of the Mamluk period, this system of state patronage had escalated to the point where "collaboration" between the state authority and religious notables had become the new norm.[22] As the following analysis will show, jurists came under increasing pressure to adapt to the circumstances of their times by allowing practices in the administration of *waqf* that would have seemed questionable at best to some of their predecessors. With the appointment of scholars to lucrative posts with fixed stipends proving such an effective mechanism of control and a "means of identifying the interests of pious circles with those of the ruling class,"[23] one might well question the motives behind the endowments. While piety and a desire to seek closeness to God (*qurba*) no doubt were motivating factors in many cases, it is difficult to explain the extraordinary proliferation of endowments that occurred during the Mamluk regime in purely religious terms.

Uses and Abuses of the *Waqf* System

The *waqf* system held certain practical advantages beyond the recognition that the founders received for serving the public good. Securing one's property in the form of an endowment ensured that one's heirs would have a share in that revenue and made it less likely that the estate would be confiscated and returned to the state after the death of the founder. As Petry observes, the policy of allotting fiefs to Mamluk officers temporarily in exchange for military service struck many Mamluks as a kind of usufruct that posed a "threat to their descendants' future prosperity, and they devised a variety of maneuvers to circumvent it—of which charitable trusts were the most reliable."[24]

[21] Joan E. Gilbert, "Institutionalization of Muslim Scholarship and Professionalization of the ʿ*Ulamāʾ* in Medieval Damascus," *Studia Islamica* 52 (1980): 114.

[22] Ira M. Lapidus, *Muslim Cities in the Later Middle Ages* (Cambridge, M.A.: Harvard University Press, 1967), 135.

[23] Donald P. Little, *History and Historiography of the Mamlūks* (London: Variorum Reprints, 1986), 172.

[24] Petry, "A Paradox of Patronage," 192. See also Sabra, *Poverty and Charity*, 5 and Makdisi, *Rise of Colleges*, 39.

Even as the system of patronage and endowments reached new heights during the Mamluk period, the old scholarly consensus of suspicion toward rulers never quite disappeared. In fact, the increase in funding and appointments granted to scholars by the state authorities eventually led to a kind of backlash in scholarly circles as the *ʿulamāʾ* struggled to come to terms with many competing interests. For example, "the availability of stipends in particular schools might lead to competition, sometimes fierce, between prospective students and teachers for succession to a lucrative post."[25]

Some scholars expressed indignation that practices once discouraged, such as collecting a salary from multiple posts in different institutions, buying and selling appointments, passing down appointments to one's sons, and appointing a substitute to carry out one's duties while still benefiting from the stipend, had all become routine by the fourteenth and fifteenth centuries (though still a source of some resentment). A scholar as respected and irreproachable as Ibn Ḥajar (d. 852/1449), for instance, was known to have held "well over a dozen" professorships during his career.[26] This state of affairs put jurists like al-Suyūṭī in the uncomfortable position of needing to justify what had become standard practice by his time, while explaining away any contradiction between his rulings and those of his earlier 'heroes' of the Shāfiʿī school, such as Ibn al-Ṣalāḥ, al-Nawawī, and ʿIzz al-Dīn b. ʿAbd al-Salām.[27]

The changing practices and the pressure to provide legal sanction for such activities contributed to a general atmosphere of anxiety and uncertainty during the later part of Mamluk rule. As Berkey points out, the "process of making appointments to paid teaching positions in academic institutions was in practice extremely fluid. Lines demarcating the limits of authority were not necessarily clear."[28] This unease within the scholarly community was reflected in society as a whole since the boundaries of authority were often

[25] Jonathan Berkey, *The Transmission of Knowledge in Medieval Cairo: A Social History of Islamic Education* (Princeton: Princeton University Press, 1992), 45.

[26] Berkey, *Transmission of Knowledge*, 45. R. Kevin Jaques examines Ibn Ḥajar's autobiographical reflections on his own highly successful career in *Ibn Hajar* (New Delhi: Oxford University Press, 2009). Interestingly, of all of his academic appointments, Ibn Ḥajar considered his post as "headmaster and financial controller" of the Baybarsiyya to be "his most important and cherished scholarly position" (Jaques, *Ibn Hajar*, 11).

[27] I will discuss this point in greater detail below.

[28] Berkey, *Transmission of Knowledge*, 106–7.

ambiguous. The economic decline under the Circassian Mamluks only exacerbated the "profound instability of the relations between the firmly corporate Mamluk elite, on the one hand, and the *ʿulamāʾ* class, on the other."[29]

Decline of the *Waqf* System

Even before the Circassian regime came to power in 784/1382, Egypt and Syria had suffered the ravages of the Black Death, which caused serious depopulation.[30] The debasement of the currency due to a shortage of silver coins and their replacement with copper dirhams only added to the instability and caused some stipends to lose much of their value.[31] To make matters worse, key industries in Egypt and Syria started to decline as European textiles and other goods came to dominate the markets.[32] Adam Sabra identifies the fifteenth century as a turning point in Egypt's economic history as "members of the Mamluk elite and their descendents privatized state resources, especially agricultural land, for their own benefit."[33] Land purchased in this way from the Treasury became a useful source of revenue for the owners and their descendents as it was converted into *waqf*, but was not as profitable for the state Treasury.

Thus, by the fifteenth century, the Mamluks increasingly were unable to finance expensive military campaigns with revenue from the Treasury, nor could they afford to continue living in the opulence and luxury to which many in the ruling class had become accustomed.[34] The shortage of revenue led naturally to changes in the way that institutions endowed with funds from the Treasury were administrated, which, in turn, had an effect on how jurists sought to rationalize such changes. It was in precisely this situation that al-Suyūṭī found himself in 1498.

[29] Haarmann, "Rather the Injustice of the Turks," 73.

[30] Eliyahu Ashtor, *A Social and Economic History of the Near East in the Middle Ages* (Berkeley: University of California Press, 1976), 301.

[31] Ashtor, *Social and Economic History*, 305. See also Sabra, *Poverty and Charity*, 11.

[32] Ashtor, *Social and Economic History*, 310. For a contemporary account of fluctuating prices and other economic concerns at the time of the Mamluks, see *Mamluk Economics: A Study and Translation of al-Maqrīzī's* Ighāthah, edited by Adel Allouche (Salt Lake City: University of Utah Press, 1994).

[33] Adam Sabra, "The Rise of a New Class? Land Tenure in Fifteenth-Century Egypt: A Review Article," *Mamlūk Studies Review* 8 (2004): 208.

[34] Little, *History and Historiography*, 167.

THE BAYBARSIYYA CONTROVERSY

Briefly, the crisis that beset the Baybarsiyya unfolded as follows: When the revenues of the institution fell into decline in the latter part of the fifteenth century, the Sufi residents of the *khānqāh* went to their shaykh, al-Suyūṭī, demanding that he intercede on their behalf and accusing him of neglecting his duties and of giving priority to some individuals over others in deciding how the stipends were to be disbursed. In a sharply worded letter, al-Suyūṭī responded that, if he were indeed showing favoritism, it was because many so-called Sufis in the institution were hardly worthy of the title, due to their low level of knowledge of the basic tenets of Sufism and, as such, were not entitled to stipends according to the stipulations of the endowment.[35]

Al-Suyūṭī reiterated his opinion, as he was wont to do, with three different legal treatises concerning the allotment of stipends,[36] in which he concludes that in times of need priority should be given to the shaykh by virtue of his learning, while those without such learning do not deserve an entitlement. Furthermore, a scholar should be entitled to his stipend from the Treasury regardless of whether or not he fulfills his stipulated duties. Unimpressed by these arguments, the Sufis of the Baybarsiyya threw their shaykh into a fountain and tried to convince the sultan that he should be killed. Al-Suyūṭī was dismissed from his position in the Baybarsiyya in 906/1501 and died four years later, having withdrawn from public life.

Al-Suyūṭī's cutting remarks about the paltry qualifications of some students were not entirely unjustified. It seems that by the fifteenth century, the Baybarsiyya was losing its stature and exclusivity as an institution of learning and devotion for Sufis, leading al-Maqrīzī to comment that "although worthy and scholarly people used to live there, they have gone, and now the *khānqāh* is occupied by insignificant people, shoemakers, and other common people."[37] As institutions became subject to economic hardship, standards began to slip, regardless of what was stipulated in the original endowment

[35] Arazi, "*Al-Risāla al-Baybarsiyya*," 347.

[36] The three treatises are *al-Inṣāf fī tamyīz al-awqāf* (the case study for this chapter), *Kashf al-ḍabāba fī masʾalat al-istināba*, and *al-Naql al-mastūr fī jawāz qabḍ al-maʿlūm maʿa ʿadam al-ḥuḍūr*. The first two are printed in *al-Ḥāwī li-l-fatāwī*, 1:150–7 and the third can be found in manuscript form (Egyptian National Library, Majāmiʿ Taymūr, 1).

[37] Sartain's translation, *Jalāl al-Dīn al-Suyūṭī*, 102. See al-Maqrīzī, *Khiṭaṭ*, 2:417.

deeds. For example, when faced with reductions in stipends, some Sufis sought positions outside the foundation. As Fernandes explains:

> To make money, other Sufis undertook the selling of their positions to outsiders, acting against the stipulations of the waqifs. As a result, khanqahs came to be filled by individuals who were for the most part unworthy of their positions. Added to this were the new practices of allowing Sufis to hold more than one position in different foundations, and the sharing of one position by two or more individuals within the same foundation.[38]

In his sweeping study of Sufism in the later Mamluk era, Éric Geoffroy remarks that the troubles that beset the Baybarsiyya lodge during al-Suyūṭī's tenure there as shaykh (891–906/1486–1501) were symptomatic of the rise and fall of the *khānqāh* as an institution.[39] By the end of the fifteenth century, the *khānqāh*'s decline was assured, as more endowments favored the less expensive *zāwiya*.[40] The decay that characterizes the institution of the *khānqāh* struck observers like al-Suyūṭī as a reflection of a broader decline in society in general and in the realm of scholarship in particular. In the end, even religious endowments were not immune from confiscation by state authorities, with or without legal sanction. Therefore, it is ironic that the same Mamluks who allowed Sufism to flourish with their support of the *khānqāh*, also, through fiscal irresponsibility, became the agents of its destruction.[41]

DISCOURSE AND POWER

Before engaging in an analysis of the texts, it is helpful to define what is meant by the term 'power relations' and its connection with the concept of discourse. Sociologists have long grappled with the notion of authority.

[38] Leonor Fernandes, *The Evolution of a Sufi Institution in Mamluk Egypt: The Khanqah* (Berlin: Klaus Schwarz Verlag, 1988), 44–5.

[39] Éric Geoffroy, *Le Soufisme en Égypte et en Syrie Sous les Derniers Mamelouks et les Premiers Ottomans: Orientations Spirituelles et Enjeux Culturels* (Damascus: Institut Français de Damas, 1995), 171.

[40] Fernandes, *Evolution of a Sufi Institution*, 111. The *zāwiya* tended to center around a particular shaykh, thus requiring a less extensive staff than the *khānqāh*. On differences between the *khānqāh, zāwiya*, and *ribāṭ* and how each institution changed over time, see Fernandes, *Evolution*, 18 and Amīn, *al-Awqāf*, 219; see also Little, "The Nature of *Khānqāhs*, *Ribāṭs* and *Zāwiyas* under the Mamlūks," 104–5.

[41] Geoffroy, *Soufisme en Égypte et en Syrie*, 175.

The sociologist Max Weber made an important contribution with his classification of authority as rational (legal), traditional, or charismatic.[42] Of particular interest to the field of religious studies is Weber's idea of the process through which an individual's charismatic authority is 'routinized' by a community of followers in order to preserve that authority for future generations. While Weber's approach is fruitful for looking at how authority functions within a community, it falls short of providing a mechanism with which to analyze the specific content of the leader's message.[43] The crucial link between the concept of power and the discourse that shapes it and is shaped by it can be found in the work of Michel Foucault.

For Foucault, 'power' is not an object in the sense that one either has it or one does not. Rather, power relations are observable in all social relations, which are, in turn, expressed in the form of discourse. As Elizabeth Castelli explains:

> Power may be analyzed by tracing its practice, it may be read in the processes by which it is articulated, but it may not be pinned down as a thing in itself. We can understand power by observing its workings, but we cannot grasp it as an object apart from its role in social relationships.[44]

Or, as Foucault puts it:

> [I]n a society such as ours, but basically in any society, there are manifold relations of power which permeate, characterize and constitute the social body, and these relations of power cannot themselves be established, consolidated nor implemented without the production, accumulation, circulation and functioning of a discourse.[45]

My intention here is not to explain Foucault's entire body of work in all of its complex and often convoluted aspects, but rather to understand how power relations function in the written word and practice of al-Suyūṭī by

[42] Sandra Hack Polaski, *Paul and the Discourse of Power* (Sheffield, England: Sheffield Academic Press, 1999), 28. Weber's theory is outlined in his *Economy and Society: An Outline of Interpretive Sociology*, 3 vols. (New York: Bedminster Press, 1968). See especially 1:215–51.

[43] Polaski, *Paul and the Discourse of Power*, 34.

[44] Elizabeth A. Castelli, *Imitating Paul: A Discourse of Power* (Louisville, Kentucky: Westminster/John Knox Press, 1991), 43.

[45] Michel Foucault, *Power/Knowledge: Selected Interviews and Other Writings 1972–1977*, edited by Colin Gordon (New York: Pantheon Books, 1980), 93.

asking a new set of questions.[46] The central question is not who is powerful and who powerless in a given society, but rather who has the authority to speak, or who controls the discourse. As Sandra Hack Polaski points out in her interesting analysis of how power relations function in the letters of the Apostle Paul:

> Discourse is less *what is said* than control over what *may be said*; control, that sometimes operates by repression or exclusion (such as censorship) but much more often operates in a positive mode, by making certain questions possible and their answers sensible, by encouraging the disciplines and institutions which in turn sustain the discourse, and by failing to generate the questions for which discourse has no answers.[47]

Thus, for Foucault, power is not merely a negative force but also a positive, productive one: "What makes power hold good, what makes it accepted, is simply the fact that it doesn't only weigh on us as a force that says no, but

[46] I am aware that a cursory treatment of Foucault's writing cannot hope to do justice to the enormous influence of his thought on research in the humanities and social sciences. As Foucault himself acknowledges, his work does not offer a comprehensive theory of power but rather a philosophical reflection on the strategies and mechanisms of power (*Power/Knowledge*, 51). For detailed analyses of Foucault's methodology, see Béatrice Han, *Foucault's Critical Project* (Stanford: Stanford University Press, 2002) and Colin Koopman, *Genealogy as Critique: Foucault and the Problems of Modernity* (Bloomington: Indiana University Press, 2013). Foucault's work advances discussions of power beyond individual agents or institutions or even economic structures and hierarchies (the focus of Marxist theories of power). As Saul Newman points out, Foucault's innovative notion that power pervades all social relations leaves unresolved the question of how one can resist relations of power (see Saul Newman, "New Reflections on the Theory of Power: A Lacanian Perspective," *Contemporary Political Theory* 3 (2004): 148–67). The important questions raised (but left unresolved) by Foucault in regards to agency, resistance, subject formation, and ethics have provided fertile ground to anthropologists interested in the ways in which women in Muslim societies negotiate power relations. A key example of such work is Lila Abu-Lughod's ethnographic study of the Awlād ʿAlī Bedouin in which she argues that local everyday forms of resistance are integral to local forms of power and that studying these forms of resistance can function as a kind of diagnostic with which to expose systems and structures of power in a particular society as it has changed over time (see Lila Abu-Lughod, "The Romance of Resistance: Tracing Transformations of Power Through Bedouin Women," *American Ethnologist* 17:1 (1990): 41–55). Saba Mahmood's groundbreaking work on the women's piety movement in Cairo draws on the writings of Foucault, Talal Asad, Judith Butler, and others to advance the discussion of power and agency even further. Mahmood challenges conceptualizations of agency that depend on subversion of existing norms and resistance to power relations and wonders if agency understood in terms of ethical formation might be more helpful in studying a group of people whose activism seems to defy liberal assumptions by seeking subordination to patriarchal norms rather than individual freedom as a primary goal. See Saba Mahmood, *Politics of Piety: The Islamic Revival and the Feminist Subject* (Princeton: Princeton University Press, 2005).

[47] Polaski, *Paul and the Discourse of Power*, 37 (emphasis in the original).

that it traverses and produces things, it induces pleasure, forms knowledge, produces discourse."[48]

Modern sociolinguistics, and in particular the subfield of Critical Discourse Analysis (or CDA), has added another perspective to the notion of discourse and power defined in terms of control. CDA tends to focus on the negative aspects of power, such as power abuse, and on how forms of injustice (racism, for example) are reproduced through discourse.[49] CDA does not, therefore, claim to be a 'neutral' science, and its practitioners express openly their desire to expose certain kinds of injustice as they appear in discourse and shape society, institutions, and even people's perceptions and opinions. Even so, CDA is grounded in the basic assumption that power can be detected through modes of discourse, i.e., through "text and talk."[50]

Those who control access to knowledge and information are able to effect change in society in ways in which those without such access cannot. It stands to reason that, in modern times, these knowledge brokers are usually part of an educated elite composed of journalists, politicians, and academics in their various disciplines. Van Dijk cautions, though, that these elites cannot work entirely independently from the patrons who maintain them. Scholarship needs sponsorship, after all. As van Dijk observes:

> Because, however, most of these elites are managed by the state or private corporations, they too have constraints on their freedom of articulation that emerge in various properties of their discourse. The voice of the elite is often the voice of the corporate or institutional master. The interests and ideologies of the elites are usually not fundamentally different from those who pay or support them.[51]

The link between scholarship as a form of "cultural capital" for educated elites and authority has not been lost on social historians of the Islamic world. Michael Chamberlain's *Knowledge and Social Practice in Medieval Damascus, 1190–1350*, for example, highlights ways in which elite households used knowledge as a means of securing and maintaining social status and power in a society that placed great value on learning as well as on the cultural practices associated with it. One area in which the struggle

[48] Foucault, *Power/Knowledge*, 119.
[49] Teun A. van Dijk, *Discourse and Power* (New York: Palgrave Macmillan, 2008), vii.
[50] Van Dijk, *Discourse and Power*, 63.
[51] Van Dijk, *Discourse and Power*, 32–3.

for social advancement and survival played out was in the competition over appointments (*manṣabs*) and the stipends or "monetized honors" that came with them.[52] Chamberlain argues that legal knowledge constituted just one aspect of a broad framework in which elites asserted power and prestige.[53]

This question of who controls the production of knowledge and 'truth,' on the one hand, and who provides the funding and means of support for scholars and their institutions, on the other, brings us back to the personal battles of al-Suyūṭī. The issue of how stipends and religious endowments were managed in fifteenth-century Cairo (and of the power relations behind these transactions) played out in al-Suyūṭī's writing and, in so doing, helped to shape his legal persona and identity. Al-Suyūṭī's own professional crisis comes at the tail end of a process in which religious endowments proliferated to a remarkable degree before sinking into inevitable decline as state revenues dwindled. The resulting conflict pitted different sectors of society against others in a power struggle to claim the same limited resources.

Analyzing Power Relations

One way to understand more fully the struggles within the Baybarsiyya during the later fifteenth century, as well as the larger conflicts within Mamluk society, is through the lens of power relations. Foucault writes that five factors must be taken into account when analyzing any given set of power relations:[54]

1. A system of differentiations
2. Objectives pursued by each of the actors
3. A means of bringing power relations into being
4. A system of institutionalization
5. Degrees of rationalization (or modes of argumentation)

My approach to al-Suyūṭī's legal opinion, *al-Inṣāf fī tamyīz al-awqāf*, is guided by these five factors. Specifically, I am interested in the discursive strategies

[52] Michael Chamberlain, *Knowledge and Social Practice in Medieval Damascus, 1190–1350* (Cambridge, U.K.: Cambridge University Press, 1994), 92.

[53] Chamberlain, *Knowledge and Social Practice*, 152.

[54] Michel Foucault, "The Subject and Power," in *Michel Foucault: Beyond Structuralism and Hermeneutics*, edited by Hubert L. Dreyfus and Paul Rabinow (Chicago: University of Chicago

that al-Suyūṭī employs in framing his arguments in order to get a clearer picture of how power functions in the text. Analyzing how power relations work in a text like *al-Inṣāf* will help to reveal not only what is going on in the text itself but also in its social and political context, or, in other words, the story behind the text.

ANALYSIS: AL-SUYŪṬĪ'S STIPEND FATWA

Question and Context of the Fatwa

The question setting up al-Suyūṭī's *al-Inṣāf fī tamyīz al-awqāf* reads as follows:

> An *amīr* endows a *khānqāh* and appoints a shaykh and Sufis to [the *khānqāh*], providing them money, oil, soap, bread and meat; then, the endowment becomes pressed [for revenue]: should the shaykh take precedence over the Sufis or should he distribute the funds amongst them in shares? Is [funding] restricted to any one of the ranks appointed by the founder and not the others, or is it given to all of the ranks appointed by the founder in shares? Is it permissible to make appointments [of deputies] to certain positions or not?[55]

The question is suggestive on a number of levels, both in regards to the complex circumstances facing institutions like the Baybarsiyya as well as to al-Suyūṭī's own concerns. First, while the query is phrased in general terms rather than in reference to a particular institution, it is noteworthy that the text specifies that the institution is a *khānqāh* housing Sufi residents (as opposed to a mosque, *madrasa*, or any other institution in which beneficiaries might receive salaries) and that the founder is an *amīr* (as Baybars al-Jāshankīr was, when the Baybarsiyya was founded).[56]

Fatwas are rarely based on hypothetical situations divorced from any real context, and this particular one is conveniently suited to fit the circumstances at the Baybarsiyya. Al-Suyūṭī includes *al-Inṣāf* in a list of disputes between him and al-Jawjarī (d. 889/1484), a merchant and scholar

Press, 1983), 221–4. Sandra Hack Polaski uses this framework in her analysis of Paul's letter to Philemon in *Paul and the Discourse of Power*, 59–72.

[55] Al-Suyūṭī, *al-Inṣāf*, 150. Translations from the fatwa are my own unless otherwise indicated.

[56] Fernandes, "The Foundation of Baybars," 24.

who shared many of the same professors but who frequently issued fatwas contradicting those of al-Suyūṭī.[57] Al-Suyūṭī no doubt composed the fatwa before al-Jawjarī's death and thus before his appointment as shaykh of the Baybarsiyya in 891/1486. However, since the fatwa fits the events of the Baybarsiyya incident so well, one should not exclude the possibility that al-Suyūṭī included the treatise after the incident to justify his claims.

The scenario presented in the fatwa is relevant to al-Suyūṭī's situation in other ways as well. Like many scholars of his day, al-Suyūṭī held multiple appointments simultaneously; there is evidence to suggest that even before adding the Baybarsiyya position, he was already receiving salaries as professor of *ḥadīth* at the Shaykhūniyya *madrasa* and as shaykh of Barqūq's tomb.[58] Sartain points out that al-Suyūṭī's posts at the mosque of Shaykhū and the Shaykhūniyya directly opposite it involved teaching, whereas his position as shaykh of Sufis at the Barqūq mausoleum and as supervisor at the Baybarsiyya appeared to be more administrative in nature.[59] After his appointment at the Baybarsiyya in 891/1486, when al-Suyūṭī was about forty-two years old, he entered a period of "semi-retirement" leading up to his complete withdrawal from public life in 906/1501.[60] Al-Suyūṭī's partial withdrawal took place after the scandal caused by his claims to be a *mujtahid* (scholar capable of independent legal reasoning) in 889/1484, but before his even more audacious claim to be the *mujaddid* (restorer of religion) for the ninth century around 896/1490–1491.

Sartain speculates that, during his semi-retirement, al-Suyūṭī may have retained his posts at the Shaykhūniyya and Shaykhū's mosque and "perhaps appointed a deputy to teach in his place, as was commonly done."[61] If al-Suyūṭī did appoint deputies for these posts, they presumably would have received his salary as well (though this point is not clear). Most importantly for the Sufis of the Baybarsiyya, however, is the fact that, after his appointment there as shaykh, al-Suyūṭī did not attend to the management of funds from the *waqf*, allowing the payment of stipends to lapse and tensions among the Sufis to increase.

[57] Jalāl al-Dīn al-Suyūṭī, *al-Taḥadduth bi-niʿmat Allāh*, edited by E.M. Sartain (Cambridge, U.K.: Cambridge University Press, 1975), 2:189.

[58] Sartain, *Jalāl al-Dīn al-Suyūṭī*, 81.

[59] Sartain, *Jalāl al-Dīn al-Suyūṭī*, 44–5.

[60] Sartain, *Jalāl al-Dīn al-Suyūṭī*, 82.

[61] Sartain, *Jalāl al-Dīn al-Suyūṭī*, 82.

While *al-Inṣāf* appears to anticipate the Baybarsiyya controversy, it also speaks to issues of the time—such as appointing deputies, holding multiple posts, and receiving a salary while not fulfilling one's duties—issues that may have had a direct bearing on al-Suyūṭī's situation. Sartain concludes that the dating of *al-Inṣāf* and *al-Naql al-mastūr* makes it unlikely that al-Suyūṭī was

> defending something that he stood to gain by at that stage. Nevertheless, the theory can be applied so beautifully to his position once he had ceased to teach that one is very tempted to suggest that, putting his theory into practice, he sought to continue taking salaries from the Shaykhūniyyah and from Shaykhū's Mosque even though he had given up teaching there.[62]

Overview of the Fatwa

To summarize the contents of the fatwa: Al-Suyūṭī begins by setting up a distinction between two types of endowment. The first type concerns the property of an individual (not a state official such as a Mamluk *amīr*) and for this type of endowment the founder's stipulations must not be violated. The second kind of endowment is linked to the state Treasury because the founder is a sultan or *amīr* whose property originates with the state.

The second type of endowment flourished during the Ayyubid and Mamluk periods. In fact, al-Suyūṭī claims, the Mamluk *amīr*s are themselves slaves belonging to the state, so any property that they own and any endowment that they establish automatically receive funding from the state. By virtue of their learning, scholars are entitled to draw stipends from these 'public' endowments even if they do not conform to the stipulations in the endowment. Since scholars had become accustomed to receiving special earmarks from the state since the time of ʿUmar b. al-Khaṭṭāb (d. 23/644), they regarded endowments established after the seventh and eighth centuries AH as replacing these earlier payments. A student is eligible for this funding so long as he is engaged in learning, and regardless of whether or not he actually attends classes. Stipends made to scholars from the Treasury

[62] Sartain, *Jalāl al-Dīn al-Suyūṭī*, 86. The third treatise, *Kashf al-ḍabāba*, was probably written after the other two since it refers to other works that al-Suyūṭī wrote on the same subject. This treatise complements *al-Inṣāf* with a fuller discussion of the appointment of deputies and a brief summary of the main points from *al-Inṣāf* regarding stipends.

through 'public' endowments should be regarded as earmarks or grants rather than as a wage earned in exchange for services rendered.

Similarly, for the second type of endowment, it is possible to appoint one's son to an endowed position as well as to give priority to the shaykh's stipend over that of other beneficiaries. In times of financial strain, stipends can be prioritized in some cases and restricted in others, based on the recipient's degree of learning and need relative to that of other ranks of beneficiaries. Since the rules concerning this second type of endowment are more lenient, the judgments of later jurists are made in consideration of the needs of their time and are not in contradiction to the opinions of earlier jurists.

DIFFERENTIATION

Three Groups: The State Official, the Scholar, and the Sufi Student

By examining the power relations articulated in *al-Inṣāf*, I hope to analyze al-Suyūṭī's motives in producing the text as well as to discover how he perceives the role of the jurist relative to other actors. The crux of al-Suyūṭī's argument lies in the system of differentiations established by the author. The question (*istiftāʾ*) introduces a series of distinctions even before al-Suyūṭī launches into his response. The *istiftāʾ* distinguishes between three distinct groups: the *amīr* who founded the institution, the shaykh, and the Sufis who receive stipends from the endowment. The *mustaftī* demands to know which takes precedence: the stipulations intended by the founder, the rights of the shaykh in claiming priority for payment, or the Sufis who expect to receive a share of the benefits?

In his answer, al-Suyūṭī must address one more distinction before considering the interests of each of the three groups. As noted above, the distinction is between two types of *waqf*: 'private' endowments that do not receive funds from the Treasury and 'public' ones that do because the founder is either a caliph or a ruler of the Ayyubid or Mamluk states.[63] For the first type

[63] Al-Suyūṭī does not use the Arabic terms for 'private' and 'public'; I have added them to clarify the point (see *al-Inṣāf*, 150). The two types are sometimes referred to as 'family' *waqf* (*ahlī* or *dhurrī*) and 'charitable' *waqf* (*khayrī*).

of endowment, the stipulations of the founder must be stringently observed, whereas for the second the rules are more flexible, according to al-Suyūṭī. Al-Suyūṭī introduces the distinction as follows:

> I say first of all (and may God grant success): Endowments are of two kinds: [For] one kind, income does not come from the Treasury. This [kind of] endowment is based on strictness and vigilance; it is not permitted to take even a little bit from [its income] without adhering to what the founder has stipulated, because it is the property of an individual and nothing can be taken out of it except in a specific manner according to the stipulations mentioned. [For] the [second] kind, income comes from the Treasury because the founder is a caliph or one of the past monarchs, such as Ṣalāḥ al-Dīn b. Ayyūb and his relatives, or it receives funding from the Treasury because it is the endowment of one of the *amīrs* of the Qalāwūn state and of those who came after them up until our present day.[64]

In his classic and thorough study of endowments during the Mamluk era, Muḥammad Amīn cautions that there was, in fact, a third type of *waqf* that combines the strictly private and the public charitable endowment.[65] As noted, Mamluk *amīrs* would ensure that, even in the case of charitable endowments that benefit public welfare, provisions were in place that would give the founder's descendants a fixed share and priority in claiming any surplus revenues. In *al-Inṣāf*, al-Suyūṭī conveniently sidesteps the issue of the founder's descendants in the case of endowments that receive funding from the Treasury.

The Entitlements of the Founder

Having introduced the crucial distinction between private and public *waqfs*, al-Suyūṭī proceeds to address the claims of each of the three groups. He turns first to the rights of the founder, who, in this case, is one of the Mamluk *amīrs*. It is here that the mufti launches into what might seem at first to be a bizarre digression from the matter at hand. He states that one reason that an endowment created by an *amīr* receives funding from the Treasury is that the *amīrs* are themselves property of the state as slaves, with the

[64] Al-Suyūṭī, *al-Inṣāf*, 150.
[65] Amīn, *al-Awqāf*, 72–3 and Berkey, *Transmission of Knowledge*, 134.

result that everything that they own also belongs to the Treasury. He adds that there is some disagreement amongst jurists as to whether or not slaves belonging to the Treasury can be manumitted. Tāj al-Dīn al-Subkī (d. 771/1370), for example, says that they can be freed, provided that the Treasury receives monetary compensation for the loss, whereas ʿIzz al-Dīn b. ʿAbd al-Salām (d. 659/1261) was strongly opposed to their manumission. Al-Suyūṭī concludes that it is not in the public interest to free Mamluks belonging to the Treasury.[66]

Sartain comments on the obvious oddness of al-Suyūṭī's argument. He seems to be making a "purely academic point," since it was normal procedure to free Mamluks after they had completed their training.[67] What then could be the reason for this somewhat unusual argument on the part of al-Suyūṭī? The reference to the great Shāfiʿī jurist and Sufi master, ʿIzz al-Dīn b. ʿAbd al-Salām, may provide a clue. For al-Suyūṭī, ʿIzz al-Dīn represents the ideal scholar activist (*ʿālim ʿāmil*), accomplished in learning and pious in action.[68] The life of ʿIzz al-Dīn, presented glowingly by Tāj al-Dīn al-Subkī in his *Ṭabaqāt al-shāfiʿiyya*[69] and by al-Suyūṭī in his *Ḥusn al-muḥāḍara fī akhbār Miṣr wa-l-Qāhira*,[70] contains many actions worthy of emulation. In addition to denying the Mamluk *amīr*s the right to free themselves from the Treasury, he also censured Sultan al-Ṣāliḥ Ismāʿīl for surrendering territory to the Franks, and he refused to allow the *amīr* Quṭuz to extract money from the populace to finance his campaign against the Mongols.[71] As a result of his protests, this "sultan of scholars"—as he was called by his student, Ibn Daqīq al-ʿĪd—endured imprisonment and exile.[72]

[66] Al-Suyūṭī, *al-Inṣāf*, 150–1.

[67] Sartain, *Jalāl al-Dīn al-Suyūṭī*, 85. Berkey confirms that, after finishing their training, the Mamluks "were freed, and entered the service of the government, or of particular Mamluks within it, in a variety of military and political capacities. From their number were drawn the sultan, who wielded considerable authority, and the amirs (military officers) of varying ranks who held the chief positions of government." See Berkey, *Transmission of Knowledge*, 10.

[68] Jean-Claude Garcin, "Histoire, Opposition Politique et Piétisme Traditionaliste dans le *Ḥusn al-Muḥāḍarat* [sic] de Suyūṭī," *Espaces, Pouvoirs et Idéologies de l'Egypte Médiévale* (London: Variorum Reprints, 1987), 78.

[69] Tāj al-Dīn al-Subkī, *al-Ṭabaqāt al-shāfiʿiyya al-kubrā*, 10 vols. (Giza: Hajr, 1992), 8:209–55.

[70] Jalāl al-Dīn al-Suyūṭī, *Ḥusn al-muḥāḍara fī akhbār Miṣr wa-l-Qāhira*, 2 vols. (Cairo: ʿĪsā al-Bābī al-Ḥalabī, 1967–1968), 1:314–16 and 2:161–3.

[71] Garcin, "Opposition Politique," 75.

[72] Al-Subkī, *al-Ṭabaqāt al-shāfiʿiyya*, 8:243.

Sultan vs. Scholar

The image of the courageous and virtuous scholar who challenges the corrupt power of the sultan is a trope in Islamic literature, especially during the 7th/13th and 8th/14th centuries. Usually, a ruler would try to appropriate funds through unjust taxation or confiscation of property (including *waqf*) to pay for his expensive military campaigns, only to be rebuffed by the righteous figure of the scholar; the ruler then either recognizes his error and backs down, or else is punished by God (often in the form of illness or other calamity). Examples of such scholars who figure prominently in al-Suyūṭī's frame of reference include al-Nawawī, ʿIzz al-Dīn b. ʿAbd al-Salām, Ibn Daqīq al-ʿĪd, and Sirāj al-Dīn al-Bulqīnī.[73] On the other side of this equation is the enduring suspicion against allowing oneself as a scholar to become co-opted by the ruling classes as a result of desire for worldly rewards. Indeed, al-Suyūṭī devotes an entire treatise to this subject.[74]

One wonders why the ruling classes bothered to solicit the approval of scholars in the first place. Clearly, the Mamluk rulers felt the need to have their authority and legitimacy recognized by the scholarly elite and, by extension, the populace. As non-Arab military officers who began their careers as slaves, the Mamluks endeavored to compensate for their questionable legitimacy in religious circles by appointing a "puppet caliph,"[75] by offering scholars attractive teaching positions and judgeships, and by spending lavish amounts of money from the Treasury on charitable foundations and stipends. At the same time, Mamluk officials were not above imposing harsh measures, such as arbitrary taxes and outright confiscation of property, measures that Petry describes as a "paradox of patronage."[76]

In the power struggle between the *umarāʾ* (rulers) and *ʿulamāʾ* (scholars), neither group sought complete dominance; the overriding attitude was one of ambivalence rather than hostility. There is evidence to suggest that some rulers did respond to the "spiritual power perceived to be vested in

[73] For a detailed account of the opposition of these and other scholars to efforts to confiscate *waqf*, see Amīn, *al-Awqāf*, 323–72.

[74] Jalāl al-Dīn al-Suyūṭī, *Mā rawāhu al-asāṭīn fī ʿadam al-majīʾ ilā al-salāṭīn* (Beirut: Dār Ibn Ḥazm, 1992).

[75] Haarmann, "Rather the Injustice of the Turks," 62.

[76] Petry, "A Paradox of Patronage," 182.

the religious classes," the Ayyubid monarch Ṣalāḥ al-Dīn being a shining example.[77] Also, in spite of the stereotypes, Mamluk officers were not, on the whole, boorish cretins with no appreciation for learning and high culture. Many Mamluks took an interest in religious learning and some even became respected scholars in their own right (despite the fact that Arabic was not their first language).[78] As Berkey points out, "Regardless of the success or lack thereof of their intellectual endeavors, the decision of individual Mamluks to endow institutions of learning must be seen against this background, as a gesture of an individual to an academic world in which, in some limited but meaningful way, he had shared."[79]

Scholar vs. Sufis

In spite of any grudging respect that al-Suyūṭī may have had toward individual Mamluks, the distinction he makes in the fatwa makes it clear which group is the favored one. Whereas Mamluk *amīrs* do not have the right to purchase their freedom from the Treasury, scholars are always entitled to support from the Treasury by virtue of their learning, even if they do not fulfill their stipulated duties. As for the third group, the Sufis, al-Suyūṭī explains their role in terms of another distinction, that between 'real' Sufis worthy of their stipend and 'fake' Sufis unqualified to receive such an entitlement.

The deciding factor for al-Suyūṭī in determining who is most deserving of endowment funds is active engagement in learning (*al-ishtighāl bi-l-ʿilm*) and not mere attendance (*ḥuḍūr*) of lectures.[80] A student can be in attendance but not actually learning; by the same token, he can be engaged in acquiring knowledge even while not physically present. Al-Suyūṭī does not consider stipends paid out of public funds to students and teachers as a remuneration for services rendered (*al-ijāra*). Rather, this type of payment falls under the category of maintenance or grants (*al-arṣād wa-l-arzāq*) for those who

[77] T. Emil Homerin, "Sufis and their Detractors in Mamluk Egypt: A Survey of Protagonists and Institutional Settings," in *Islamic Mysticism Contested*, edited by Frederick De Jong and Bernd Radtke (Leiden: Brill, 1999), 230.

[78] Berkey, *Transmission of Knowledge*, 147.

[79] *Transmission of Knowledge*, 160.

[80] Makdisi presents a useful explanation of the difference between *ishtighāl* and *ḥuḍūr*. See his *Rise of Colleges*, 207–9.

benefit society through their scholarship.[81] Furthermore, al-Suyūṭī contends that such 'earmarks' had been set aside for scholars since the reign of ʿUmar b. al-Khaṭṭāb (r. 634–644) up to the time of the Caliph al-Mustaʿṣim (r. 1242–1258). Therefore, scholars came to regard endowments from public funds as replacing yearly payments that had been made in the past but that had been discontinued.[82] Still, the fact remains that some residents of the Baybarsiyya who expected a handout did not, in al-Suyūṭī's view, meet the requirement of learning that would qualify them to receive such funding.

Al-Suyūṭī is certainly not alone in criticizing the poor academic standards of Sufis in *khānqāh*s during the late Mamluk period. For example, Tāj al-Dīn al-Subkī was known for his strict reproof of 'fake' Sufis who take advantage of the institution for worldly ends. In his *Muʿīd al-niʿam wa-mubīd al-niqam*, he states clearly that any person who comes to the *khānqāh* in pursuit of material gain rather than devotion to God and retreat from worldly desires is forbidden from benefiting from an endowment designated for Sufis, since he does not qualify as one.[83]

Al-Subkī's *Muʿīd al-niʿam* describes what the 8th/14th-century author thinks are laudable and contemptible qualities in a broad range of public figures, from the sultan and his underlings to the beggar in the street. This work suggests that when a writer like al-Suyūṭī distinguishes between *amīr*s, scholars, and Sufis he does so for polemical purposes, whereas, in reality, the situation was more complex. The ruling power was represented not only by the sultan himself but also by a vast staff of bureaucrats. The title of 'Sufi' was clearly contested. Even the educated elite or *ʿulamāʾ* were "not a distinct class, but a category of persons overlapping other classes and social divisions, permeating the whole of society."[84]

[81] Here, al-Suyūṭī appears to agree with the Ḥanbalī jurists Ibn Taymiyya (d. 728/1328) and Abū Yaʿlā (d. 458/1065). See Makdisi, *Rise of Colleges*, 58.

[82] According to Sartain, al-Suyūṭī qualifies this statement in *al-Naql al-mastūr*, saying that "scholars did not receive anything from the public treasury in Umayyad and ʿAbbasid times, unless they frequented the *wazīr* or caliph and did what they asked, and most scholars refused to do this. Later, Nūr al-dīn b. Zangī and Ṣalāḥ al-dīn b. Ayyūb began to set aside properties belonging to the public treasury to provide for scholars, students, Ṣūfīs, poor people, and others." See *Jalāl al-Dīn al-Suyūṭī*, 85–6.

[83] Tāj al-Dīn al-Subkī, *Muʿīd al-niʿam wa-mubīd al-niqam* (Cairo: Maktabat al-Khānjī, 1993), 125. See also Makdisi, *Rise of Colleges*, 177–9 and Geoffroy, *Soufisme en Égypte et en Syrie*, 170–1.

[84] Lapidus, *Muslim Cities*, 108.

OBJECTIVES

The second factor required by Foucault when analyzing power relations in discourse is the objectives of the actors involved. The answer to the obvious question—did al-Suyūṭī have anything material to gain from his rulings on endowment funds?—is far from clear in *al-Inṣāf*. As mentioned, in his personal life al-Suyūṭī did face issues that may have had a bearing on his motives, such as giving priority to some ranks over others in the disbursement of stipends and the appointment of successors or deputies to public posts.

In his letter to the Sufis of the Baybarsiyya, al-Suyūṭī defends himself from suspicions regarding his personal motivations and attempts to find alternative explanations for his attitude and behavior. First, he acknowledges that there was a period during which he did not attend to the affairs of the Sufis because he saw disagreements and conflicts of interest amongst them, but he knew that by acting according to the law that it would anger a lot of people because the 'Truth' (*al-ḥaqq*) can be bitter.[85] Al-Suyūṭī explains that he was faced with a choice: He could either please people by giving them what they wanted (stipends in equal shares), or he could do what is right in accordance with the Law (*al-sharᶜ*).

The Scholar Represents the Law

In what is a relatively short letter, al-Suyūṭī mentions several times that his actions regarding the disbursement of funds at the Baybarsiyya were carried out in adherence to the Law and the Sunna. At times, al-Suyūṭī's interpretation of the Law trumps even the stipulations set down in the endowment deed. For example, he says that he is well within his rights, as stipulated in the *waqf* deed, to collect his entire salary as shaykh even during times of economic hardship, but he did not do so. Furthermore, if he had chosen to treat the residents according to the stipulations of the founder, that would have harmed many of them, since the founder specified that the money go to Sufis and the majority do not fit that description. If most of them were asked

[85] Arazi, "*Al-Risāla al-Baybarsiyya*," 344.

twenty questions about the basic tenets of Sufism, they would not even have an answer, much less a detailed understanding of the issues.[86] If the Sufis are not prepared to accept his judgment about whose stipends should be given priority and whose delayed, and if they are not prepared to treat him and his representative with respect and decorum, then they should not blame him if he neglects their interests and delegates the matter to someone else.[87]

Al-Suyūṭī insists that his main objective in this affair is to respect the Law and honor knowledge and people of learning. No manner of attack or insult could persuade him to act against the Law. There have always been scholars who resolve to keep the law and uphold the Sunna, even if it means defying the rulers, without regard for opposition. After all, when the shaykh ʿIzz al-Dīn b. ʿAbd al-Salām performed his great acts of resistance on his own and without support from any helper except God, could anyone harm him?[88] Again, the reference to this paragon of Sufi scholarly resistance to despotism, ʿIzz al-Dīn b. ʿAbd al-Salām, is telling of al-Suyūṭī's desire to emulate this important figure.

I would argue, therefore, that al-Suyūṭī's main objective in his writing regarding *waqf* and the Baybarsiyya is moral rather than material in nature. By casting himself as the voice of the Law (*al-sharʿ*) and of the Sunna, al-Suyūṭī claims the right to interpret the will of God in this situation, and it is his knowledge (*ʿilm*) that gives him the moral authority to do so. Furthermore, al-Suyūṭī shows himself to be blameless of any wrongdoing.

The Scholar Controls the Discourse

This use of power on the part of al-Suyūṭī touches on one of the fundamental questions posed by Critical Discourse Analysis (CDA): Who can speak? The scholar, al-Suyūṭī, controls the means of discursive production in this case because he is the one writing the fatwas. We hear from the Sufis only through al-Suyūṭī's representation of their position in his letter and fatwa, and from Ibn Iyās's description of the physical act of throwing their shaykh in a fountain. By denying that the Sufis have knowledge, al-Suyūṭī effectively denies them a voice in the debate, since only scholars can issue fatwas.

86 Arazi, "*Al-Risāla al-Baybarsiyya*," 347.
87 Arazi, "*Al-Risāla al-Baybarsiyya*," 348.
88 Arazi, "*Al-Risāla al-Baybarsiyya*," 345.

MEANS OF BRINGING POWER RELATIONS INTO BEING

As the voice of moral authority in the Baybarsiyya controversy and *waqf* dispute, al-Suyūṭī's means of realizing this authority are primarily persuasive. Unlike the ruler, who has the threat of force at his disposal, al-Suyūṭī must rely on his ability to influence social formation through language. As a jurist, the source of al-Suyūṭī's persuasive power is his degree of learning and ability to interpret the law. While it must be remembered that a fatwa is a non-binding opinion, it carries the moral weight of its author's reputation as a privileged knower and speaker. When a jurist like al-Suyūṭī issues a fatwa, he is taking part in an ongoing negotiation of meaning. In order to be considered authoritative, his opinion must take into account the opinions of respected jurists who came before him and should anticipate future developments as well. At the same time, a legal opinion must be relevant to the current social context in which it is produced in order to be effective.

Putting Knowledge into Action

As al-Suyūṭī makes clear, possessing knowledge and keeping it to oneself does not give one authority as a jurist. The simple possession of knowledge is not sufficient to command authority. Rather, this knowledge must be expressed through authoritative forms of discourse (such as fatwas) and then realized through lived experience.

Al-Suyūṭī identifies with ʿIzz al-Dīn b. ʿAbd al-Salām, for example, as someone who embodies the ideal persona of the jurist both through his level of knowledge (*ʿilm*) and through his practice and action in society (*ʿamal*). It is al-Suyūṭī's firm belief, as articulated in his writing, that the jurist's duty is to uphold the Law, even if it puts him at odds with the ruler. As Khaled Abou El Fadl explains: "Muslim jurists' rhetorical and moral power was grounded in the fact that they could plausibly argue that ruler and ruled are normatively bound by God's law. The legitimacy of any political or social institution should and must be evaluated according to its compliance with God's law."[89]

[89] Khaled Abou El Fadl, *Speaking in God's Name: Islamic Law, Authority and Women* (Oxford: Oneworld Publications, 2001), 13.

One example of how al-Suyūṭī uses power is his stubborn refusal to go up to the Citadel to collect his stipend. After arguing at great length in *al-Inṣāf* and in his other treatises on endowments that scholars are entitled to their stipends from the Treasury by virtue of their learning, al-Suyūṭī deliberately angered Sultan Qāytbāy by refusing to make the trip to the Citadel to collect his own stipend. Al-Suyūṭī's student, al-Shādhilī, records that Qāytbāy sent multiple envoys to the shaykh to try to persuade him to change his mind. All of these efforts were rebuffed.[90]

Al-Suyūṭī justifies his refusal to meet with Qāytbāy by arguing that he is following the practice of early Muslims who avoided visiting kings except when absolutely necessary. Al-Suyūṭī composed his *Mā rawāhu al-asāṭīn fī ʿadam al-majīʾ ilā al-salāṭīn* as a reproach to the Sultan and made a point of resigning from his post of shaykh at Barqūq's tomb (an endowment linked to Qāytbāy). Meanwhile, the Sultan's rancor was kindled further by another one of al-Suyūṭī's enemies, Ibn al-Karakī, who tried to convince the ruler to punish the shaykh for his insolence. Luckily for al-Suyūṭī, Qāytbāy became ill and died in 901/1496, thus defusing what could have been a dangerous situation.

Sartain interprets this incident as another example of al-Suyūṭī's firm belief in the soundness of his argument and conviction that God would protect him against danger. Indeed, al-Suyūṭī argued that the fire in the Citadel and Qāytbāy's illness were "punishments inflicted by God upon the sultan for his treatment of him," and thus, "it would seem that his enormous self-confidence, so far from being shaken, was actually bolstered by this episode."[91] Notwithstanding the inconvenience of leaving his studies to go up to the Citadel every month, al-Suyūṭī seems to have resented the expectation that a scholar like himself would collect his payment like any other employee of the state.[92] No doubt al-Suyūṭī's unwillingness to collect his own salary also had an effect on the stipends of the Sufis at the Baybarsiyya, though he does suggest that the Sultan continued to pay them even while

[90] Sartain provides a translation of al-Shādhilī's abridgement of al-Suyūṭī's account of this episode in *Jalāl al-Dīn al-Suyūṭī*, 87–90.

[91] Sartain, *Jalāl al-Dīn al-Suyūṭī*, 91.

[92] Sartain, *Jalāl al-Dīn al-Suyūṭī*, 90–1.

withholding his salary.[93] Sartain concludes from this episode that al-Suyūṭī's "refusal to call upon Qāytbāy at the beginning of every month is more likely to have been regarded as stubborn arrogance than as an example of pious humility; certainly al-Suyūṭī's fellow scholars seem to have had no such scruples about keeping on good terms with the sultan, or receiving money from his hands."[94]

It is worth nothing that even though al-Suyūṭī's stubbornness caused him to run afoul of three different sultans, he had no such conflict when it came to the caliph.[95] He was on especially good terms with al-Mutawakkil (r. 1479–1497) who had been a student of al-Suyūṭī's father. It was al-Mutawakkil who allegedly facilitated his appointment as shaykh of the Baybarsiyya[96] and who later attempted to reinstate the position of chief judge (*qāḍī al-quḍāt*) to accommodate al-Suyūṭī, though he was forced to abandon the plan due to the outcry and opposition of the scholarly community.[97] It is likely that al-Suyūṭī's frustrated ambition to seize control of the Egyptian judiciary colored his view of the role of the scholar in relation to the state. Certainly, it was easier for al-Suyūṭī to claim moral superiority as a scholar independent of material and political interests than to acknowledge his own failed attempts to exploit the caliph's favor for his personal gain.

Objective Achieved

Al-Suyūṭī's moral objective to cast himself as a pious scholar uncorrupted by worldly rewards and to live out this role through practice was not a complete failure, however. Another one of al-Suyūṭī's students, ʿAbd al-Wahhāb al-Shaʿrānī (d. 973/1565), presents an admiring biography of his shaykh in

93 Sartain, *Jalāl al-Dīn al-Suyūṭī*, 88.

94 Sartain, *Jalāl al-Dīn al-Suyūṭī*, 91.

95 The Mamluks under al-Ẓāhir Baybars reinstated the ʿAbbasid line of caliphs after its destruction by the Mongols in an attempt to bolster the religious legitimacy of their military regime. As Jonathan Berkey observes, though, the attempt was "a mere feint, a gesture to past political realities: their caliphate was not widely recognized as legitimate outside the Mamluk realm, and even within played at best a marginal political role," *The Formation of Islam: Religion and Society in the Near East, 600–1800* (New York: Cambridge University Press, 2003), 210.

96 ʿAbd al-Raḥmān al-Sakhāwī, *al-Ḍawʾ al-lāmiʿ*, 12 vols. (Cairo: Maktabat al-Qudsī, 1934–6), 4:69. See also Garcin, "Opposition Politique," 36.

97 Al-Sakhāwī, *al-Ḍawʾ al-lāmiʿ*, 37 and Sartain, *Jalāl al-Dīn al-Suyūṭī*, 91–4. The incident is recorded in Ibn Iyās, *Badāʾiʿ al-zuhūr*, 3:339.

which he reiterates the information from al-Shādhilī's account and adds a positive spin to the controversies described, including the Baybarsiyya incident. He writes approvingly of al-Suyūṭī's refusal to seek favor from the sultan, especially after his full retirement from public life in 906/1501. At this time, the new sultan, Qānṣūh al-Ghawrī (r. 906–922/1501–1516), tried to convince him to accept honorary posts and gifts of money but al-Suyūṭī turned down all offers.[98] Al-Shaʿrānī warns that those who have tried to persecute scholars and saints often suffer a painful death, implying that this was the case with al-ʿĀdil Ṭūmānbāy (whose death al-Suyūṭī predicted to the day).[99]

INSTITUTIONALIZATION AND RATIONALIZATION

The fourth characteristic of power relations outlined by Foucault is that of institutionalization, which can take the form of a family, a government, a legal system, or some other structure with its own set of regulations and hierarchy. As a jurist, al-Suyūṭī positions himself as part of the formidable institution of Islamic law as it had developed over the centuries. When al-Suyūṭī claims to represent 'the Law' (*al-sharʿ*) and the Sunna, this is what he means. The legal structure demands that the individual jurist frame his opinion within the bounds established by earlier generations of jurists according to a hierarchy and using a particular methodology and set of stylistic conventions. In other words, the various modes of argumentation are an integral part of the system itself. It is for this reason that I have grouped together Foucault's fourth and fifth factors, institutionalization and rationalization, because in the context of *iftāʾ* one cannot exist without the other. With these factors in mind, I will take a closer look at the legal arguments in al-Suyūṭī's *Inṣāf*.

[98] ʿAbd al-Wahhāb al-Shaʿrānī, *al-Ṭabaqāt al-ṣughrā* (Cairo: Maktabat al-Thaqāfa al-Dīniyya, 2005), 17–18.

[99] Al-Suyūṭī's reputation as Sufi saint receives additional support in al-Shaʿrānī's account of the miracles that he is said to have performed, such as seeing visions of the Prophet while awake, traveling from Cairo to Mecca instantaneously, and predicting the fall of Egypt to the Ottomans in 923/1517. See al-Shaʿrānī, *al-Ṭabaqāt al-ṣughrā*, 15–17. On the miracles attributed to al-Suyūṭī, see further Geoffroy, *Soufisme en Égypte et en Syrie*, 296–7.

'Public' vs. 'Private' *Waqf*

One can learn much about the power relations surrounding the administration of endowments during al-Suyūṭī's time by closely examining how these power relations are institutionalized and justified through argumentation in a text like *al-Inṣāf*. As noted, al-Suyūṭī's legal argument hinges on his distinction between two kinds of *waqf*: those in which funds do not originate from the Treasury and those in which they do. For the first type, the stipulations of the founder must be strictly followed in all cases, whereas for the second type, the stipulations can be handled more leniently, especially during times of economic hardship. Al-Suyūṭī says that he is not alone in making this distinction; Walī al-Dīn al-ʿIrāqī made a similar distinction regarding the issue of transferring an appointment to one's son and al-Adhraʿī may have preceded him in that view. Furthermore, al-Bulqīnī argued during the council conducted by al-Ẓāhir Barqūq that students and teachers are entitled to funds from the Treasury.[100]

However, it is clear from al-Suyūṭī's rhetoric in *al-Inṣāf* that the legality of an endowment created by a sultan with funds from the Treasury was not a foregone conclusion but was, rather, a topic of debate among earlier jurists.[101] For example, al-Nawawī argues that a sultan may purchase land from the Treasury and use it to endow a foundation such as a school or hospital, because the Treasury serves the benefit of Muslims (*li-maṣāliḥ al-muslimīn*).[102] As Amīn points out, this precedent allowed later sultans, like Qāytbāy, to take advantage of their access to funds belonging to the Treasury, including using state holdings to create special earmarks for scholars.[103] Naturally, it was in the scholars' interest to approve such a move.

[100] Al-Suyūṭī, *al-Inṣāf*, 151.

[101] The issue of proper and improper use of funds from the Treasury came up during al-Suyūṭī's time as well. For a monograph-length study on this subject, see Muḥammad b. Muḥammad al-Balāṭunusī (d. 936/1529), *Taḥrīr al-maqāl fī mā yaḥill wa-yaḥrum min bayt al-māl* (al-Manṣūra: Dār al-Wafāʾ, 1989).

[102] Muḥyī al-Dīn al-Nawawī, *Fatāwā al-Imām al-Nawawī* (Beirut: Dār al-Kutub al-ʿIlmiyya, 1982), 105–6.

[103] Amīn, *al-Awqāf*, 95. See also Sabra, *Poverty and Charity*, 71.

Earlier vs. Later Jurists

Al-Suyūṭī argues that jurists at the time of al-Nawawī (d. 676/1277) and Ibn al-Ṣalāḥ (d. 643/1245) tended to be very strict in their fatwas regarding endowments, whereas later scholars like al-Subkī (d. 771/1370) and al-Bulqīnī (d. 805/1403) were more lenient in their opinions. Al-Suyūṭī explains that:

> there is no contradiction between these later scholars and al-Nawawī; rather, each one speaks in accordance with the reality (*al-wāqiʿ*) of his time. Most of the endowments from the time of al-Nawawī and Ibn al-Ṣalāḥ were private, whereas the endowments of the Turks started at the end of the seventh century [AH] and increased during the eighth century [AH], which was the age of al-Subkī and those after him.[104]

This statement by al-Suyūṭī demonstrates in clear terms the ability of Islamic law as an institution to change and adapt to new circumstances.[105]

Al-Suyūṭī's assertion that earlier jurists tended to be stricter in their opinions regarding the administration of *waqf* is largely correct, although the private/public distinction may not have been as simple as he describes. As the creation of religious endowments expanded under the Ayyubids and then exploded under the Mamluks, new situations arose that required juristic attention. Another example of the initial strictness on the part of the early 7th/13th-century jurists are the opinions by ʿIzz al-Dīn b. ʿAbd al-Salām, al-Nawawī, and Ibn al-Ṣalāḥ all affirming that if a founder stipulates in the deed that a *madrasa* or other institution is to follow a certain *madhhab* (legal school), then it is not permissible to deviate from that condition, even if the majority in a certain region belong to a different school. Similarly, an imam cannot change his affiliation from one school to another to accommodate the *waqf*. If no such conditions are known, then custom (*al-ʿāda*) must be followed.[106]

[104] Al-Suyūṭī, *al-Inṣāf*, 151.

[105] Al-Suyūṭī's statement also seems to support Wael Hallaq's thesis that the fatwa, as both a "legal discourse" and a "social instrument," played "a considerable role in the growth and gradual change of Islamic substantive law." See his "From *Fatwās to Furūʿ*: Growth and Change in Islamic Substantive Law," *Islamic Law and Society* 1:1 (1994): 31.

[106] See al-Nawawī, *Fatāwā al-Imām al-Nawawī*, 107; and ʿIzz al-Dīn b. ʿAbd al-Salām al-Sulamī, *Fatāwā Shaykh al-Islām ʿIzz al-Dīn b. ʿAbd al-Salām* (Beirut: Muʾassasat al-Risāla, 1996), 444–6 and

All of these opinions by Shāfiʿī jurists favored the status quo of Shāfiʿī dominance in Egypt and Syria under the Ayyubids. The system was turned on its head, however, in 663/1265 when Sultan al-Ẓāhir Baybars decided that a chief *qāḍī* should be appointed from each of the four legal schools. Although this decision ultimately helped to introduce more flexibility into the legal system,[107] it was also regarded by many Shāfiʿīs as an objectionable attempt by the ruler to control the *ʿulamāʾ* and to break Shāfiʿī dominance in favor of the Ḥanafī school preferred by the Mamluks.[108] Al-Suyūṭī, for instance, praises Ibn Bint al-Aʿazz (d. 665/1267), the Shāfiʿī chief *qāḍī*, for his resistance to Baybars' power play.[109] In any case, the Mamluks' promotion of the Ḥanafī school in mostly Shāfiʿī Egypt and Syria would change the way *madrasas* and *khānqāhs* were structured, regardless of the original stipulations of the founders, and these changes naturally necessitated accommodation from the legal system and the jurists.

It is also the case, as al-Suyūṭī says, that later jurists tended to be more lenient in general regarding rules for *waqf*, though there were occasional exceptions. Tāj al-Dīn al-Subkī and Ibn Taymiyya, for example, were both critical of scholars who held simultaneous appointments in multiple institutions, even though the practice had become "all but institutionalized" by this time.[110] Despite Ibn Taymiyya's censure of "those who took multiple posts with salaries beyond their needs, and those who hired substitutes to work in their place for a fraction of the pocketed salary,"[111] the fact was that the appointment of a successor or deputy, which had become a common practice, served the interests of the *ʿulamāʾ*, allowing them to "replicate their own power, wealth, and position in their offspring."[112]

Ibn al-Ṣalāḥ al-Shahrazūrī, *Fatāwā wa-masāʾil Ibn al-Ṣalāḥ*, 2 vols. (Beirut: Dār al-Maʿrifa, 1986), 2:633–44.

107 For an analysis of the legal implications of this decision, see Yossef Rapoport, "Legal Diversity in the Age of *Taqlīd*: The Four Chief *Qāḍīs* Under the Mamluks," *Islamic Law and Society* 10:2 (2003): 210–28.

108 Jørgen S. Nielsen, "Sultan al-Ẓāhir Baybars and the Appointment of Four Chief *Qāḍīs*, 663/1265," *Studia Islamica* 60 (1984): 171–2. See also Leonor Fernandes, *The Evolution of a Sufi Institution in Mamluk Egypt*, 1.

109 Garcin, "Opposition Politique," 70. See also al-Suyūṭī, *Ḥusn al-muhāḍara*, 2:165–7.

110 Berkey, *Transmission of Knowledge*, 113.

111 Makdisi, *Rise of Colleges*, 169.

112 Berkey, *Transmission of Knowledge*, 125.

At the same time, these later jurists were realistic about the status of endowed institutions and the position of scholars in them. For example, by the 8th/14th century, the practice of *istibdāl* (the sale or exchange of an already existing *waqf*, often under a new set of conditions) was widely tolerated by the judiciary.[113] Later jurists were forced to consider economic hardship and diminishing revenues as factors in the administration of endowments. Ibn Taymiyya, for one, allowed students to pursue sources of funding outside of their stipulated stipends if their financial needs were not being met, since providing adequate support to scholars is a universal duty under the Law and should be considered as a religious matter and not as a wage in the secular sense.[114]

Rules for Students

Could a student's poor attendance at lectures or his low level of learning disqualify him from receiving a stipend from an endowed institution? Or was a student's entitlement to be based solely on financial need regardless of his academic performance? As Makdisi notes, these "were questions which arose early in the history of endowed colleges and continued down through the centuries."[115] Ibn al-Ṣalāḥ's early opinion on this issue anticipates al-Suyūṭī's later interpretation, but is a bit more qualified in distinguishing between different ranks of students and citing custom (*al-ʿurf*) as a reason to expect attendance from students if the stipulations are not already clear from the endowment deed.[116] For al-Suyūṭī, a student's level of learning (and, to some extent, his financial need) was the determining factor. Also, al-Suyūṭī makes the decision a function of whether or not the endowment funds come from the Treasury or from a private source, an issue that had not yet been addressed by Ibn al-Ṣalāḥ.

[113] Fernandes, *Evolution*, 45–6. On *istibdāl*, see further Amīn, *al-Awqāf*, 341–54.

[114] Ibn Taymiyya, *Majmūʿ fatāwā Shaykh al-Islām Aḥmad b. Taymiyya*, 37 vols. (Beirut: Maṭābiʿ Dār al-ʿArabiyya, 1977–1978), 31:12–15.

[115] Makdisi, *Rise of Colleges*, 185.

[116] Makdisi, *Rise of Colleges*, 186. For Ibn al-Ṣalāḥ's fatwa, see *Fatāwā wa-masāʾil Ibn al-Ṣalāḥ*, 1:372 and Ibn Ḥajar al-Haythamī, *al-Fatāwā al-kubrā al-fiqhiyya*, 4 vols. (Beirut: Dār al-Kutub al-ʿIlmiyya, 2008), 3:183–4.

Rules for Teachers

The question of giving priority to the shaykh is more problematic, however. Again, al-Suyūṭī distinguishes between the two different kinds of *waqf*. His argument is as follows:

> For the first kind [of *waqf*], no one is given priority over anyone else except with the written consent of the founder. The second kind is subject to examination: If the shaykh, by virtue of his learning, is entitled to [funding] from the Treasury and the rest of the ranks are not, then the shaykh is certainly given priority when the endowment becomes pressed for funds, because he alone merits entitlement (*munfarid bi-l-istiḥqāq*). If everyone is of equal learning and the shaykh is the most needy, then he is given priority, just as priority is given in order of need when the Treasury becomes pressed for funds. If everyone is equal in both learning and need, then they are given funding according to shares, without preference.[117]

That al-Suyūṭī does not cite any other jurists who held this opinion suggests that the matter is far from being settled. He also declines to mention any jurists whose views on giving priority conflict with his own, though such views did exist and were probably known to him. Ibn Taymiyya, for example, acknowledges that jurists were in disagreement about this issue but "declared that the principle of giving priority to the professor of law, or to someone else, was invalid; and that he knew of no reliable jurisconsult who adhered to such a principle, or anything like it, even though it had been enforced by qadis."[118] In a related opinion, he held against giving priority to a *waqf* supervisor because there was nothing in the stipulations of the endowment to allow it.[119]

Actual practice seems to favor some degree of prioritization, albeit not in favor of the shaykh. Berkey suggests that, from the point of view of the founder, the most important groups to be supported in times of need are the founder's own relatives and those responsible for the basic upkeep of the buildings. Prayer leaders and preachers are considered more essential than teachers and students, according to endowment deeds like the one for

[117] Al-Suyūṭī, *al-Inṣāf*, 152. [118] Makdisi, *Rise of Colleges*, 67.
[119] Ibn Taymiyya, *Majmūʿ fatāwā Shaykh al-Islām Aḥmad b. Taymiyya*, 31:66–7.

the *madrasa* of Sulṭān Ḥasan.[120] In any case, by al-Suyūṭī's time standards for both teachers and students had become considerably more lax, while their sense of entitlement had only increased. The pervasive practice of appointing deputies (*al-istināba*) made it easier for shaykhs to avoid attending to their duties, essentially "allowing the shaykhs benefit from a salary without having to work for it."[121]

CONCLUSION

We may never know the details of what transpired between al-Suyūṭī and the Sufis of the Baybarsiyya *khānqāh* in the late 9th/15th century. However, by examining al-Suyūṭī's legal writing, it is possible to discover intriguing strands in an impressive network of power relationships that characterized late Mamluk Egypt. This mode of inquiry also reveals much about al-Suyūṭī's perception of himself as a jurist in relation to other jurists, to the state authority, and to the Sufi students under his supervision. We also begin to get a clearer picture of how these relations shaped al-Suyūṭī's larger narratives of self-representation.

Some initial observations may be made: First, al-Suyūṭī believes in a social hierarchy that, contrary to what one might suppose for a traditional context, does not give top priority to the ruler. Instead, moral authority lies in the hands of the scholar by virtue of his learning and ability to benefit society through knowledge and ethical witness. Therefore, the scholar is entitled to preferential treatment and respect in the form of earmarks and maintenance. The problem is that by the Mamluk period these earmarks increasingly were under the control of the Treasury, which gave the ruler much greater power over the scholars. It was the sultan who determined who was appointed to certain desirable positions and it was the sultan who dismissed a scholar if he became troublesome.

In short, scholars were in danger of becoming petty public officials and of losing their special privileges as representatives and interpreters of God's

[120] Berkey, *Transmission of Knowledge*, 19–20.
[121] Fernandes, *Evolution of a Sufi Institution*, 51.

Law and Sunna. The ultimate manifestation of this threat, for al-Suyūṭī, was the intolerable indignity of requiring the scholar to climb up to the Citadel every month to collect his salary like a common state employee. Following in the footsteps of the great ʿIzz al-Dīn b. ʿAbd al-Salām, al-Suyūṭī refused to subordinate himself to the authority of the ruler. This refusal nearly cost him his life.

The deterioration of relations between the ruler and the *ʿulamāʾ*, coupled with economic upheaval and political instability, created a tenuous state of affairs in late Mamluk society. Once considered a reliable way to protect one's estate, *waqf* became subject to corruption and unlawful appropriation by the ruler, causing a subsequent decrease in funding for stipends. At the same time, al-Suyūṭī laments what he sees as a general decline in the standards of scholarship, with the result that once illustrious educational institutions came to be filled with ignorant Sufi poseurs and riffraff. It is no wonder, then, that al-Suyūṭī often adopts an apocalyptic tone in his writings.

Faced with the risk of irrelevancy, jurists like al-Suyūṭī came under pressure to justify, in legal terms, changes in the way that *waqf* was administrated. These jurists had to situate themselves within the institutional parameters of the Islamic legal structure and they had to conform to its accepted modes of argumentation. For al-Suyūṭī, this meant making a crucial distinction between different kinds of *waqf*, a distinction that allowed him to pay respect to the views of earlier Shāfiʿī greats like Ibn al-Ṣalāḥ and al-Nawawī and that provided the flexibility needed to re-negotiate some of their ideas in light of changed circumstances. It is this discursive ability to negotiate and to interpret the Law in response to new situations that gives the scholar a meaningful role in the power relations that govern society: Therein lies the true power of the jurist.

2

Authority by Association: Consensus vs. Ignorance in al-Suyūṭī's Legal Opinion on Logic

INTRODUCTION

In the year 889/1484, Jalāl al-Dīn al-Suyūṭī sent waves of furor rippling through the scholarly community by declaring that he had attained the level of *ijtihād* (independent legal reasoning) in the fields of law, *ḥadīth*, and the Arabic language. Al-Suyūṭī's enemies, especially someone to whom al-Suyūṭī refers only as "the Ignoramus," seized on a controversial legal opinion that he wrote as a young student condemning the study of logic to allege that the author was deficient in his knowledge of logic and thus not qualified to claim the rank of *mujtahid*. To bolster their assault, they used a famous statement by the renowned jurist al-Ghazālī (d. 505/1111) that one who does not know logic cannot be trusted in his scholarship to suggest that proficiency in logic and the rational sciences was a requirement for *ijtihād*.

Al-Suyūṭī responded to the latest round of attacks on his reputation by issuing yet another fatwa on the subject of logic, entitled *al-Qawl al-mushriq fī taḥrīm al-ishtighāl bi-l-manṭiq* ("An Enlightening Statement Prohibiting Preoccupation with Logic").[1] In the text, the author tries to accomplish several complex rhetorical goals. First, al-Suyūṭī is faced with the delicate task of showing himself to be well versed in an area of study that he and others have already declared prohibited. At the same time, the author must try to

[1] Jalāl al-Dīn al-Suyūṭī, *Al-Qawl al-mushriq fī taḥrīm al-ishtighāl bi-l-manṭiq* in *al-Ḥāwī li-l-fatāwī* (Beirut: Dār al-Kutub al-ʿIlmiyya, 2000) 1:244–6.

The Legal Thought of Jalāl al-Dīn al-Suyūṭī: Authority and Legacy. Rebecca Skreslet Hernandez.

discredit his opponent without casting any blame on his hero and exemplar within the Shāfiʿī legal school, al-Ghazālī. Ultimately, al-Suyūṭī hopes to position himself as a *mujtahid* whose opinions are in line with other authorities within his community of scholars.

The main argument of this chapter is that al-Suyūṭī's logic fatwa is a plea on the part of the author to gain recognition from his community of scholars as a *mujtahid* and one of the leading scholars of his age. At the same time, it is a polemic directed not solely against the study of logic per se but also against those who would use the logic debate as a weapon with which to damage al-Suyūṭī's own reputation and authority. The analysis of the text takes into account both linguistic factors internal to the text as well as external contextual factors.

Starting with the internal factors, the chapter examines how al-Suyūṭī uses the stylistic conventions of the fatwa genre such as the question and answer frame device and the citation of authorities from each of the four legal schools to perform a dual function. First, the author creates a clear opposition between the correct righteous opinion of himself and his exemplars versus the ignorant and heretical views of his enemies. Second, al-Suyūṭī seeks to derive transitive authority from his predecessors within his "community of practice" of fellow jurists, particularly from such paragons of learning as Ibn Taymiyya, Ibn al-Ṣalāḥ, and al-Ghazālī. The particular linguistic strategies that al-Suyūṭī employs in the fatwa allow him to appeal to deeper narratives within the scholarly community. These themes include the limits of *ijtihād* in an age of *taqlīd*, preservation of learning against the threat of growing ignorance, and the perceived superiority of some means of acquiring knowledge over others.

In order to assess how successful al-Suyūṭī is in meeting his objectives, I turn to external evidence from the larger context, including the opinions of other jurists before, during, and after al-Suyūṭī's time, to understand how their arguments match up (or not) with those of al-Suyūṭī. Finally, this chapter looks at the broader historical tension within Islamic thought between suspicion toward Greek-inspired disciplines such as logic on the one hand, and the gradual acceptance of logic as part of the curriculum for Islamic scholars (including al-Suyūṭī) on the other. I question whether or not al-Suyūṭī's condemnation of logic represents the "mainstream" view—as he implies in the fatwa—or whether, at least as far as the logic debate is concerned, he is on the wrong side of history.

APPROACH TO THE TEXT

This chapter examines al-Suyūṭī's fatwa condemning the study of logic from the standpoint of literary and discourse analysis. An instructive model for this approach is Kristen Brustad's article analyzing al-Suyūṭī's autobiography, *al-Taḥadduth bi-niʿmat Allāh* (as expertly edited by Sartain).[2] I take a brief look first at how al-Suyūṭī constructs and defends his authority in the autobiography through his use of language before turning to the fatwa itself. The analysis adds to Brustad's literary approach sociolinguistic tools and theories (such as interdiscursivity, framing, and communities of practice) to better understand how al-Suyūṭī uses language to accomplish his pragmatic goals.

Brustad approaches *al-Taḥadduth bi-niʿmat Allāh* "in light of questions raised by modern scholarship surrounding individuality, textual cohesion and coherence, and public versus private in medieval Arabic autobiography," paying particular attention to recurring tropes and "conventions of representation" in the account.[3] Brustad considers both internal textual evidence as well as external information to argue that al-Suyūṭī sought, through the use of literary conventions characteristic of medieval Arabic autobiography, to "impose his authority as the leading scholar of his day."[4]

Authority Construction and Self-Representation

The overall goal of al-Suyūṭī's autobiography, according to Brustad, is one of authority construction. Therefore, if al-Suyūṭī neglects to mention some topics it is because such matters do not serve the larger purpose of the text. For example, Brustad calls into question the seeming lack of tension

[2] E.M. Sartain, *Jalāl al-Dīn al-Suyūṭī: Biography and Background*, 2 vols. (Cambridge, U.K.: Cambridge University Press, 1975). Volume 2 contains the edited text of al-Suyūṭī's *al-Taḥadduth bi-niʿmat Allāh*.

[3] Kristen Brustad, "Imposing Order: Reading the Conventions of Representation in al-Suyūṭī's Autobiography," *Edebiyāt* 7:2 (1997): 327.

[4] Brustad, "Imposing Order," 328.

between the "private" and "public" self that has caused some modern critics to judge medieval autobiographies as dry and lacking in personal details and emotional depth. As Brustad points out, the medieval Arabic autobiography differs in many ways from what we today understand by genres of self-narrative.[5] She notes, for example, al-Suyūṭī's avoidance of any information regarding his wives or children (though he does name several women in connection with his study of *ḥadīth*). Brustad concludes from this, not that al-Suyūṭī refrains from delving into family matters out of a sense of prudishness or modesty, but that this aspect of his life is not considered relevant to the goal of the text, namely, to prove the intellectual authority of the author himself.[6] Al-Suyūṭī makes his emotions known through his autobiography through the cultural and literary conventions of his time and social context rather than through an emphasis on personal reflection and self-discovery that the modern reader might expect.

Several scholars have pointed out that al-Suyūṭī's use of the phrase, *al-taḥadduth bi-niʿmat Allāh* ("recounting God's blessings") speaks to the literary conventions and expectations associated with the autobiographical genre and is, at the same time, performative in the sense that use of the phrase hints at underlying intentions on the part of the author. Looking at the phrase from a sociolinguistic perspective, Devin Stewart argues that, as a rhetorical strategy, the phrase falls under the category of "linguistic prophylaxis" intended to shield the speaker from accusations of boastfulness and arrogance.[7] Drawing inspiration from al-Suyūṭī, al-Shaʿrānī (d. 973/1565) also makes use of the phrase *al-taḥadduth bi-niʿmat Allāh* and begins his autobiographical work with a meditation on the ethical implications of writing about oneself, presenting a

[5] On the differences between Arabic autobiography and modern autobiographical genres, see Franz Rosenthal, "Die arabische Autobiographie," *Studia Arabica* 1 (1937): 1–40; David Reisman, "Medieval Arabic Medical Autobiography," *Journal of the American Oriental Society* 129:4 (2009): 559–69; and the introduction and essays presented in *Interpreting the Self: Autobiography in the Arabic Literary Tradition*, edited by Dwight F. Reynolds (Berkeley: University of California Press, 2001).

[6] Brustad, "Imposing Order," 330.

[7] Devin J. Stewart, "Recounting God's Blessings: Linguistic Prophylaxis and Self-Representation in Arabic Autobiography," *Al-ʿArabiyya* 40/41 (2007–2008): 207. The strategy may not always be successful, however. Stewart writes: "The pious and social impulse to efface the self, to avoid putting oneself above the interlocutor is countered, however, by strong impulses in the opposite direction. No one can come away from al-Suyūṭī's autobiography without thinking that this man had an absolutely colossal ego, and was not afraid to let it be known" (217).

spirited defense of the practice.[8] Brustad suggests that the phrase in the title of al-Suyūṭī's work is linked to the final passage in which al-Suyūṭī expresses hope that the "blessing" in store for him will be recognition of his rank as the renewer of religious thought for the past century.[9]

Both Sartain and Brustad interpret the autobiography as a whole as a kind of last-ditch effort by a scholar toward the end of his career to gain the respect and recognition of his peers that he feels that he deserves but that has eluded him up to the point of writing. Begun at a time when al-Suyūṭī had more or less retired from public life (and left uncompleted), the text reads as an attempt by the author to set the record straight, so that not only can he have the last word in the many disputes that plagued him throughout his career, but also that he may one day be acclaimed as the renewer of his age, much like his heroes before him.

When speaking of "authorial intent" and self-representation in the autobiography, one is reminded of Bakhtin's notions of interdiscursivity and the "dialogic" nature of language, or the idea that all utterances are built on past utterances and anticipate future ones. As Bakhtin suggests, an author can even use "double-voiced" discourse to strike a "polemical blow" at another person's speech.[10] Thus, as Brustad observes, al-Suyūṭī's autobiography "shows the author's recognition of the performative nature of the act of self-representation. Not only is the past viewed from the standpoint of the present of writing, it is also viewed with an eye to the future."[11] In other words, self-representation is not limited to the self but is used to comment on others' utterances as well.

"Transitivity" and "Exemplarism"

One method through which al-Suyūṭī appeals to the cultural and literary conventions of the day to aid his project of authority construction is through

[8] Dwight F. Reynolds, "Shaykh ʿAbd al-Wahhāb al-Shaʿrānī's Sixteenth-Century Defense of Autobiography," *Harvard Middle Eastern and Islamic Review* 4: 1–2 (1997–1998): 122–37.

[9] Brustad, "Imposing Order," 337.

[10] Mikhail Bakhtin, *Discourse in Dostoevsky's Poetics*, edited and translated by Caryl Emerson (Minneapolis, Minnesota: University of Minnesota Press, 1984), 195.

[11] Brustad, "Imposing Order," 343.

what Michael Cooperson has called "transitivity."[12] In an intellectual context in which scholars were considered (ideally) the heirs of the Prophet, the author found it part of his mission to associate himself with his forerunners in the tradition. Paired with this idea of transitivity is that of "exemplarism"; al-Suyūṭī cites anecdotes relating to his heroes, such as al-Shāfiʿī (d. 204/820), al-Ghazālī (d. 505/1111), and Ibn Ḥajar al-ʿAsqalānī (d. 852/1449), in the hopes that he might himself be placed in the same class of intellect and religiosity as his esteemed predecessors. As Brustad puts it: "The fact that most of the figures he invokes are renowned for their piety and scholarship points to al-Suyūṭī's view of his role in God's Plan as one who leads in the expansion of religious knowledge. By emulating exemplary figures, he becomes one."[13]

Offensive and Defensive Use of Language

One need not infer passionate conviction in al-Suyūṭī's autobiography from literary conventions alone. Rather, Sartain and Brustad acknowledge moments in the narrative when raw emotion bubbles to the surface. Never is this phenomenon more vivid than when al-Suyūṭī describes his enemies and their relentless attacks upon both his personal and professional reputation.[14] Both Sartain and Brustad find remarkable the more informal register employed by al-Suyūṭī in portraying these disputes as well as the intensity of the bitterness and resentment behind the words.[15] For example, Brustad

[12] See Michael Cooperson, "Aḥmad Ibn Ḥanbal and Bishr al-Ḥāfī: A Case Study in Biographical Traditions," *Studia Islamica* 86 (1997): 95. For a fuller discussion of Cooperson's theories on religious authority, see his *Classical Arabic Biography: The Heirs of the Prophets in the Age of al-Maʾmūn* (Cambridge, U.K.: Cambridge University Press, 2008) in which he compares four exemplars all of whom claim authority as symbolic heirs of the Prophet, including an ʿAbbasid caliph, a Shiʿi Imam, a Sunni scholar, and a "proto-Sufi" ascetic.

[13] Brustad, "Imposing Order," 336.

[14] The hostility expressed in al-Suyūṭī's autobiography stands in contrast to the tone used by Ibn Ḥajar (d. 852/1449), a respected scholar of the preceding generation, in his own autobiographical writing. R. Kevin Jaques observes that, despite his high profile success as a scholar in the fluid political environment of late Mamluk Egypt, Ibn Ḥajar had very few enemies and was, for the most part, respectful in his writing in regards to his colleagues. Jaques interprets Ibn Ḥajar's self-reflection, not as a vain ploy to extoll his own virtues and accomplishments, but as a sincere attempt "to portray and understand the mysteries of God's blessing and his own role in the unfolding of Muslim religious history." See R. Kevin Jaques, *Ibn Hajar* (New Delhi: Oxford University Press, 2009), 4.

[15] Brustad, "Imposing Order," 340. Sartain writes: "The lively descriptions of al-Suyūṭī's disputes with other scholars, which are written in a very conversational, almost colloquial, style,

highlights a passage in which al-Suyūṭī switches from third to second person pronouns to address the reader directly, saying: "By God, those of you with intelligence, *look* [*unẓurū*] at someone who has reached this degree of paucity of intellect."[16] The author emerges as a victim in the narrative unfairly wronged by his opponents, much as the early Muslims (*salaf*) were sent enemies by God to confront them and to test their faith. Even al-Suyūṭī must have sensed, however, that his career had sparked more conflict and exchanges of abuse than was common to most scholars, thus putting him in the defensive position of having to explain that he is not trying to disagree with people just for the sake of being ornery but strives only for impartial truth.[17]

As Brustad suggests, by taking the offensive in his narrative against his enemies, al-Suyūṭī ends up appearing on the defensive: "It is here that the author most vehemently emphasizes his authority, and here that the final authority of the text most escapes him, because he controls his words but not the reception of them which will ensue."[18] While the majority of al-Suyūṭī's enemies represent named historical figures (Ibn al-Jawjarī, Ibn al-Karakī, and al-Sakhāwī, to name a few), one opponent is considered too contemptible even to be cited by name and is instead referred to as either *abū jahl* or *al-jāhil*, "the Ignoramus." As Brustad points out, al-Suyūṭī had already spent three chapters describing the origins of his own name and thus "The absence of the antagonist's name stands in sharp contrast to the narrator's lengthy establishment of his own, and represents al-Suyūṭī's attempt to impose anonymity upon the 'ignoramus.'" "The Ignoramus," although most likely a real person,[19] becomes for the purposes of the narrative a kind of generic opponent for the author to refute. Rather than simply ignoring the man's attacks as beneath his notice, al-Suyūṭī goes to great lengths to defend his point of view and to correct what he sees as gross errors on the part of the enemy.

are particularly valuable, and such revealing personal statements as we find here are rare in Arabic autobiographical writing, of which impersonality is one of the main characteristics," (*Jalāl al-Dīn al-Suyūṭī*, viii).

[16] Brustad, "Imposing Order," 342 (Brustad's translation and emphasis).

[17] Al-Suyūṭī, *al-Taḥadduth bi-niʿmat Allāh*, 20; Brustad, "Imposing Order," 341–2.

[18] Brustad, "Imposing Order," 340.

[19] Sartain deduces that *al-jāhil* was probably someone by the name of Shams al-Dīn al-Ṭūlūnī, who fits the description based on the sparse biographical details provided (*Jalāl al-Dīn al-Suyūṭī*, 56–7).

THE LOGIC FATWA

Many of the discursive techniques governing al-Suyūṭī's use of language in his autobiography come back in full force in his fatwas. Although legal opinions fall under a different literary genre entirely, they nevertheless contain many of the same pragmatic uses of language as the autobiographical narrative. Never are these techniques more pronounced than in al-Suyūṭī's fatwa concerning the study of logic, *al-Qawl al-mushriq fī taḥrīm al-ishtighāl bi-l-manṭiq*, or "An Enlightening Statement Prohibiting Preoccupation with Logic."[20] Like Brustad, I will consider both internal and external evidence to examine the text, paying particular attention to the author's pragmatic use of language (including cultural and literary conventions of representation) and what it might reveal about the goals of the producer of the discourse. The aim is to get beyond what the text *says* in order to accede what it *means* both for the author and within its broader social and intellectual context.

The Frame Device

First, it must be stated that the fatwa follows a standard question and answer format common to legal opinions, where the issue is outlined under the heading "*mas'ala*" and the answer given as "*al-jawāb*." Hallaq, for example, has pointed out that there is no reason to assume that this format was not based on a real question presented by an actual questioner rather than a purely hypothetical device created by the jurist.[21] The fact that the questioner's name was usually omitted indicates that the fatwa "was not merely an ephemeral legal opinion or legal advice given to a person for immediate and mundane purposes but also an authoritative statement of the law that was considered to transcend the individual case and its mundane reality."[22] It should be noted also that many of the fatwas (especially those regarding

[20] The text that I am using comes from al-Suyūṭī's fatwa collection, *al-Ḥāwī li-l-fatāwī*, (Beirut: Dār al-Kutub al-ʿIlmiyya, 2000), 244–6. Therefore, all comments concerning the format and content of the text are based on this print edition unless otherwise specified. Quotations in English from the logic fatwa are from my own translation of the text.

[21] Wael B. Hallaq, "From *Fatwās* to *Furūʿ*: Growth and Change in Islamic Substantive Law," *Islamic Law and Society* 1:1 (1994): 33.

[22] Ibid., 34.

controversial or contested issues) in al-Suyūṭī's fatwa collection, *al-Ḥāwī li-l-fatāwī*, were in fact stand-alone treatises that were later incorporated into the collection. *Al-Qawl al-mushriq* is such a treatise and, as such, exists in manuscript form separate from the other fatwas and treatises in *al-Ḥāwī*.[23]

The question setting up the frame device for al-Suyūṭī's logic fatwa reveals immediately some rather perplexing inconsistencies. Mufti Ali, one of the few contemporary scholars to address the contents of the fatwa to any degree of detail, presents a somewhat odd portrayal of the question. Stating first that al-Suyūṭī gives no "information about the identity of the questioner," he then suggests that the statements defending logic that al-Suyūṭī refutes one by one in the fatwa were attributed to al-Ghazālī.[24] This reading of the question does not seem to agree with the latter part of the fatwa, in which al-Suyūṭī passionately upholds al-Ghazālī's reputation as a jurist and denounces the questioner as a sinner and a fool. Earlier in his analysis, Ali suggests: "one understands that this treatise was written in answer to a question about the study of logic and the status of the knowledge of logic as a condition of undertaking *ijtihād*,"[25] an interpretation that appears much more likely in light of the text itself.

In the print edition of the fatwa, al-Suyūṭī's lead-up to the question consists simply of the statement: "There is a person claiming legal expertise who says" (*fī shakhṣ yaddaʿī fiqhan yaqūl*) without mentioning any names. He then lists seven claims made by this person, four of which relate directly to logic and three that seem unrelated to the issue of logic but are nevertheless lumped into the same list. The statements relating to logic are as follows:

1. Monotheism (*tawḥīd*) rests on the knowledge of the science of logic.
2. The study of logic is an individual duty (*farḍ ʿayn*) for every Muslim.
3. To learn it in all its detail is [the equivalent of] ten good deeds.
4. He who does not learn [logic] is not correct in his faith and he who issues rulings but does not know [logic] is wrong in his rulings.

[23] The manuscript is listed in the collection of the Egyptian National Library (Dār al-Kutub) in Majāmiʿ Qawwāla, 25. See Sartain, *Jalāl al-Dīn al-Suyūṭī*, 220.

[24] Mufti Ali, *Muslim Opposition to Logic and Theology in Light of the Works of Jalāl al-Dīn al-Suyūṭī (d. 911/1505)*, Ph.D. Diss. (University of Leiden, 2008), 156.

[25] Ibid.

The other three statements included in the question are as follows:

5. Anyone who uses *ḥashīsh* is an unbeliever.
6. The *mujtahid* makes allowed the prohibited and prohibits the allowed.
7. Abū Ḥāmid al-Ghazālī was not a jurist but rather an ascetic.

The variety of these statements leaves open the question whether they were all made by the same person or were grouped together either by al-Suyūṭī himself or by a later editor. In any case, it is clear from the text of the reply that al-Suyūṭī not only considers the statements themselves to be false, but the person who made them "a man of extreme ignorance and stupidity and depravity" who deserves to be beaten with a whip and imprisoned in order to deter others from making such dangerous claims.[26]

Timing of the Fatwa

Like the autobiography, this particular fatwa was composed fairly late in al-Suyūṭī's life. We can conclude this based on references in the text to earlier works by al-Suyūṭī on the same subject. He mentions an abridgement that he made of Ibn Taymiyya's *al-Radd ʿalā manṭiq al-Yūnān*[27] as well as a volume condemning logic in which he quotes statements from the religious authorities on the topic, most likely in reference to his *Ṣawn al-manṭiq wa-l-kalām ʿan fann al-manṭiq wa-l-kalām*. In the introduction to *Ṣawn al-manṭiq*, al-Suyūṭī recalls a treatise that he wrote many years before (about 867–8/1461–2)[28] in which he condemned logic and cited Ibn Taymiyya's book, even though he was not able to obtain an actual copy of the manuscript until twenty years later[29]—the same year in which he declared himself to have attained the rank of *mujtahid* (889/1484).[30] Al-Suyūṭī describes his purpose in writing

[26] Al-Suyūṭī, *al-Qawl al-mushriq*, 245–6.

[27] This abridgement, entitled *Jahd al-qarīḥa fī tajrīd al-Naṣīḥa*, has been edited and translated by Wael Hallaq as *Ibn Taymiyya Against the Greek Logicians* (Oxford, U.K.: Clarendon Press, 1993).

[28] Al-Suyūṭī describes the uproar that arose after this pamphlet was made public as the first of his many disputes (Sartain, *Jalāl al-Dīn al-Suyūṭī*, 32). Clearly, the controversy had not abated by the time he composed *Jahd al-qarīḥa* and *Ṣawn al-manṭiq* twenty years later.

[29] Al-Suyūṭī, *Ṣawn al-manṭiq wa-l-kalām ʿan fann al-manṭiq wa-l-kalām*, edited by ʿAlī Sāmī al-Nashshār (Egypt: Maktabat al-Khānjī, 1947), 1.

[30] Sartain, *Jalāl al-Dīn al-Suyūṭī*, 59.

Ṣawn al-manṭiq as both a refutation of the claim brought against him that one of the conditions for achieving *ijtihād* is a knowledge of logic (the implication being that al-Suyūṭī was deficient in this regard) as well as a defense of the famous and highly disputed fatwa of Ibn al-Ṣalāḥ al-Shahrazūrī (d. 643/1245) denouncing the study of logic, which was still evidently receiving criticism in al-Suyūṭī's time.[31]

As Sartain observes, al-Suyūṭī's claim to *ijtihād* provided his enemies with "fresh ammunition for their attacks on him"[32] and rekindled the dispute about logic that had plagued him as a student—except that this time, the stakes were higher. When someone used al-Ghazālī's statement in his famous introduction to the science of logic in *al-Mustaṣfā* that one who is not well-versed in the rational sciences cannot be trusted in his scholarship[33] to suggest that al-Suyūṭī did not fulfill the conditions for *ijtihād*, the scholar was therefore "in the awkward position of having to demonstrate his knowledge of the subject, while of course maintaining his view that it was a 'forbidden' discipline."[34] Not only does al-Suyūṭī set out to show his own familiarity with arguments by previous generations of scholars against the study of logic, philosophy, and theology in his *Ṣawn al-manṭiq*, he also derides his opponents for criticizing what they do not understand by trying to debate the use of logic without employing it in their own work.

Many of the same issues come back yet again in al-Suyūṭī's fatwa, which is the latest of his writings on logic. It is interesting that a scholar with three known works on the subject of logic (an early treatise, an abridgement, and a full-length book) would feel compelled to write yet another treatise on the subject in the form of a fatwa. One surmises that *Ṣawn al-manṭiq* did not put matters to rest, as the author intended, since some of the same accusations resurface in the fatwa along with new claims that al-Suyūṭī felt also needed to be countered.

[31] Al-Suyūṭī, *Ṣawn al-manṭiq*, 1–3. See also Mufti Ali, "Jalāl al-Dīn al-Suyūṭī Against Logic and *Kalām*: Analysis and Significance of *Ṣawn al-manṭiq wal-kalām ʿan fannay* [sic.] *al-manṭiq wal-kalām*," *Hamdard Islamicus* 28:2 (2005): 24.

[32] Sartain, *Jalāl al-Dīn al-Suyūṭī*, 69.

[33] Abū Ḥāmid al-Ghazālī, *al-Mustaṣfā min ʿilm al-uṣūl* (Cairo: Dār al-Baṣāʾir, 2007), 10.

[34] Sartain, *Jalāl al-Dīn al-Suyūṭī*, 69.

Audience and Opponent

In addition to Cooperson's notions of "transitivity" and "exemplarism," the concept of communities of practice as outlined by Etienne Wenger[35] and others is helpful in determining the intended audience of the text and the pragmatic rhetorical strategies employed by the author in appealing to that audience. According to Wenger, members of a community of practice are united by mutual engagement, a joint enterprise, and a shared repertoire (of tools, concepts, or symbols).[36] Individuals participate in an ongoing "negotiation of meaning" both by being actively engaged in the social practice of the community (participation) and by helping to define the terms and character of the community (reification). Taking part in a joint enterprise "gives rise to relations of mutual accountability among those involved."[37] This "regime of mutual accountability" is not expressed usually as formal rules as much as it exists as a set of unspoken expectations governing appropriate practice within the community, which is itself subject to further negotiation.

As noted above, the immediate context for the fatwa appears to be al-Suyūṭī's attempt to refute specific remarks made by an unnamed person whom he considers to be both ignorant and sinful. The author uses this person's claims as the frame device for his response, returning time after time to condemn the person and to declare each claim to be more misguided than the last. Therefore, it seems that, like so many of al-Suyūṭī's treatises, the text bears an element of personal grudge but, at the same time, its intended impact is not limited to a private exchange between two individuals but includes a wider community as well. A major element of al-Suyūṭī's audience probably consisted of his peers within the scholarly community—the same colleagues who fiercely contested al-Suyūṭī's own claims to *ijtihād* and *tajdīd*.

When al-Suyūṭī came out with his claim of having attained the rank of *mujtahid*, he challenged the expectations of his community of scholars and provoked a heated discussion and renegotiation of what it meant to be a *mujtahid* as defined by the shared practice of the community. In seeking to

[35] See Etienne Wenger, *Communities of Practice: Learning, Meaning and Identity* (New York: Cambridge University Press, 1998).

[36] Ibid., 73. [37] Ibid., 81.

convince his fellow scholars of his identity as a *mujtahid*, al-Suyūṭī makes full use of the repertoire of his community, including the statements of past authorities (such as Ibn al-Ṣalāḥ, al-Ghazālī, and Ibn Taymiyya). At the same time, he strives to counter rival interpretations of the same references by his opponents.

The fatwa acts as a vehicle for the jurist who aims to negotiate his own identity within the community through participation in practice. The authority of the fatwa (which represents the reified opinion of the jurist and the consensus of the legal school) depends on the authority of the speaker as defined through practice. In order to be considered worthy of the title of *mujtahid*, al-Suyūṭī must *do ijtihād*, as the concept has been defined and interpreted by the community. One of the ways in which an individual jurist could practice *ijtihād* in the post-formative era was to issue legal opinions that must then be accepted as authoritative by his peers.

List of Scholars Opposed to Logic

One strategy that al-Suyūṭī uses to appeal to an audience of fellow scholars is to show that his opinion is in line with that of other jurists, especially those within his own Shāfiʿī legal school. Here, al-Suyūṭī employs heavily Cooperson's idea of "transitivity" and "exemplarism" (described above) to suggest that he is the natural intellectual heir of these great luminaries and that anyone who questions this consensus is, at best, ignorant and, at worst, a heretical betrayer of the tradition. A lengthy portion of the fatwa is taken up with a list of names of "the leaders of the faith and legal scholars (*aʾimmat al-dīn wa-ʿulamāʾ al-Sharīʿa*)" who have written against logic. Mufti Ali helpfully provides a list of these names in his study of the fatwa, indicating which individuals were also included in al-Suyūṭī's earlier works on logic.[38]

Although I agree with Ali that these lists provide "rich prosopographical data which shed light on the history of logic and theology in the Islamic

[38] Ali, *Muslim Opposition to Logic*, 157–60. There are a few inconsistencies between the names as they appear in the print edition of the fatwa and those listed by Mufti Ali. For example, the fatwa includes the name Ibn Rushd, which Ali lists as Ibn Rashīd al-Sibtī (d. 721/1322) and Ibn Abī Jamra, which Ali includes as Ibn Abī Ḥamza (d. 695/1296). Jamra and Ḥamza have the same *rasm* in the Arabic script, which may account for the discrepancy. For more on Ibn Rashīd, see Mufti Ali, *Muslim Opposition to Logic*, 45.

world as well as of the opposition to both,"[39] I would submit that such data must be approached with caution and that taking al-Suyūṭī's citations at face value may, in fact, distort the results more than it helps to elucidate them. For example, as Ali notes, an overwhelming proportion of scholars listed are Shāfiʿīs (twenty-eight) in comparison to Mālikīs (twelve), Ḥanafīs (two), and Ḥanbalīs (three). One cannot conclude from this, however, that Shāfiʿīs were necessarily more opposed to logic than their counterparts in other schools, since it would be expected that al-Suyūṭī, as a proud Shāfiʿī scholar, would be more familiar with and thus more likely to cite authorities within his own school. Also, while the individuals listed do cover a large geographical area,[40] again, it is likely that al-Suyūṭī would be most familiar with the work of scholars in Egypt and Syria, even though he clearly (albeit to a lesser degree) had access to more far-flung resources as well. Furthermore, it is ultimately in al-Suyūṭī's interest to show that a majority of Shāfiʿī scholars support his opinion, so bulging the ranks of Shāfiʿīs in the list would aid this goal.

The list of scholars has interesting implications in terms of timing. The list begins with al-Shāfiʿī (d. 204/820), who is the only one of the four school founders to be mentioned in the text.[41] Presumably, this is meant to be consistent with al-Suyūṭī's assertion in the fatwa that logic did not enter Islam until the year 180 AH (796 CE) even though in his *Ṣawn al-manṭiq* he quotes Abū Ismāʿīl al-Anṣārī al-Harawī (d. 481/1089)[42] in listing five generations of scholars before al-Shāfiʿī, all of whom, he says, opposed speculative theology and heretical innovation (though not logic explicitly). The majority of names listed in the fatwa are of scholars who lived from the 7th–8th/13th–14th centuries, which is significant given that by the 8th/13th century logic was fully entrenched as a tool in the field of theology and "an established

[39] Ibid., 164. [40] Ibid., 160.

[41] For al-Suyūṭī to claim that al-Shāfiʿī has laid down stipulations against logic is rather a stretch. For instance, Roger Arnaldez draws a connection between al-Shāfiʿī's early formulations of juridical logic, especially the concept of analogy (*qiyās*), and Greek thought, noting the influence of Aristotle's *Topics*. See R. Arnaldez, "Manṭiḳ," in *The Encyclopaedia of Islam*, Second Edition (Brill Online, 2010).

[42] A Sufi and staunch Ḥanbalī scholar, al-Harawī was known for issuing "polemics against the theologians," and, as a result, was "threatened with death on five occasions and was thrice exiled." See S. de Beaurecueil, "al-Anṣārī al-Harawī," *Encyclopaedia of Islam*, Second Edition (Brill Online, 2010).

part of the official curriculum for training theological students in the *madrasah*"[43]—even as it continued to draw opposition in some circles.

Also, in some cases, the individuals in the fatwa are not listed in strict chronological order. For instance, directly after al-Shāfiʿī, al-Suyūṭī mentions Imām al-Ḥaramayn [al-Juwaynī] (d. 478/1085) followed by al-Ghazālī (d. 505/1111) before al-Qushayrī (d. 469/1077), Ibn al-Ṣabbāgh (d. 477/1085), and Naṣr al-Maqdisī (d. 490/1098). It is difficult to say why al-Suyūṭī chose to put al-Juwaynī and al-Ghazālī at the top of the list after Shāfiʿī, though perhaps he considers them to have attained a higher rank within the school and are thus worthy of preferential treatment. The list ends with the Ḥanbalīs and the illustrious Ibn Taymiyya (d. 728/1328), giving al-Suyūṭī an opportunity to mention his abridgement of Ibn Taymiyya's work as well as his own volume condemning logic, which he considers to be an example of independent reasoning and inference (*ʿalā ṭarīqat al-ijtihād wa-l-istidlāl*).[44]

Al-Suyūṭī accomplishes two pragmatic goals with this list. First, he attempts to show that there is a consensus amongst the leading Sunni authorities within the four legal schools against the study of logic and philosophy. Second, he associates himself with these scholars whom he sees as his exemplars, especially within his own community of Shāfiʿī jurists. With this reasoning in mind, however, the fatwa omits many individuals, including some who appear much stronger in their opposition to logic than those who do make the list. First of all, as Ali notes, neither the fatwa nor any of al-Suyūṭī's other works on logic include the work of non-Sunni scholars condemning logic. For example, he does not include statements condemning logic by key Shiʿi figures such as Jaʿfar al-Ṣādiq (d. 148/764) and Ḥasan b. Mūsā al-Nawbakhtī (d.c. 310/922), nor does he include the Zaydī scholar Ibn al-Wazīr al-Ṣanʿānī (d. 840/1374) or the Muʿtazilī Ibn al-Shirshīr (d. 293/905).[45]

[43] Nicholas Rescher, *The Development of Arabic Logic* (Pittsburgh: University of Pittsburgh Press, 1964), 62. Khaled El-Rouayheb shows that by the thirteenth and fourteenth centuries Arabic logicians and theologians were engaged in an active debate regarding the subject matter of logic. Some scholars chose to defend Avicenna's views on the issue while others opted for new interpretations. See Khaled El-Rouayheb, "Post-Avicennan Logicians on the Subject Matter of Logic: Some Thirteenth- and Fourteenth-Century Discussions," *Arabic Sciences and Philosophy* 22 (2012): 69–90.

[44] Al-Suyūṭī, *Ṣawn al-manṭiq*, 3.

[45] Mufti Ali, "A Statistical Portrait of the Resistance to Logic by Sunni Muslim Scholars Based on the Works of Jalāl al-Dīn al-Suyūṭī (849–909 [sic.]/1448–1505)," *Islamic Law and Society* 15:2 (2008): 250–1 and 256.

Even if one considers just the Shāfiʿīs in the list, one encounters some notable absences. In his list of Syrian scholars, for example, al-Suyūṭī does not include anyone from the prominent Subkī family in the fatwa, even though he does refer to three of them (Zayn al-Dīn, Taqī al-Dīn, and Tāj al-Dīn) in his much earlier treatise.[46] It could be that al-Suyūṭī was trying to minimize the length of the fatwa by not including a comprehensive list of scholars, but when one examines the statements by Taqī al-Dīn and Tāj al-Dīn about logic, they are not conclusive in their condemnation of the discipline. Tāj al-Dīn (d. 771/1370), for example, seems to recognize that logic can be used for good by those with a firm grounding in the religious sciences even as it can become dangerous in the hands of those with inferior training.[47] Elsewhere, he is quoted as saying that logic is "like a sword, which may be used in fighting for Islam and in a highway robbery."[48]

Similarly, al-Suyūṭī omits mention of Sayf al-Dīn al-Āmidī (d. 631/1233) who was "heavily involved in the study of logic alongside the traditional sciences."[49] Also missing from this list is al-Suyūṭī's own respected contemporary, the judge Zakariyyāʾ al-Anṣārī (d. 926/1520), who defends logic in his commentary on the most popular and widely studied handbook on logic during al-Suyūṭī's time, the *Īsāghūjī* of Athīr al-Dīn al-Abharī (d. 633/1264).[50]

As a framing device, al-Suyūṭī's list is telling both in terms of which names the author chooses to include as well as which he omits. In her work on how frames operate in discourse, Tannen explains that frames act as a filter through which we perceive information. She looks for certain kinds of linguistic evidence that point to the expectations of the speaker. If a speaker

[46] Ali, "Statistical Portrait," 266.

[47] Cited in Mufti Ali, "Statistical Portrait," 264 and in Ignaz Goldziher, "The Attitude of Orthodox Islam Toward the Ancient Sciences," in *Studies on Islam*, edited and translated by M.L Swartz (New York: Oxford University Press, 1981), 207. This famous article by Goldziher was first published as "Stellung der alten islamischen Orthodoxie zu den antiken Wissenschaften," *Abhandlung der Königlichen Akademie der Wissenschaften*, 8 (1915): 3–46. All references here are from the English translation cited above.

[48] Cited in Khaled El-Rouayheb, "Sunni Muslim Scholars on the Status of Logic, 1500–1800," *Islamic Law and Society* 11:2 (2004): 219. This quotation of al-Subkī is taken from a fatwa in favor of logic by Ibn Ḥajar al-Haythamī (d. 973/1566). Tāj al-Dīn echoes a similar statement made by Taqī al-Dīn al-Subkī (d. 756/1355) in an earlier fatwa. See Franz Rosenthal, *The Classical Heritage in Islam* (Berkeley: University of California Press, 1965), 81–2.

[49] Wael Hallaq, "Logic, Formal Arguments and Formalization of Arguments in Sunnī Jurisprudence," *Arabica* 37 (1990): 327.

[50] El-Rouayheb, "Sunni Muslim Scholars," 216.

omits information, for example, it could indicate that the speaker finds that detail unremarkable and thus not worth reporting, or the speaker has chosen to leave out information that might contradict his or her interpretation of events.[51]

In this case, al-Suyūṭī presents his audience with a list of authorities all of whom, he says, have written in opposition to logic. While al-Suyūṭī does include al-Ghazālī with the qualification that he opposed logic "toward the end of his life," he omits others whose more nuanced views on logic might contradict his otherwise monolithic framing of the issue. He frames the debate as one in which a consensus exists amongst Sunni scholars against the study of logic when, in reality, the situation was more complicated.

TWO EXEMPLARS IN THE CROSSFIRE: IBN AL-ṢALĀḤ AND AL-GHAZĀLĪ

Two important members of al-Suyūṭī's historical community of practice whose opinions have a bearing on al-Suyūṭī's own reputation (and who thus play a key role in the polemic behind the logic fatwa) are Ibn al-Ṣalāḥ and al-Ghazālī. These two stand out as having driven much of the debate about the permissibility of logic within the community of Shāfiʿī jurists over the ages, and support of one over the other appears to have acted as a kind of litmus test to determine a given jurist's stance on logic. Similarly, the desire to defend both Ibn al-Ṣalāḥ and al-Ghazālī in the debate about logic (as al-Suyūṭī attempts to do) tends to result in complex linguistic and conceptual maneuverings in the discourse.

Ibn al-Ṣalāḥ's Harsh Critique

Al-Suyūṭī declares in the introduction to his *Ṣawn al-manṭiq* an intention to prove the correctness of Ibn al-Ṣalāḥ when he denied the permissibility of pursuing the studying and teaching of logic.[52] This famous fatwa of Ibn

[51] Deborah Tannen, "What's in a Frame?" in *Framing in Discourse*, edited by Deborah Tannen (New York: Oxford University Press, 1993), 41.
[52] Al-Suyūṭī, *Ṣawn al-manṭiq*, 3.

al-Ṣalāḥ carries an even more hostile tone than al-Suyūṭī's toward people who study logic and philosophy. While al-Suyūṭī directs most of his wrath against a single person whose claims he dismisses as ignorant and misguided, Ibn al-Ṣalāḥ goes further in actually calling for the authorities to punish those currently teaching philosophy by removing them from their positions, arresting them, and threatening them with execution.[53]

As Goldziher points out, Ibn al-Ṣalāḥ also employs some polemic against al-Ghazālī in his harsh condemnation of the "use of the terminology of logic in the investigation of religious law" and of "those who think that they can occupy themselves with philosophy and logic merely out of personal interest or through belief in its usefulness."[54] Ibn al-Ṣalāḥ clearly felt the need to react against a trend that had started to grow more and more pervasive after al-Ghazālī—namely, the use of the terminology of logic in fields other than philosophy and *kalām*, including grammar and law. As Goldziher also notes, it was not in fact unheard of for scholars during Ibn al-Ṣalāḥ's time to experience persecution and removal from their teaching positions on charges relating to the teaching of philosophy and related disciplines, as happened to his contemporary, Sayf al-Dīn al-Āmidī (d. 631/1233). Indeed, the historian Michael Chamberlain portrays Ibn al-Ṣalāḥ's intellectual environment as one of frequent *fitna* and upheaval amongst the scholarly elites (though rarely did these disputes require direct intervention by state authorities in order to suppress heresies).[55]

The severity of Ibn al-Ṣalāḥ's critique of the teaching of logic as a discipline as well as his indirect but biting allusion to al-Ghazālī made this fatwa the go-to text "to which the enemies of logic referred."[56] It also put the onus on later Shāfiʿī scholars in particular to explain the basis for Ibn al-Ṣalāḥ's criticisms on the one hand, while, at the same time, showing some deference to al-Ghazālī as a leading authority in Shāfiʿī *fiqh* whose own stance on logic is equivocal and far from straightforward.

[53] Ibn al-Ṣalāḥ al-Shahrazūrī, *Fatāwā Ibn al-Ṣalāḥ* (Cairo: Maktabat Ibn Taymiyya, [1980?], 42–3. Goldziher provides a translation of the text of the fatwa (omitting the question) in his "Ancient Sciences," 205–6.

[54] Goldziher, "Ancient Sciences," 205–6.

[55] Michael Chamberlain, *Knowledge and Social Practice in Medieval Damascus, 1190–1350* (Cambridge, U.K.: University of Cambridge Press, 1994), 171.

[56] Goldziher, "Ancient Sciences," 206.

Al-Ghazālī's Challenging Legacy

In his *Radd ʿalā manṭiq al-Yūnān* (abridged by al-Suyūṭī), Ibn Taymiyya (d. 728/1328) confronts al-Ghazālī's difficult legacy in the logic debate head on. He notes that the method of the logicians "has become widespread since the time of Abū Ḥāmid [al-Ghazālī]" and lists al-Ghazālī's compositions in the field of logic, including his *Miʿyār al-ʿilm, Miḥakk al-naẓar*, the treatise *al-Qisṭās al-mustaqīm*, and the introduction to *al-Mustaṣfā* in which is recorded the notorious statement that "the learning of those who do not know this logic is not to be trusted."[57] Ibn Taymiyya then goes on to insist that al-Ghazālī, toward the end of his life, refuted the views of the logicians and "showed that their method, which is more erroneous than that of the speculative theologians, contains so much ignorance and heresy that it must be censured."[58] This defense of al-Ghazālī based on his changing attitudes toward logic over the course of his career is taken up again by al-Suyūṭī in his early treatise against logic[59] and alluded to in the fatwa, where he includes al-Ghazālī's name near the top of the list of scholars who have written against logic with the important qualification: "toward the end of his life" [*fī ākhiri amrihi*].

Recent scholarship on al-Ghazālī casts doubt on the idea that al-Ghazālī's views on logic changed in any substantive way over the course of his career. ʿAzmi T. Al-Sayyed Ahmad surveys al-Ghazālī's works dealing with logic, making the observation that "it is striking to find that al-Ghazālī's attitude toward logic is invariable and the changes in his outlook, which occurred during the course of his life, only added greater clarity and firmness to this."[60] R.M. Frank adds that, despite the great diversity in both form and focus that his works took over the years, "there is a basic, integrated theoretical system that underlies al-Ghazālī's logical and theological writings, orders them, and gives them consistency" and that al-Ghazālī's works are "to be viewed together as the essentially consistent, albeit rhetorically

[57] Hallaq, *Ibn Taymiyya*, 111.
[58] Hallaq, *Ibn Taymiyya*, 112.
[59] Mufti Ali, *Muslim Opposition to Logic*, 169. Ali also suggests that al-Suyūṭī purposefully limited Ibn Taymiyya's negative references to al-Ghazālī in his abridgement of *al-Radd*.
[60] ʿAzmi T. Al-Sayyed Ahmad, *Al-Ghazālī's Views on Logic*, Ph.D. Diss. (University of Edinburgh, 1981), 27.

modulated, address to his fellow Shāfiʿites and to the *ʿulamāʾ* at large."[61] These authors see in al-Ghazālī's works a grand design in which he attempts a gradual separation of the discipline of logic from philosophy in order to integrate it as a tool in his broader scheme to revive the religious sciences, which includes legal theory and methodology (*uṣūl al-fiqh*) in particular.

Al-Ghazālī begins his project with *Maqāṣid al-falāsifa*, a work in which he outlines the views of the philosophers (focusing primarily on Ibn Sīnā)[62] so that he can refute some of those views in his next work, *Tahāfut al-falāsifa*. First, it is important to note that both works reference 'the philosophers' (*al-falāsifa*) rather than being set up as an attack on philosophy itself (implying that the discipline is not entirely blameworthy and does have some value). In the introduction to the *Maqāṣid*, in which al-Ghazālī clearly expresses his own views, he states that his intention is to present the theories of the philosophers in four different fields of knowledge without distinguishing between those that are true and those that are false, but then goes on to judge the rational sciences (i.e., logic) as being predominantly of a sound methodology (*ʿalā manhaj al-ṣawāb*) with errors occurring only rarely.[63] Al-Ghazālī suggests that it is not the substance of the rational sciences that contradicts correct thinking, but only how the discipline is conceptualized in terms of its technical vocabulary. Even in the *Tahāfut* one gets the impression that al-Ghazālī's primary objection to the philosophers' views on logic is that they try to claim a sort of discursive monopoly on the field, when, in reality, it has been used as a basis for disputation and reflection on rational matters by the theologians for a long time.[64] As al-Ghazālī says:

> Their [the philosophers'] statement that the rules of logic are necessary is correct, but logic (*al-manṭiq*) is not exclusive to them. Rather, it is the subject that we classify in the field of *kalām* under the 'section of theoretical inquiry' (*kitāb al-naẓar*) – they changed its name to 'logic' in order to sound intimidating.

[61] R.M. Frank, *Al-Ghazālī and the Ashʿarite School* (Durham: Duke University Press, 1994), 86–7.

[62] For important background on Ibn Sīnā's integration of key aspects of the Aristotelian tradition into his philosophical works, see Dimitri Gutas, *Avicenna and the Aristotelian Tradition: Introduction to Reading Avicenna's Philosophical Works*, Second Edition (Leiden: Brill, 2014).

[63] Abū Ḥāmid al-Ghazālī, *Maqāṣid al-falāsifa*, edited by Maḥmūd Bījū (Damascus: 2000), 10.

[64] In a later polemical work refuting doctrines of the Ismāʿīlīs, al-Ghazālī even goes so far as to argue that, when conceptualized as a criterion or a just balance with which to judge between truth and falsehood, logical syllogisms exist in the Qurʾān itself. See al-Ghazālī, *al-Qisṭās al-mustaqīm*, edited by Maḥmūd Bījū (Damascus: 1993).

> I have referred to it under the 'section of disputation' (*kitāb al-jadal*) and the 'perceptions of the intellects' (*madārik al-ʿuqūl*). When a gullible enthusiast hears the word 'logic,' he might think that it is an entirely new field unknown to the *mutakallimūn*, pursued by the philosophers alone . . . [65]

In the *Tahāfut* and in the first of his books devoted specifically to logic, *Miʿyār al-ʿilm*, al-Ghazālī agrees to adopt some of the terminology of the logicians for the time being (avoiding temporarily the language of the theologians and jurists) so that he can confront their ideas on their own terms.[66] The *Tahāfut* and the *Miʿyār* are linked, with the *Miʿyār* serving as a kind of appendix or accompanying logic manual to aid the reader's understanding of the *Tahāfut*.[67] The *Miʿyār*, in turn, anticipates its companion work, the *Mīzān al-ʿamal*, further reinforcing the notion that the author is following a master plan rather than shifting capriciously between writing styles, technical vocabularies, and viewpoints. Finally, in *Miḥakk al-naẓar fī l-manṭiq*, al-Ghazālī completes the transition to a neutral terminology and a voice that demonstrates his independence from any single school of thought.[68] Certainly, efforts to confine the accomplished polymath to any sort of ideological box are likely to be frustrated. At the same time, it is easy to see how the fluidity of al-Ghazālī's discourse gives rise to the criticism that he displays a "certain ambivalence" at times such that "one cannot be everywhere certain whether or not al-Ghazālī is speaking in his own voice or whether, when he cites the *falāsifa* explicitly or the *mutakallimūn*, he agrees or disagrees with what he says they say."[69]

Al-Suyūṭī bypasses the majority of al-Ghazālī's complex and often "ambivalent" legacy in his *Ṣawn al-manṭiq*, preferring to quote selectively from two of al-Ghazālī's works written toward the end of his career. The first quotation is from al-Ghazālī's *Fayṣal al-tafriqa bayna al-islām wa-l-zandaqa*[70] and the

[65] Al-Ghazālī, *Tahāfut al-falāsifa*, edited by Sulaymān Dunyā (Cairo: Dār al-Maʿārif, 1962), 85. For alternate translations of this passage, see Al-Sayyed Ahmad, *Al-Ghazālī's Views on Logic*, 30 and the translation by Sabih Ahmad Kamali published as *Al-Ghazali's* Tahafut al-Falasifah (Lahore: Pakistan Philosophical Congress, 1963), 10.

[66] Al-Ghazālī, *Miʿyār al-ʿilm*, edited by Sulaymān Dunyā (Cairo: Dār al-Maʿārif, 1961), 60–1.

[67] Frank, *Al-Ghazālī and the Ashʿarite School*, 93.

[68] Frank, *Al-Ghazālī and the Ashʿarite School*, 94–5.

[69] Frank, *Al-Ghazālī and the Ashʿarite School*, 93.

[70] For an annotated translation of this work, see Sherman A. Jackson, *On the Boundaries of Theological Tolerance in Islam: Abū Ḥāmid al-Ghazālī's* Fayṣal al-tafriqa bayna al-Islām wa al-zandaqa (New York: Oxford University Press, 2002).

second is from *Iḥyāʾ ʿulūm al-dīn*. Neither passage mentions logic specifically, but they do warn against those who base their faith on *kalām* rather than on transmitted texts and who use their knowledge of *kalām* to accuse others of unbelief.[71]

Al-Ghazālī acknowledges in the passage from *al-Fayṣal al-tafriqa* that the purpose of *kalām* is to preserve correct belief and that, while immersing oneself in it is prohibited in most cases, it is permissible in two types of person: one who is plagued by doubts that will not dissipate any other way, and a person who is of strong mind and well rooted in his faith who wants to use *kalām* to refute the attacks and temptations of dangerous innovators.[72] It is also worth noting that, in the passage from *al-Fayṣal al-tafriqa* in particular, al-Ghazālī uses mystical language to describe the correct means with which to pursue enlightenment and soundness of faith, including references to purifying the inner self (*al-bāṭin*) from the murkiness of the world and embracing the knowledge that comes from opening oneself to the light of God—a kind of knowledge that cannot be attained through the weakness of *kalām*.[73] This more nuanced viewpoint stands in contrast to Ibn al-Ṣalāḥ's rather hostile call to arrest teachers of *kalām* and to denounce them as unbelievers.

Al-Ghazālī's legacy in the debate on logic and *kalām* is double-edged in the sense that his work helped to insure the survival of logical studies in eastern Islam by effectively exempting it as a methodological tool from the attacks made against philosophy,[74] even as it helped to fuel a trend of anti-logic rhetoric in Islamic thought that would continue "in theological and philosophical circles long after the twelfth century"[75] in the writings of Ibn Taymiyya, al-Suyūṭī, and others. The difference, though, is that while Ibn Taymiyya tries to refute the claims of the philosophers one by one in a systematic and substantive manner, by al-Suyūṭī's time the arguments have

[71] For the two relatively brief passages from al-Ghazālī quoted in *Ṣawn al-manṭiq*, see al-Ghazālī, *Al-Fayṣal al-tafriqa bayna al-islām wa-l-zandaqa*, edited by Sulaymān Dunyā (Cairo: Dār Iḥyāʾ al-Kutub al-ʿArabiyya, 1961), 202–4 and *Iḥyāʾ ʿulūm al-dīn*, 4 vols. (Cairo: Al-Maṭbaʿa al-Azhariyya al-Miṣriyya, 1898), 1:37.

[72] Al-Suyūṭī, *Ṣawn al-manṭiq*, 186–7.

[73] Al-Suyūṭī, *Ṣawn al-manṭiq*, 188.

[74] Rescher, *The Development of Arabic Logic*, 53.

[75] Majid Fakhry, *A History of Islamic Philosophy*, Third Edition (New York: Columbia University Press, 2004), 324.

already been made, and thus he finds it necessary to repeat them in what Hallaq calls "a shallow and ineffective critique which lacked a respectable methodology or theoretic."[76]

A CLOSER LOOK AT THE ARGUMENTS

After establishing the intellectual context of the logic fatwa within the author's community of practice, I would like to return to the text itself to analyze in more detail the specific arguments of the author. Looking at al-Suyūṭī's arguments will allow an expansion from the micro level of linguistic analysis to the macro level of broader narratives that spring from the text. These larger narratives include the rhetoric of *ijtihād* and *taqlīd*, learning versus ignorance, and hierarchies of knowledge.

The Rhetoric of *Ijtihād* and *Taqlīd*

One of the great ironies behind al-Suyūṭī's logic fatwa is that, while it was written as part of the author's defense of his claims of *ijtihād*, the arguments in the text predominantly support an attitude of *taqlīd*. Or, to put it differently, al-Suyūṭī distinguishes between the *ijtihād* of Shāfiʿī and "those leading authorities of the four schools whom we have named [above], those who set down jurisprudence and demonstrated how to issue legal opinions, those who are the guardians of religion" and the *ijtihād* of his own time. He protests vehemently against the notion that "if one does not know logic then his legal opinions are not correct," arguing that the Companions and Followers got along just fine without the use of formal logic. He evokes the name of Shāfiʿī to suggest that this great early eponym was aware of what logic had to offer and rejected it, even though logic as a discipline within Islamic thought was nowhere near developed by the beginning of the 3rd/9th century.

Similarly, al-Suyūṭī's defense of al-Ghazālī in the fatwa is not based on the latter's ideas as such but on his standing and authority within the *madhhab*. He denounces the claim that "Abū Ḥāmid al-Ghazālī was not a jurist but

[76] Hallaq, *Ibn Taymiyya*, xlix.

rather an ascetic," not by arguing that the two are not mutually exclusive, but by stating that al-Ghazālī must be a jurist because the entire edifice of Shāfiʿī *fiqh* rests on his works in jurisprudence. After listing al-Ghazālī's contributions in the form of "*al-Basīṭ* and *al-Wasīṭ* and *al-Wajīz* and *al-Khulāṣa*" he then makes the point that the books of the two shaykhs (*kutub al-shaykhayn*) rely on al-Ghazālī's works in an allusion to the two pillars of later Shāfiʿī *fiqh*, al-Nawawī (d. 676/1277) and al-Rāfiʿī (d. 623/1226). Therefore, the implication is that anyone who casts doubt on one aspect of al-Ghazālī's reputation undermines all of it, which is completely unacceptable to someone like al-Suyūṭī who sees himself as the natural heir of his esteemed predecessors within the Shāfiʿī school of law. Al-Suyūṭī responds to such accusations by recommending beating and imprisonment "so that no ignoramus would have the insolence to speak about one of the leaders of Islam words that reveal any failing [on their part]."[77]

Finally, there is no better argument for *taqlīd* (or for *ijtihād* within the confines of the *madhhab*) than al-Suyūṭī's highly revealing statement at the end of the logic fatwa to the effect that:

> The *mujtahid* does not make permissible that which is forbidden and does not make forbidden that which is permissible, for prohibition and permission is God's alone and no other's. In fact, the opinion does not even come from the jurist himself; rather, his job is to examine the statements of those who came before him and to choose an opinion for which there is evidence for its being preferable.[78]

This conceptualization of the role of the *mujtahid* contrasts significantly with that which the author mentions just a few lines earlier—the *mujtahidīn* during the first few centuries of Islam, or "those who set down jurisprudence and demonstrated how to issue legal opinions" as an example for subsequent generations to follow.

Thus, al-Suyūṭī is careful to portray his own role in the debate within the parameters that he has set up in the text. On the one hand, he begins his answer by stating unequivocally that the "discipline of logic is a harmful and reprehensible discipline with which it is forbidden to occupy oneself," but then quickly adds: "All of what I mentioned has been expressed by the

[77] Al-Suyūṭī, *al-Qawl al-mushriq*, 246. [78] Al-Suyūṭī, *al-Qawl al-mushriq*, 246.

leaders of the faith and legal scholars." In other words, while he is making the assertion that preoccupying oneself with the study of logic is *ḥarām*, he also wants to make it clear that this opinion is based on the precedent set by the leading authorities both within his own school of law and by scholars from other schools throughout the centuries of Islamic thought. Al-Suyūṭī casts his own stance as a continuation of the views of the *mujtahids* of old, thus seeking to claim a place in the hierarchy for himself.

Learning vs. Ignorance

One of the narratives that resonates quite strongly throughout al-Suyūṭī's logic fatwa is that of the learned against those who are ignorant. Rather than naming his questioner, al-Sūyūṭī refers to him simply as "this ignorant person" (*hādha al-jāhil*). Al-Suyūṭī portrays this person as someone who does not know what he is talking about and who may even be lying outright to serve some malicious intention. At one point, al-Suyūṭī goes so far as to accuse his questioner of polytheism on the grounds that "he said that monotheism rests on the knowledge of [logic] though he does not yet know logic." The questioner's views are contrasted with those of people "who have examined and who know logic." Indeed, it is the repeated references to the "ignorant person" and his outrageous statements that serve as the common theme tying together what would otherwise be seemingly random topics (including everything from the study of logical principles to the use of *ḥashīsh*).

Of course, the central contention (and inherent contradiction) of the fatwa and of al-Suyūṭī's other works on logic is that one must be well versed in a prohibited discipline in order to refute its study. When al-Suyūṭī's enemies took al-Ghazālī's famous statement that the knowledge of one who does not know logic cannot be trusted in his scholarship and interpreted it to mean that a knowledge of logic is a requirement for attaining the rank of *ijtihād*, they put al-Suyūṭī in the uncomfortable position of having to prove his familiarity with the discipline while at the same time having to uphold his early condemnation of it as *ḥarām*.

In his characteristically frank and acerbic introduction to *Ṣawn al-manṭiq*, al-Suyūṭī's asserts:

> In the year that I spoke of what God had endowed upon me in reaching the rank of *ijtihād*, someone mentioned that one of the conditions for *ijtihād* is a knowledge of the art of logic, meaning that this condition was lacking in me according to his claim. What the pathetic person did not realize was that I know it better than those who claim to know it and use it in their disputes. I know its principles and foundations and [how much] of the knowledge of the teachers of logic now is drawn from it; only our teacher Muḥyī al-Dīn al-Kāfiyajī [knows more].[79]

Al-Suyūṭī then sets out to prove his knowledge of logic by listing a plethora of statements from scholars against logic and *kalām*, which make up the text of *Ṣawn al-manṭiq*.

It is significant that in the passage above, al-Suyūṭī mentions his own teacher, al-Kāfiyajī, because it brings to mind the author's account of his own education in the rational sciences as described in his autobiography. He explains that as a youth he studied the *Īsāghūjī* and even composed an abridgement of al-Juwaynī's *Waraqāt*. Then, a *qāḍī* from Tarsus came to stay with al-Kāfiyajī at the Shaykhūniyya *madrasa* and took al-Suyūṭī's abridgement and left, perhaps with the intention of attributing the work to himself back in his own land. Al-Suyūṭī says that he studied some aspects of law with this person and found him lacking in knowledge, so he began to hate logic in general. After seeing statements from scholars against it including the fatwa of Ibn al-Ṣalāḥ, al-Suyūṭī became utterly opposed to logic.[80] According to this account, al-Suyūṭī's distaste toward logic began as a personal problem between him and a teacher whose training he did not respect and then became an ideological issue once he found sources to support his opinion.

Al-Suyūṭī's account of his own conversion from one who occupied himself with logic to one who was completely opposed to the discipline bears a striking similarity to Ibn al-Ṣalāḥ's own early struggle with logic as reported in the biographical work of Ibn Khallikān (and quoted in al-Subkī's *Ṭabaqāt al-shāfiʿiyya*). Both accounts also contain echoes of al-Ghazālī's alleged change of heart later in life in regards to the sciences of logic and philosophy. Indeed,

[79] Al-Suyūṭī, *Ṣawn al-manṭiq*, 1–2. For Mufti Ali's translation of this passage, see his "Jalāl al-Dīn al-Suyūṭī Against Logic and *Kalām*," 24.

[80] Al-Suyūṭī, *al-Taḥadduth bi-niʿmat Allāh*, 241. Sartain provides a translation of this passage in *Jalāl al-Dīn al-Suyūṭī*, 32.

Ibn al-Ṣalāḥ and al-Suyūṭī's accounts are so alike that one suspects a literary *topos* or motif at work. According to this narrative, Ibn al-Ṣalāḥ traveled to Mosul to study logic with the great master of the rational sciences, Kamāl al-Dīn b. Yūnus. However, Ibn al-Ṣalāḥ found himself incapable of learning the discipline and was counseled to abandon it before damaging his reputation to no avail.[81] As Goldziher points out: "Not only did Ibn al-Ṣalāḥ give up the study of logic which proved to be too difficult for him. In the name of religion, he came forward as its archenemy"[82] in his fatwa declaring the study of logic to be *ḥarām* and calling for the arrest and dismissal by the state authority of those who currently teach logic in the schools. One difference between the two accounts is that, while Ibn al-Ṣalāḥ's brain refused to absorb logic, al-Suyūṭī was perfectly capable of producing enviable works in the discipline but declined to do so.[83]

A Hierarchy of Knowledge

At the very end of the account from al-Suyūṭī's autobiography where he describes his early flirtation with logic and subsequent rejection of it, the author adds: "Therefore I gave it up, and God gave me in compensation the science of *ḥadīth*, which is the noblest of all branches of knowledge."[84] So, like Ibn al-Ṣalāḥ, al-Suyūṭī's lack of expertise in the morally questionable field of logic is more than made up for by his brilliance in the irreproachable discipline of *ḥadīth*. This view of a ranking of disciplines by their relative merits is not limited to al-Suyūṭī's autobiography but comes out quite clearly in several of his works, including the fatwa on logic. When faced with the assertion that "logic is an individual duty of every Muslim," al-Suyūṭī retorts: "the

[81] Goldziher recounts this story in his "Ancient Sciences," 204–5.

[82] Goldziher, "Ancient Sciences," 205.

[83] Dwight Reynolds points out that Ibn Sīnā (d. 428/1037) in his autobiography also admits to failing initially to understand Aristotle's *Metaphysics*. Reynolds observes that youthful confessions of failings are "probably the single most enduring theme of childhood in the pre-modern Arabic autobiographical tradition." See Dwight Reynolds, "Childhood in One Thousand Years of Arabic Autobiography," *Edebiyāt* 7:2 (1997): 384–5. Devin Stewart affirms that the tendency on the part of medieval scholars to express shortcomings in childhood is relatively safe as a rhetorical strategy since it implies modesty but does not cast any blame on the autobiographer once he has reached the moral responsibility required in adulthood. See Stewart, "Recounting God's Blessings," 213–14.

[84] Sartain's translation, *Jalāl al-Dīn al-Suyūṭī*, 32.

sciences of exegesis, *ḥadīth* and jurisprudence—the most noble sciences—are not an individual duty [*farḍ ʿayn*] by consensus but rather a collective duty [*farḍ kifāya*]. So, how could logic be greater than those [sciences]?"[85]

Of course, exegesis (*tafsīr*), *ḥadīth* and jurisprudence (*fiqh*) hold a privileged place in the catalogue of Islamic sciences because they are closely linked to the sacred textual sources of the Qurʾān and Prophetic traditions, whereas rational sciences like logic, mathematics, astronomy, and medicine are seen as foreign in origin and distant from the textual sources, relying instead on the human faculty of reason.[86] Therefore, accomplishments in the preferred fields did more to enhance the reputation of scholars who mastered them than proficiency in the rational sciences. In fact, a preoccupation with the rational sciences was more likely to attract accusations of heretical innovation and dangerous philosophical tendencies for the practitioner.

This tension tended to spill over into theological disputes within Sunni Islam (especially between Muʿtazilī and Ashʿarī schools of thought) involving the omnipotence of God and the correct means with which to find absolute truth. Al-Suyūṭī alludes to some of these disputes in the fatwa when he states at the beginning of the opinion that logic is "based on talk of 'primary matter' that [amounts to] unbelief." He goes on to assert: "the proofs of logic are based on universals that do not exist outside of it and do not indicate a particular at all." Both of these arguments can be found in Ibn Taymiyya's *Radd ʿalā manṭiq al-Yūnān*. For example, Ibn Taymiyya refutes the idea of the philosophers that "matter independent of form subsists outside the mind, and that this matter is the primary matter (*hayūlā*) on the basis of which they have constructed the doctrine of the eternity of the World. The majority of scholars have proven them wrong on this score."[87] Also, Ibn Taymiyya

[85] Al-Suyūṭī, *al-Qawl al-mushriq*, 245.

[86] As Goldziher observes, the *ʿulūm al-awāʾil* or the "sciences of the ancients" included "those branches of learning in the literature of Islam that found their way into the sphere of Muslim culture through the direct influence or mediation of works (*kutub al-awāʾil*) that had been taken over from Hellenistic literature... Since the cultivation of these fields of learning followed the Neoplatonic tradition, occult practices and various types of witchcraft (not to mention astrology) were included in the *ʿulūm al-awāʾil* and the sciences of the philosophers" in "Ancient Sciences," 185. Franz Rosenthal provides a helpful overview of the array of sciences from the classical tradition that were incorporated into Islamic thought thanks to the work of translators in the eighth and ninth centuries. See his *The Classical Heritage in Islam* (Berkeley: University of California Press, 1965).

[87] Hallaq, *Ibn Taymiyya*, 25.

is highly critical of sciences like mathematics and metaphysics that rely on concepts (or universals) that exist only in the mind but that "have no reality in the external world."[88]

Al-Suyūṭī likewise dismisses the notion that one's faith or belief in the Oneness of God (*tawḥīd*) is dependent on one's ability to draw logical inferences. Al-Suyūṭī distinguishes between the kind of inference that is based on the principles of logic and the faculty of deduction (*al-istidlāl*) that is innate to all human beings, regardless of their rank or status as intellectuals. He remarks that this absolute faculty of deduction is in the nature of every person:

> even in the nature of the elderly, the Bedouins, and the youth, such as the ability to deduce from the stars that they have a Creator or from the heavens, or the rivers or from fruits and so forth—and this does not require logic or anything like it. The masses and the common people are all believers in this manner.[89]

Therefore, al-Suyūṭī tries to show that one does not need to master the principles of logic in order to comprehend the Oneness of God and to be a true believer.

Surely it is no coincidence that while al-Suyūṭī rejects firmly the notion that knowledge of logic is a requirement for *ijtihād*, he does allow for one to achieve the rank of *mujtahid* in areas in which he himself excels, namely religious law (*al-aḥkām al-sharʿiyya*), Prophetic traditions (*al-ḥadīth al-nabawī*), and the Arabic language (*al-ʿarabiyya*).[90] Furthermore, al-Suyūṭī states that these three were not united in anyone after Taqī al-Dīn al-Subkī (d. 756/1355) except in him.[91] As Sartain observes, it was rather unusual for al-Suyūṭī to speak of attaining the rank of *mujtahid* in fields other than law, which he then had to justify by trying "to define the degree of knowledge in Prophetic tradition and Arabic language which entitles one to claim the rank of *mujtahid*."[92]

Although I discuss al-Suyūṭī's concept of *ijtihād* in more detail in Chapter 3, suffice it to say for now that logic is not included in al-Suyūṭī's list of fields in which he excelled to varying degrees of proficiency. Rather,

[88] Hallaq, *Ibn Taymiyya*, 151.
[89] Al-Suyūṭī, *al-Qawl al-mushriq*, 245.
[90] Al-Suyūṭī, *al-Taḥadduth*, 205.
[91] Al-Suyūṭī, *al-Taḥadduth*, 205.
[92] Sartain, *Jalāl al-Dīn al-Suyūṭī*, 63.

he makes a point of saying that his accomplishments in these fields were reached "according to the way of the great Arab scholars and not according to the methods of the non-Arabs and philosophers."[93] Elsewhere in the autobiography he asserts even more clearly: "As for logic and the philosophical sciences, I do not occupy myself with them because they are *ḥarām*, as al-Nawawī and others have stated, and, even if they were permissible, I would not prefer them to the religious sciences."[94] In short, one cannot ignore the fact that al-Suyūṭī's hierarchy of disciplines was likely not purely a theoretical typography but had a distinctly personal aspect to it as well. Therefore, the idea that knowledge of the science of logic was a requirement for *ijtihād* contradicted al-Suyūṭī's view of himself as a jurist and a *mujtahid*.

THE LARGER CONTEXT: WHAT IS "MAINSTREAM"?

Al-Suyūṭī frames his logic fatwa to suggest that there is a consensus amongst scholars from each of the four Sunni legal schools against the study of logic as a discipline that is both suspiciously foreign in origin and unnecessary as a means of acquiring knowledge. In fact, the situation is considerably more complicated than al-Suyūṭī would have his readers believe. The discourse on logic in Islamic thought (to which al-Suyūṭī is a fairly late contributor) is most often portrayed in the secondary literature as a struggle between the "mainstream" Sunni view and dissenting opinion from a minority opposition. The issue, however, is that both medieval and modern scholars differ as to what the majority and minority opinions are in the case of the permissibility of logic. In this section, I will examine some of the key arguments in the secondary literature about the logic controversy before stating my own interpretation of where al-Suyūṭī fits into this debate based on both external and internal evidence from the text.

The secondary literature on the status of logic in Islamic thought takes as a starting point the influential article by Ignaz Goldziher first published in 1916 and translated into English under the title: "The Attitude of Orthodox Islam Toward the 'Ancient Sciences.'" Goldziher lays out the history of opposition

[93] Al-Suyūṭī, *al-Taḥadduth*, 203.

[94] Sartain's translation, *Jalāl al-Dīn al-Suyūṭī*, 33.

to the *ʿulūm al-awāʾil* as foreign in origin, even though they received patronage at times, particularly from some of the ʿAbbasid caliphs.[95] Following a brief discussion of mathematics and astronomy, Goldziher moves to logic, explaining that:

> While orthodoxy expressed its distrust of these other fields of Greek learning simply by showing a certain preventative concern, the battle against logic was an opposition of fundamental importance. It (orthodoxy) maintained that the recognition of Aristotle's methods of proof was a serious threat to the validity of religious doctrines.[96]

As Goldziher points out, much of the perceived danger surrounding the study of logic lay in its link to theological disputes. Al-Ghazālī changed the terms of the debate by, as Hallaq says, making sure logic "was sifted out of Aristotelian philosophy and thus cleared of its 'non-theistic' tendencies"[97] and bringing it into the field of legal methodology as a tool with which to derive rulings from scripture. Goldziher suggests that it was after al-Ghazālī's time, in the 7th/13th century, that opposition to logic "made decisive progress."[98] He focuses on Ibn al-Ṣalāḥ (d. 643/1245), Ibn Taymiyya (d. 728/1328) and finally al-Suyūṭī (d. 911/1505) as representative of a general current of hostility toward logic amongst Sunni orthodox scholars after the thirteenth century.

However, it is important to note that even Goldziher at the end of his article admits that his sources indicate that "the viewpoint of those who condemned logic was not victorious in the educational system of Islamic theology."[99] He notes that the great rationalist theologian Fakhr al-Dīn al-Rāzī (d. 606/1210) frequently used Aristotelian philosophy "as a methodological tool."[100] Al-Abharī (d. 663/1264) produced a logic textbook (*al-Īsāghūjī*) that became a standard of the theological curriculum and that continued to be used well into al-Suyūṭī's time. Finally, Goldziher acknowledges:

> Just how little impact the anathema of Ibn al-Ṣalāḥ al-Shahrazūrī against logic had, has only recently become evident in the theology of the North African Sanūsī (d. 982/1490) who employed the methods of Greek philosophy and

[95] Goldziher, "Ancient Sciences," 185. [96] Goldziher, "Ancient Sciences," 198.
[97] Hallaq, "Logic," 315. [98] Goldziher, "Ancient Sciences," 204.
[99] Goldziher, "Ancient Sciences," 208. [100] Goldziher, "Ancient Sciences," 208.

whose theology achieved a position of dominance within the orthodox schools of Islam.[101]

In fact, al-Sanūsī was a close contemporary of al-Suyūṭī.

Khaled El-Rouayheb makes an important contribution to the debate surrounding the status of logic in "mainstream" Sunni Islamic thought, particularly in regards to the period between 1500 and 1800 CE.[102] He brings in a new corpus of evidence to challenge Goldziher's assertion that opposition to logic was the prevailing attitude amongst Sunni scholars after the 7th/13th century. By focusing on the roots of pro-logic opinion that led to its flourishing between 1500 and 1800, El-Rouayheb seeks to show that "hostility to logic was indeed a minority view in scholarly circles throughout his period" and even questions "whether hostility to logic was ever a predominant view amongst Sunnī scholars, at least between the endorsement of the discipline by Abū Ḥāmid al-Ghazālī (d. 505/1111) and the rise of the Salafiyya in the nineteenth and twentieth centuries."[103]

El-Rouayheb's article begins with a look at three influential Egyptian jurists, Zakariyyā' al-Anṣārī (d. 926/1520), Shihāb al-Dīn Aḥmad al-Ramlī (d. 957/1550), and Ibn Ḥajar al-Ḥaythamī (d. 973/1566), all of whom indicated that "logic was permissible, indeed praiseworthy and necessary"[104] in contrast to al-Suyūṭī's condemnation of it as prohibited less than a generation before. By the sixteenth century, jurists were still quoting al-Ghazālī's famous remark that he who has no knowledge of logic cannot be trusted in his scholarship and including knowledge of logic as a precondition for *ijtihād*, even as they tried to explain away the objections of Ibn al-Ṣalāḥ by saying that he prohibited the "logic of the philosophers" as opposed to the benign logic of their time.[105]

Although most of these scholars criticized al-Suyūṭī indirectly by attacking his position but not mentioning his name, al-Sanūsī's commentator, the Moroccan scholar al-Ḥasan al-Yūsī (d. 1102/1691), explicitly rejects many

[101] Goldziher, "Ancient Sciences," 208.

[102] El-Rouayheb, "Sunnī Muslim Scholars on the Status of Logic, 1500–1800," *Islamic Law and Society* 11:2 (2004): 213–32.

[103] El-Rouayheb, "Sunnī Muslim Scholars," 215.

[104] El-Rouayheb, "Sunnī Muslim Scholars," 219.

[105] El-Rouayheb, "Sunnī Muslim Scholars," 217–18.

of al-Suyūṭī's claims. For example, he considers laughable al-Suyūṭī's assertion that logic should be prohibited because it relies on universals that do not indicate existing particulars, arguing that all sciences necessarily use universals and to suggest otherwise betrays al-Suyūṭī's ignorance of the discipline.[106] El-Rouayheb notes that al-Yūsī's discussion is clearly a direct response to al-Suyūṭī's fatwa and that he "seems to have been unaware of the much longer and more formidable attack on logic by Ibn Taymiyyah."[107]

El-Rouayheb makes the point that, not only did the Maghribī scholars al-Sanūsī and al-Yūsī exert considerable influence through the large number of commentaries produced on their work, they also trained generations of scholars who would later carry the Maghribī expertise in the field of logic back to Egypt in what amounted to a revival of the study of logic in Egypt during the eighteenth century.[108] This trend is reflected, for instance, in the work of the prominent Egyptian scholars Aḥmad al-Mallawī (d. 1181/1767) and Aḥmad al-Damanhūrī (d. 1192/1778).[109] Al-Mallawī, al-Damanhūrī and ᶜAlī al-ᶜAdawī al-Ṣaᶜīdī (d. 1189/1775) all agree that the type of logic about which there was disagreement was that which was linked with philosophy, whereas the logic of their day was not harmful in any way and, in fact, constituted a communal duty (*farḍ kifāya*).[110]

It is interesting that the scholars of present-day North Africa should be considered particularly accomplished in the logical sciences given al-Suyūṭī's statements in the logic fatwa. In his list of authorities that wrote in opposition to logic, al-Suyūṭī includes under the Mālikī school "most of the North African jurists" (*ᶜāmmat ahl al-maghrib*). This assertion would seem to be in direct contradiction to the evidence presented in El-Rouayheb's research where he shows that, by the end of the seventeenth century, Maghribī scholars had acquired "a reputation for brilliance in the field"[111] that must have had roots during the time of al-Sanūsī and al-Suyūṭī, since such a reputation would presumably have taken a few generations to develop. Nicholas Rescher suggests

[106] El-Rouayheb, "Sunnī Muslim Scholars," 225.
[107] El-Rouayheb, "Sunnī Muslim Scholars," 226.
[108] El-Rouayheb expands on this idea in his subsequent article: "Was There a Revival of Logical Studies in Eighteenth-Century Egypt?" in *Die Welt des Islams* 45:1 (2005): 1–19.
[109] El-Rouayheb, "Sunnī Muslim Scholars," 226.
[110] El-Rouayheb, "Sunnī Muslim Scholars," 227.
[111] El-Rouayheb, "Revival of Logical Studies," 12.

that, as far as Muslim Spain was concerned, logical studies experienced a decline by the thirteenth century after a period of intense activity during the twelfth century. The locus of logical studies shifted back to the East and flourished in Persia, while, by "the year 1300 the fine logical tradition of al-Andalus, which had preserved the work and the standards of al-Fārābī and which produced the magnificent commentaries of Averroes, was extinct."[112] However, the link between the rise and fall of logic in al-Andalus and its apparent revival in North Africa (which later influenced Egypt) is still unclear.

Another important later figure to emerge out of El-Rouayheb's research on logic is Murtaḍā al-Zabīdī (d. 1205/1791).[113] This famous lexicographer and *ḥadīth* scholar enjoyed enormous popularity during his life to the point that he was called "the Suyūṭī of his time."[114] Al-Zabīdī's attitude toward the study of logic is quite revealing in terms of which of al-Suyūṭī's ideas he chose to support and which he chose to reject. El-Rouayheb describes al-Zabīdī's position, "formulated in opposition to the views of Yūsī," as "a qualified defense of Suyūṭī's condemnation of logic."[115] While not declaring logic to be prohibited, he shares al-Suyūṭī's suspicion toward the discipline as encouraging dangerous innovation and contributing to the decline of the study of *ḥadīth* (which was a concern in both centuries). Also, like al-Suyūṭī, he affirms that logic is not essential to faith and that an awareness of the Oneness of God (*tawḥīd*) comes through a more direct experience of the divine rather than through logical demonstration.[116] El-Rouayheb comments that: "Zabīdī's hostility to logic was not representative of Islamic religious scholars of the eighteenth century," in which logic continued as an accepted field of instruction and scholarship.[117]

Opposition to logic did make a comeback, though, according to El-Rouayheb, in the nineteenth and twentieth centuries with the rise of the

[112] Rescher, *The Development of Arabic Logic*, 65.

[113] Stefan Reichmuth, "Murtaḍā az-Zabīdī (d. 1791) in Biographical and Autobiographical Accounts: Glimpses of Islamic Scholarship in the 18th Century" in *Die Welt des Islams*, 39:1 (1999): 66. More information about al-Zabīdī's life can be found in Reichmuth's excellent study: *The World of Murtaḍā al-Zabīdī (1732–91): Life, Networks and Writings* (Cambridge, U.K.: Gibb Memorial Trust, 2009).

[114] Reichmuth, "Glimpses of Islamic Scholarship," 66.

[115] El-Rouayheb, "Revival of Logical Studies," 4.

[116] El-Rouayheb, "Sunnī Muslim Scholars," 228.

[117] El-Rouayheb, "Revival of Logical Studies," 5.

Salafiyya movement. This movement, which he identifies as "inspired in part by the Yemeni scholars Muḥammad b. Ismāʿīl al-Amīr (d. 1182/1768) and Muḥammad al-Shawkānī (d. 1250/1834), and in part by the Wahhābī movement of central Arabia" revived the ideas of Ibn Taymiyya as central to their enterprise, including his condemnation of logic.[118] Even though al-Suyūṭī and his fellow Sunni scholars opposed to logic may have represented a minority view during the pre-modern period, their ideology did gain ground in the more recent *salafī* and Wahhābī movements, which "were so influential that they could hardly be called an 'undercurrent.' "[119]

In a recent article, Mufti Ali criticizes El-Rouayheb's thesis and defends Goldziher's contention that resistance to logic began in the 2nd/8th century and reached a peak in the thirteenth and fourteenth centuries. Ali bases his conclusions on the "rich prosopographical data" found in al-Suyūṭī's four works on logic.[120] While the background information that Ali provides concerning the composition and content of these works is laudable, and the table listing the authorities cited by al-Suyūṭī is also extremely useful, the conclusions that he draws from the data require careful examination. First, the individuals are given equal weight in Ali's analysis whether they composed a whole volume specifically condemning logic or if they mentioned philosophy in passing. Also, it should be noted that the list includes only works known to al-Suyūṭī and, of those, only those that he chose to record. As mentioned earlier, it is problematic to assume that the majority of scholars who opposed logic were Shāfiʿīs based in Egypt and Syria, since those would automatically be the group most known to al-Suyūṭī and closest to his own community of practice. So, although Mufti Ali's research presents a valuable set of data, he does not go far enough in questioning some of the motives behind al-Suyūṭī's account and its larger significance.[121]

[118] El-Rouayheb, "Sunnī Muslim Scholars," 230. For more on al-Suyūṭī's connection to the *salafī* scholars of Yemen, especially al-Shawkānī, see Chapter 3.

[119] El-Rouayheb, "Sunnī Muslim Scholars," 231.

[120] Mufti Ali, "Statistical Portrait," 253.

[121] Aaron Spevack adds a third interpretation occupying a middle ground between Ali and El-Rouayheb in his "Apples and Oranges: The Logic of the Early and Later Arabic Logicians," *Islamic Law and Society* 17 (2010): 159–84. He argues that the period between the thirteenth and fifteenth centuries marked a transition in the thought of Sunni scholars in which neither opposition to logic nor support thereof achieved predominance. Spevack criticizes Ibn Taymiyya and al-Suyūṭī for taking a "monolithic" stance that lumped together two different

A broader view of the history of logic in Islamic thought suggests an ebb and flow of two parallel strains—one accepting of logic and one in opposition to it. Rescher outlines the development of logic as following more or less distinct phases where the locus of creative output in the logical sciences shifted geographically in response to political events in different time periods. While instances of violence against logicians and their works did occur,[122] this undeniable current of hostility did not succeed in stamping out logic as a field of study in Islamic scholarship. The watershed moment came with the work of al-Ghazālī, who did the most to separate logic as a tool from that which was associated with philosophy, thus allowing its gradual incorporation into the fields of theology and law.[123] Even the loud and persistent protests of Ibn al-Ṣalāḥ and Ibn Taymiyya did not manage to stem the tide advocating the permissibility of logical studies. As Tony Street puts it, Ghazālī's "achievement was not the end of all opposition to logic among Muslim scholars, though future attacks on logic never seriously affected the study of the discipline."[124] By the 7th/13th century, logical studies had become an accepted sub-discipline of religious instruction as students memorized handbooks as part of their education.[125]

CONCLUSION

The aim of this chapter is to demonstrate a method with which to gain access to the meaning behind a text like al-Suyūṭī's fatwa prohibiting the study of logic. As with Brustad's approach to al-Suyūṭī's autobiography, I attempt to acquire insight into the pragmatic goals and motivations driving the arguments of the author through an analysis of both internal linguistic evidence and external historical evidence from the immediate and broader social

approaches to logic practiced by earlier and later logicians. While earlier logicians tended to incorporate ideas from Greek philosophy into the realm of logic, later logicians generally did not include these elements.

[122] See, for example, recorded instances of book burning, exile and threats made against scholars in Rescher, *The Development of Arabic Logic*, 59–60.

[123] Rescher, *The Development of Arabic Logic*, 53.

[124] Tony Street, "Arabic Logic" in *Handbook of the History of Logic*, edited by Dov M. Gabbay and John Woods, 7 vols. (Amsterdam: Elsevier B.V., 2004), 1:559.

[125] Rescher, *The Development of Arabic Logic*, 63.

context in which the text was produced. Identifying certain themes and narratives that underlie the framing of the text not only helps to explain the significance of this particular fatwa, but will prove useful in looking at other parts of al-Suyūṭī's legal discourse as well. This approach allows me to make a number of observations regarding the role of the jurist in al-Suyūṭī's fatwa and where the author might envision himself within that framework.

First, even though the fatwa does prohibit the study of logic, that is not its primary function. The frame device of the fatwa allows al-Suyūṭī to reply to specific challenges to his authority as a *mujtahid*. The most serious of these claims is the contention that knowledge of logic is necessary both for correct faith and for authoritative legal rulings. Al-Suyūṭī's rejection of logic was clear even from the age of eighteen when he produced his first statement on the subject (much to the disgust of some of his fellow scholars). It was his claim to be a *mujtahid* that was still under fiercely critical discussion toward the end of his life, and the logic debate only helped to fuel the ongoing controversy.

In answering his questioner, al-Suyūṭī frames the argument as one of the pious and learned against the sinful and ignorant. He uses phrases like "this ignorant person" to diminish the status of his opponent and even goes so far as to recommend flogging and imprisonment as punishment for the person's offensive statements. In contrast, the author portrays himself as the latest in a list of experts and leaders of the faith who have reached the same conclusion regarding logic after careful and informed study. Thus, al-Suyūṭī appeals to his community of jurists by showing his own opinion to be in accordance with the scholarly consensus. In order to do this, he has to resort to some rhetorical posturing, such as his support of both al-Ghazālī and Ibn al-Ṣalāḥ (even though their views on logic conflicted to a large extent). Also, in order to prove his own knowledge of the discipline, al-Suyūṭī has to demonstrate an understanding of principles that he has just declared to be forbidden.

Internal and external evidence from al-Suyūṭī's logic fatwa reveal it to be the final desperate effort of a scholar to gain the recognition of his peers in the face of criticism and attack. Al-Suyūṭī provides a defense of his own early and forceful opposition to the study of logic by arguing that it is consistent with the opinion of other leading scholars of law, especially within his own

Shāfiʿī school (omitting reference to Shāfiʿīs like al-Āmidī who did not support this view). Through the discussion on logic, al-Suyūṭī seeks to influence the broader debate surrounding the role and qualifications of the *mujtahid*. He casts the *mujtahid* as one who shows a high level of achievement in what he considers to be the superior sciences of *ḥadīth* and *tafsīr*, while denying such a distinction in inferior and morally questionable foreign fields such as logic (in contrast to al-Ghazālī in his *Mustaṣfā*). Moreover, he frames the *mujtahid* of the 9th/15th century as one who does not deviate from precedent but rather selects preferable opinions from those that already exist, thereby re-defining what it means to do *ijtihād*. Therefore, al-Suyūṭī sets out to define the role of the *mujtahid* as one that he himself fulfills, while his enemies and detractors are left to occupy the positions of ignorant fools and dangerous heretics.

3

Authority by Articulation: The Language of Religious Revival and Reform in al-Suyūṭī's *Tajdīd* Genre

INTRODUCTION

Jalāl al-Dīn al-Suyūṭī is above all else known for his claims to be a *mujtahid* (scholar capable of independent legal reasoning) as well as the *mujaddid* (renewer or restorer of religion) at the turn of the ninth century AH. Indeed, Sartain does not exaggerate when she says that these claims made al-Suyūṭī "the most controversial figure of his time."[1] It is no surprise, then, that this aspect of his legal persona has also received the most attention in the secondary literature. In fact, it would be difficult to write about al-Suyūṭī's legal thought and portrayal of himself as a jurist without including a discussion of *ijtihād* and *tajdīd* and what those two important concepts mean to the 9th/15th century author. Al-Suyūṭī's status as a *mujtahid* and *mujaddid* represents the linchpin of his self-framing enterprise and it is these elements of his legal persona that bear the most significant implications for his legacy.

There can be little doubt that *ijtihād* and *tajdīd* are closely linked in al-Suyūṭī's frame of reference. Hallaq and others have been swift to point out that al-Suyūṭī considered attaining the rank of *mujtahid* a prerequisite to claiming the title of *mujaddid*,[2] which is clear from his autobiography where al-Suyūṭī prefaces a chapter on *tajdīd* with a chapter entitled: "A record of God's favor in granting me mastery over the sciences and attaining the rank

[1] E.M. Sartain, *Jalāl al-Dīn al-Suyūṭī: Biography and Background*, 2 vols. (Cambridge, U.K.: Cambridge University Press, 1975), 1:72.

[2] Wael B. Hallaq, "Was the Gate of Ijtihād Closed?" *International Journal of Middle East Studies* 16 (1984): 27.

The Legal Thought of Jalāl al-Dīn al-Suyūṭī: Authority and Legacy. Rebecca Skreslet Hernandez.

of *ijtihād*."[3] The author does not limit his claims to the autobiography but repeats them for good measure either directly or indirectly in a number of different instances,[4] perhaps in the hopes that his assertions would gain greater acceptance through repetition. Sartain notes that it was a habit of al-Suyūṭī when challenged in a dispute to issue an angry treatise (or two or three) declaring the correctness of his opinion and the ignorance of his opponents, striving to have the last word on the matter in question.[5] Even when his initial claims to the rank of *mujtahid* were poorly received by his colleagues, al-Suyūṭī's "confidence in his ability was such that he went ahead undaunted to make the more serious claim to be the awaited *mujaddid*."[6]

Despite the strong link between the rank of *mujtahid* and *mujaddid* in al-Suyūṭī's writings, there are some important differences between the two concepts as well. The secondary literature focuses on the fact that, "whereas the concept of *ijtihād* was extensively discussed, developed and systematized by Muslim scholars, that of *tajdīd* was not."[7] This observation leads Ella Landau-Tasseron to conclude "that *tajdīd* was not a central concept in the evolution of medieval Islamic thought; it was rather an honorific title bestowed on individuals over the ages, and the conceptual aspect was secondary, involving mainly the qualifications of the candidates."[8] In a similar but slightly different vein, after arguing that the concept of *tajdīd* "appeared initially in Islam under the influence of Jewish sources," Hava Lazarus-Yafeh goes on to say: "its appearance in Arabic literature never became very frequent, and it is questionable whether it has ever served in classical Islam as

[3] Jalāl al-Dīn al-Suyūṭī, *al-Taḥadduth bi-niʿmat Allāh*, edited by E.M. Sartain (Cambridge, U.K.: Cambridge University Press, 1975), 203. Al-Suyūṭī's chapter on *tajdīd* is titled *Dhikr al-mabʿūthīn ʿalā raʾs kull miʾa* ("A Record of Those Sent at the Turn of Every Century") and the date given in the autobiography is 896 AH. In 899, al-Suyūṭī issued a longer treatise containing many of the same sources and arguments as the *tajdīd* chapter but with more emphasis on the coming apocalypse as well as a much more forceful statement of the author's own accomplishments as a potential *mujaddid*. This treatise has been published as: al-Suyūṭī, *al-Tanbiʾa bi-man yabʿathuhu Allāh ʿalā raʾs kull miʾa*, (Mecca: Dār al-Thiqa li-l-Nashr wa-l-Tawzīʿ, 1990).

[4] For example, in a short treatise entitled *Taqrīr al-istinād fī tafsīr al-ijtihād* (Alexandria: Dār al-Daʿwa li-l-Ṭabʿ wa-l-Nashr wa-l-Tawzīʿ, 1983), al-Suyūṭī outlines the levels and qualifications for the *mujtahid* before including the section, "The *mujtahid* is a *mujaddid* for the religion in every century," in which he argues that all of the designated *mujaddids* were also *mujtahids* in their time (59–62) and that *ijtihād* has never ceased (66).

[5] Sartain, *Jalāl al-Dīn al-Suyūṭī*, 53. [6] Sartain, *Jalāl al-Dīn al-Suyūṭī*, 71–2.

[7] Ella Landau-Tasseron, "The 'Cyclical Reform': A Study of the *Mujaddid* Tradition," *Studia Islamica* 70 (1989): 83.

[8] Landau-Tasseron, "Cyclical Reform," 84.

the stimulus for a movement or a concrete action."[9] Hamid Algar also admits the relatively undeveloped ideas surrounding *tajdīd* in the medieval Islamic context: "The attention paid to the *mujaddid* in Islamic history has, however, been remarkably uneven; it cannot be said that even the pious have regularly attempted to identify the *mujaddid* of their age at each turn of the century."[10]

Although the secondary literature interprets this difference between *ijtihād* and *tajdīd* in different ways, much of the confusion seems to lie in the elusiveness and fluidity of the *tajdīd* concept itself as well as its subtle changes in meaning over time. The concept of *tajdīd* in Islamic thought has accumulated meaning over time in the sense that scholars working in different eras have molded it to address the concerns of their particular contexts. At the same time, though, *tajdīd* remains rooted in certain common themes, symbols, ideologies, and modes of expression. In this way, the scholar uses the *tajdīd* framework much in the same way that Bakhtin suggests that a great author uses genre. As he puts it: "Genres (of literature and speech) throughout the centuries of their life accumulate forms of seeing and interpreting particular aspects of the world. For the writer-craftsman the genre serves as an external template, but the great artist awakens the semantic possibilities that lie within it."[11] The individual scholar taps into the potential stored within the existing framework, supplementing and shaping it "to give it more roundness and finality."[12] The artist frees the concept from the captivity of the past to imbue it with new meaning for the future.

This chapter argues that al-Suyūṭī as an individual played a pivotal role during a key transitional era in Islamic thought by striving to recapture the classical concept of *tajdīd* from possible obscurity and transforming its potential as a tool in later discussions about reform and orthodoxy in the early modern and modern eras. In a period of great anxiety and instability, al-Suyūṭī affirmed the need for an unbroken chain of *mujtahid*s for every

[9] Hava Lazarus-Yafeh, "*Tajdīd al-Dīn*: A Reconsideration of Its Meaning, Roots and Influence in Islam," in *Studies in Islamic and Judaic Traditions*, edited by William M. Brinner and Stephen D. Ricks (Atlanta: Scholars Press, 1986), 99.

[10] Hamid Algar, "The Centennial Renewer: Bediüzzaman Said Nursi and the Tradition of *Tajdīd*," *Journal of Islamic Studies* 12:3 (2001): 297.

[11] M.M. Bakhtin, "Response to a Question from the *Novy Mir* Editorial Staff," in *Speech Genres and Other Late Essays*, edited by Caryl Emerson and Michael Holquist, translated by Vern W. McGee (Austin: University of Texas Press, 1986), 5.

[12] Bakhtin, "Response to a Question," 6.

age and declared in bold terms the imperative to restore the community to correct belief and practice and to fight against the threat of intellectual stagnation and corruption.

Although al-Suyūṭī's framing of himself as the *mujaddid* of the ninth Islamic century failed to convince many of his contemporaries, his legacy spread as later champions of *ijtihād* and *tajdīd* continued to find meaning in his works. These later reformers built on the legacy of past scholars adding their own significant contributions to what can be termed a "*tajdīd* genre" in Islamic thought. This chapter traces the development of the *tajdīd* genre as it existed before, during, and after al-Suyūṭī's time. Looking at which themes changed and which remained consistent over time, I argue that al-Suyūṭī succeeded in liberating the classical concept from the shackles of the past and in helping to unlock its potential for future generations almost in spite of his own efforts.

TAJDĪD BEFORE AL-SUYŪṬĪ

Eschatological Implications of the Tradition

The Prophetic *ḥadīth* that provides the textual basis for the *mujaddid* tradition can be found in the *Sunan* of Abū Dāwūd: "God will send to this community at the turn of every century someone to renew for it its religion."[13] The placement of the text in Abū Dāwūd's *Kitāb al-malāḥim* (book of battles, or portents of the end of the world) has prompted a debate in the secondary literature about the possible eschatological context for the tradition. Yohanan Friedmann, for example, postulates a link between the appearance of the centennial renewer and postponement of the Day of Judgment, but admits that this may not have been the tradition's primary role,[14] while Landau-Tasseron is more skeptical about the eschatological connection citing limited evidence.[15] Landau-Tasseron and Algar are probably right in suggesting that the apocalyptic context in which the *ḥadīth* appears depends on the "circumstances

[13] Algar observes that this tradition is absent from the Shiʿi collections, though one does run across the occasional list of Shiʿi renewers ("The Centennial Renewer," 292 n. 3).

[14] Yohanan Friedmann, *Prophecy Continuous: Aspects of Aḥmadī Religious Thought and Its Medieval Background* (New Delhi: Oxford University Press, 2003), 97.

[15] Landau-Tasseron, "Cyclical Reform," 80.

of the times and places in question, not to the conditions under which the Hadith first entered circulation."[16] It is likely not a coincidence that the role of the *mujaddid* in delaying the Day of Judgment would crop up in the eighth century AH in the writings of Zayn al-Dīn al-ʿIrāqī (d. 806/1404) when anxieties about the end of the Islamic millennium were starting to run rampant.[17]

The eschatological connotations of the tradition are similarly important for al-Suyūṭī, who was writing at a time when scholars were actively debating how many years the community had left before the coming of the Mahdī. Al-Suyūṭī devotes a sizeable section of his *Tanbiʾa* to this question, chronicling all of the trials and disasters that the community has faced at the turn of each century.[18] Some of the disasters listed include plagues, political and doctrinal corruption, invasions by foreign powers such as the Mongols and the Franks, and of course the deterioration of scholarship in general, leading to a dangerous scarcity of *mujtahids*. He argues in accordance with Ibn ʿAsākir's interpretation that, since the trial (*miḥna*) affects the whole community, the mission of the renewer must also be of universal benefit. As is so often the case, al-Suyūṭī's remarks are "double-voiced" in response to critics who would argue that the imminent apocalypse and arrival of the Mahdī eclipses the need for a ninth *mujaddid*.[19]

The *Ahl al-Bayt* Factor

A variant of the same tradition reads: "God will send to this community at the turn of every century a man from my family [*min ahl baytī*] to renew their religion for them."[20] The mention of the Prophet's family strengthens

[16] Algar, "The Centennial Renewer," 293.

[17] Landau-Tasseron, "Cyclical Reform," 80. See also al-Suyūṭī, *al-Taḥadduth*, 227. In his study of authority in the work of Ibn Qāḍī Shuhbah (d. 851/1448), R. Kevin Jaques observes that an ideology of crisis and decline seems to permeate late Mamluk historiography. In addition to a general sense of anxiety reflected in the work of scholars from this time period, Jaques detects signs of popular resentment against jurists for failing to guide the community in times of peril. This resentment spilled over into debates about the existence of *mujtahids* and the need for legal reform. See R. Kevin Jaques, *Authority, Conflict, and the Transmission of Diversity in Medieval Islamic Law* (Leiden: Brill, 2006), 2–3.

[18] Al-Suyūṭī, *al-Tanbiʾa*, 69–71.

[19] On this point, see also al-Suyūṭī's *al-Kashf ʿan mujāwazat hādhihi al-umma al-alf* in *al-Ḥāwī li-l-fatāwī*, 2 vols. (Beirut: Dār al-Kutub al-ʿIlmiyya, 2000), 2:81–6.

[20] Cited in Tāj al-Dīn al-Subkī, *al-Ṭabaqāt al-shāfiʿiyya al-kubrā*, 8 vols. (Giza: Hajr, 1992), 1:200; also cited in al-Suyūṭī, *al-Taḥadduth*, 216 but with slightly different wording.

the case for the first two renewers, ʿUmar b. ʿAbd al-ʿAzīz (d. 101/720) and Muḥammad b. Idrīs al-Shāfiʿī (d. 204/820) but complicates the matter for later *mujaddids* who could not claim such descent. This issue occasioned some creative interpretations of who could rightfully be considered to be from the Prophet's family. For example, Tāj al-Dīn al-Subkī (d. 773/1371) in his famous biographical dictionary, *al-Ṭabaqāt al-shāfiʿiyya*, acknowledges that it is more difficult to speak of a *mujaddid* after the second century who fits this criterion, but explains that most of the renewers are from the Shāfiʿī legal school and were sent to fulfill the task of strengthening the school at the turn of every century.[21] Al-Subkī suggests that being a Shāfiʿī scholar and working in the interests of the school amounts to the same function as claiming descent from the Prophet's family. While medieval jurists like al-Subkī tried to explain away the *ahl al-bayt* factor or modify it to suit their own polemical purposes, this aspect of the *tajdīd* genre was never completely forgotten and would resurface later in connection to ideas about the emergence of the Mahdī.[22]

Soundness of the Tradition

The great authorities on *ḥadīth* criticism, al-Ḥākim al-Nīsābūrī (d. 405/1014) and Ibn Ḥajar al-ʿAsqalānī (d. 852/1449) evaluate the *mujaddid* tradition as sound, based on the reliability of its transmitters as well as on statements attributed to Ibn Shihāb al-Zuhrī (d. 124/742) and Aḥmad b. Ḥanbal (d. 241/855). Ibn Ḥajar, for instance, notes that al-Zuhrī preceded Ibn Ḥanbal in affirming that ʿUmar was the *mujaddid* for the first century, which to him indicates that the tradition was known already in the first century, thus strengthening its authority.[23] Al-Suyūṭī records several different statements by Ibn Ḥanbal, all affirming ʿUmar's status and praising al-Shāfiʿī as the renewer at the turn of the second century.

[21] Al-Subkī, *al-Ṭabaqāt al-shāfiʿiyya*, 1:200 and al-Suyūṭī, *al-Taḥadduth*, 218. See also Ignaz Goldziher, "Ignaz Goldziher on al-Suyūṭī," edited and translated by John Hunwick, *The Muslim World* 68:2 (1978): 81–2.

[22] Algar, "The Centennial Renewer," 295. A sizeable section of al-Suyūṭī's *Tanbiʾa* deals with the *ahl al-bayt* factor (34–45). Al-Suyūṭī even hints at one point that his own genealogy includes a possible connection to the Prophet's family (67).

[23] Al-Suyūṭī, *al-Taḥadduth*, 216.

Of course, it is prudent to consider these statements with some degree of skepticism. First, although Ibn Ḥanbal was certainly familiar with al-Shāfiʿī and his work, and "despite the abundance in the biographies linking the two, it does not seem that they were well acquainted."[24] At a time when orthodoxy and innovation had yet to be fully defined, it is safe to say that al-Shāfiʿī and Ibn Ḥanbal were not always in agreement and in fact differed considerably in their legal methodologies.[25] Indeed, Ibn Ḥanbal has even been cast as critical of al-Shāfiʿī's use of opinion (*raʾy*) in his works.[26] Also, the *mujaddid* tradition as a concept was not regularly cited by Muslim scholars until much later, becoming more frequent during the 5th/11th century.[27] It is therefore possible that Ibn Ḥanbal's endorsement of al-Shāfiʿī reflects a need on the part of later scholars both to validate al-Shāfiʿī as an orthodox *mujaddid* as well as to render greater authority and legitimacy to the Shāfiʿī school in general.

Polemical Implications of the Tradition

It is clear that pro-Sunni, pro-Shāfiʿī and pro-Ashʿarī polemics played a key role in the development of the *tajdīd* genre prior to the time of al-Suyūṭī. One of the fundamental functions of the *mujaddid* is to promote correct and proper practice (*sunna*) and to eradicate heresy and dangerous innovations (*bidʿa*). One might even say that during the 4th/10th and 5th/11th centuries and beyond the device of naming a *mujaddid* for the turn of each century acted as a kind of proxy in the larger theological and doctrinal debates occupying legal scholars. Landau-Tasseron, for example, notes that "the mere names of the *mujaddidūn* served as an argument in the Sunnite polemics against the Muʿtazila."[28]

Two sources that al-Suyūṭī cites regarding the *mujaddid* are Tāj al-Dīn al-Subkī's *Ṭabaqāt* and Abū al-Qāsim b. ʿAsākir's (d. 571/1153) *Tabyīn kadhib al-muftarī ʿalā Abū al-Ḥasan al-Ashʿarī*, both of which have been identified by George Makdisi as "Ashʿarite propaganda."[29] Al-Suyūṭī quotes extensively from

[24] E. Chaumont, "al-Shāfiʿī," *Encyclopaedia of Islam*, Second Edition (Brill Online, 2010).
[25] Christopher Melchert, *Aḥmad Ibn Ḥanbal* (Oxford, U.K.: Oneworld Publications, 2006), 79.
[26] Landau-Tasseron, "Cyclical Reform," 109.
[27] Lazarus-Yafeh, "*Tajdīd al-Dīn*," 101.
[28] Landau-Tasseron, "Cyclical Reform," 113.
[29] George Makdisi, "Ashʿarī and the Ashʿarites in Islamic Religious History I," *Studia Islamica* 17 (1962): 57.

al-Subkī but the reference to Ibn ʿAsākir is contained within a long quotation from a source that al-Suyūṭī is not able to identify but which Sartain has traced to Badr al-Dīn al-Ahdal's (d. 855/1451) *al-Risāla al-marḍiyya fī nuṣrat madhhab al-Ashʿariyya* (which could also be described as pro-Ashʿarī polemic).[30] Al-Ahdal notes that Ibn ʿAsākir, for example, prefers Ashʿarī as the *mujaddid* for the third century over Ibn Surayj (d. 306/918) as well as Abū Bakr al-Bāqillānī (d. 403/1013) who, in spite of being a Mālikī jurist and not a Shāfiʿī like the majority of the renewers, was nevertheless a strong supporter of Ashʿarī theology.[31]

Makdisi speaks of a broader struggle within Sunni Islamic thought starting around the 5th/11th century in Baghdad and Khurāsān and later moving toward Damascus that went beyond a simple clash of Ashʿarī and Muʿtazilī theological schools.[32] Instead, he describes a conflict within the Shāfiʿī school itself between rationalist and traditionalist forces as Ashʿarism started to take hold. This infiltration of Ashʿarism into the Shāfiʿī school was not as smooth as later pro-Ashʿarī sources (like al-Subkī) suggest, but rather "proved for the Ashʿarites a very hard nut to crack."[33] This debate played into another controversy within the ranks of Shāfiʿī scholars and beyond about the role of rationalist *kalām* in the Islamic sciences versus the primacy of *ḥadīth* in which the renowned Abū Ḥāmid al-Ghazālī (d. 505/1111) played a key role.[34] Interestingly, al-Ghazālī is overwhelmingly recognized by Shāfiʿī sources as the *mujaddid* for the fifth century AH. Remnants of these discussions were still alive in the scholarly community during al-Suyūṭī's time, forcing him to situate his own claims to be a *mujtahid* and *mujaddid* within this highly sensitive arena.[35]

The Importance of al-Ghazālī

Al-Ghazālī is also significant in the history of the development of the *tajdīd* genre because he is the only scholar before al-Suyūṭī to claim the rank for

[30] Sartain, *Jalāl al-Dīn al-Suyūṭī*, 213; al-Suyūṭī, *al-Taḥadduth*, 224. The source is identified in the *Tanbiʾa*, 61.
[31] Al-Suyūṭī, *al-Taḥadduth*, 224.
[32] Makdisi, "Ashʿarī and the Ashʿarites," 47.
[33] Makdisi, "Ashʿarī and the Ashʿarites," 47–8.
[34] Makdisi, "Ashʿarī and the Ashʿarites," 56.
[35] For a discussion of al-Suyūṭī's views concerning philosophy, *kalām*, and especially logic and his claims to be a *mujtahid*, see Chapter 2.

himself (in addition to having it conferred upon him by others).[36] Naturally, he does so in a suitably indirect and humble fashion. In al-Ghazālī's "spiritual autobiography," *al-Munqidh min al-ḍalāl*, he reflects upon his decision to return to teaching after an eleven-year absence. He explains that his return in the year 499 AH was pre-ordained by God because God promised to revive (*bi-iḥyāʾ*) His religion at the turn of every century.[37]

There are a number of noteworthy sentiments contained within al-Ghazālī's statements. First, it has been suggested that al-Ghazālī's use of the term *iḥyāʾ* may reflect a deliberate choice on his part in order to draw a connection with his own masterpiece, *Iḥyāʾ ʿulūm al-dīn*.[38] It is clear from the passage in question that al-Ghazālī saw his own task in terms of imparting knowledge (*ʿilm*), not in the pursuit of glory, but in the interests of reforming himself first and then others.[39] Also, al-Ghazālī is not the last to use the term *iṣlāḥ* in relation to reform and renewal, though the term would come to take on meanings and significance for reformers in later Islamic thought that al-Ghazālī could not have anticipated.[40] Finally, al-Ghazālī is careful to characterize his decision to return to teaching not as a personal one made on the basis of practical or mundane considerations, but as one that was ordained by God and then communicated to him by righteous persons who had in turn come to the idea through recurring dreams and visions.[41]

Thus, al-Ghazālī provides three different justifications for his return and desire to implement a revivification and reform of the religious sciences: the will of God, the favorable opinion of his contemporaries, and instruction through dreams. Al-Ghazālī's interpretation of the *tajdīd* genre would find

[36] Kenneth Garden argues persuasively that al-Ghazālī's works reflect a systematic attempt by the author to promote a revivalist agenda using "the language of revival and renewal." Garden casts al-Ghazālī as a politically savvy scholar fully aware of his own intellectual and religious authority. See Garden, *The First Islamic Reviver: Abū Ḥāmid al-Ghazālī and his* Revival of the Religious Sciences (New York: Oxford University Press, 2014). For another interesting reading of al-Ghazālī's thought, especially in relation to the Saljuk political authorities of the time, see Omid Safi, *The Politics of Knowledge in Premodern Islam: Negotiating Ideology and Religious Inquiry* (Chapel Hill: University of North Carolina Press, 2006).

[37] Al-Ghazālī, *al-Munqidh min al-ḍalāl* (Egypt: Maktabat al-Anjlū al-Miṣriyya, 1962), 190. Al-Suyūṭī quotes this section of al-Ghazālī's *Munqidh* in his *Tanbiʾa* (47–8).

[38] Lazarus-Yafeh, "*Tajdīd al-Dīn*," 103.

[39] Al-Ghazālī, *al-Munqidh*, 190–1.

[40] See John O. Voll, "Renewal and Reform in Islamic History: *Tajdid* and *Islah*," in *Voices of Resurgent Islam*, edited by John L. Esposito (New York: Oxford University Press, 1983), 32.

[41] Al-Ghazālī, *al-Munqidh*, 190.

resonance not only with al-Suyūṭī but also with reformers after him, particularly those inclined toward Sufism. It remains a matter for debate, however, how aware al-Ghazālī was of the *mujaddid* tradition at the end of the 5th/11th century that had yet to be fully developed. Lazarus-Yafeh, for instance, writes: "although al-Ghazālī considered himself destined to be a messenger of religious renewal, and therefore wrote this book [the *Iḥyāʾ*], there is no indication that he believed that this was the special task of a specific person at the end of every century—a conviction that was subsequently consolidated in Islam."[42]

Still, for al-Ghazālī, the assertion paid off in the sense that he was recognized quite decisively as the most influential Shāfiʿī scholar of his generation, whereas for other *mujaddids* the process was not resolved so neatly and "no formal method of appointing a *mujaddid* ever evolved."[43] This ambiguity in the historical process of identifying *mujaddids* has given rise to some debate in the secondary literature. For example, Goldziher in his classic article asserts:

> The mujaddid was to be recognized not through a majority of votes in authoritative circles; rather he would owe this distinction to his popularity and, as we have noted, to the *vox populi*, on which no influence could generally have been exerted and certainly, in most cases, not until after the death of the person recognized as the regenerator would there arise a general manifestation of this.[44]

Landau-Tasseron disputes the notion that a general consensus was the determining factor but insists rather that the claim must first be made and "it depended on *ijmāʿ* whether or not it was accepted."[45] Landau-Tasseron also points out that the claim was generally put forward by a person's disciples or by a small circle of students, often during their master's lifetime.[46] Al-Suyūṭī elected to take his cue from al-Ghazālī and "did not wait for public opinion but with due (false) modesty expressed the hope that God had chosen him to be the ninth *mujaddid*."[47]

[42] Lazarus-Yafeh, "*Tajdīd al-Dīn*," 103.
[43] Landau-Tasseron, "Cyclical Reform," 86.
[44] Goldziher, "Ignaz Goldziher on al-Suyūṭī," 81.
[45] Landau-Tasseron, "Cyclical Reform," 86; see also Friedmann, *Prophecy Continuous*, 97.
[46] Landau-Tasseron, "Cyclical Reform," 88.
[47] Landau-Tasseron, "Cyclical Reform," 87.

Rhyming Lists of *Mujaddids*

One popular method of naming scholars as *mujaddids* before al-Suyūṭī was by composing lists, often in poetic form. Such lists appealed to the tendency in medieval literature to produce texts that were easy to memorize and to communicate orally across several generations. They also helped to codify past learning and to build on it as later scholars contributed verses and added to the record. One of the earliest lists of preferred restorers was that of Ibn ʿAsākir (d. 571/1153) in his previously mentioned pro-Ashʿarī polemic. Tāj al-Dīn al-Subkī is again instrumental in bringing together previous lists, explaining any discrepancies or disagreements concerning some of the candidates and including new names—all in one long poem in his *Ṭabaqāt.*[48]

Al-Suyūṭī uses al-Subkī's text as a starting point for his listing, presenting a slightly abridged version in his own work.[49] The quotation from al-Subkī and other supporting evidence brings al-Suyūṭī's account up to the seventh *mujaddid*, Ibn Daqīq al-ʿĪd. The next long quotation is from Zayn al-Dīn al-ʿIrāqī, who adds some alternate names for previous centuries and suggests that the eighth renewer could be the Mahdī, since the Muslim community is already starting to see signs of the last days, such as the disappearance of outstanding scholars.[50] Al-Suyūṭī's clinching argument is from the scholar that he is unable to identify in the autobiography, Badr al-Dīn al-Ahdal. Al-Ahdal is crucial to al-Suyūṭī's narrative because, coming a generation after al-ʿIrāqī, he is able to attest to the fact that al-ʿIrāqī's prediction has not come to pass and that "it is possible that there could still be a ninth at the turn of the ninth century that we are in currently and that the Mahdī or ʿĪsā b. Maryam could [come] in the tenth century at the end of the [millennial] cycle and the Arabic numeration."[51] This introduction sets the stage for the final statement in al-Suyūṭī's chapter in the autobiography in which he

[48] Al-Subkī, *al-Ṭabaqāt al-shāfiʿiyya*, 1: 203.
[49] Al-Suyūṭī, *al-Taḥadduth*, 217–21. Al-Suyūṭī also composed his own rhyming list of *mujaddids* entitled *Tuḥfat al-muhtadīn bi-akhbār al-mujaddidīn*. The poem can be found in Muḥammad Shams al-Ḥaqq al-ʿAẓīmābādī, *ʿAwn al-maʿbūd fī sharḥ Sunan Abī Dāwūd*, 14 vols. (Medina: al-Maktaba al-Salafiyya, 1969), 11: 393–4. Al-Suyūṭī's *Urjūza* (as it is also called) appears at the end of his *Tanbiʾa* (74–5).
[50] Al-Suyūṭī, *al-Taḥadduth*, 221–4.
[51] Al-Suyūṭī, *al-Taḥadduth*, 226.

claims that not only is a ninth *mujaddid* a possibility, but that he hopes to be that person.

TAJDĪD AND AL-SUYŪṬĪ

Al-Suyūṭī's major contribution to Islamic scholarship in general is based on his extraordinary ability to gather vast amounts of information and to synthesize it in such a way that it is accessible to later generations who may not possess the same encyclopedic scope as that of their predecessors. Al-Suyūṭī's consolidating efforts were by no means mindless collections of data but represented a selective skill on the part of the author that was of direct benefit to his students (as much as it was indirectly self-serving). The concept of *tajdīd* offers a valuable case study of al-Suyūṭī's role as a scholar, both as he imagined it and expressed it pragmatically through his writings, as well as how this role was interpreted by his contemporaries and by later generations. It is characteristic of al-Suyūṭī that very often the two aspects were in conflict and the *tajdīd* debate is no exception.

The secondary literature seems to agree on the idea that, regardless of the original context or purposes of the *mujaddid* tradition in medieval Islam, by al-Suyūṭī's time the rank had more or less become an honorary title bestowed on the person who was thought to be the most outstanding scholar of his age in terms of adherence to the Sunna, rejection of *bidʿa*, and of the benefit derived from his works. For example, Lazarus-Yafeh concludes that al-Suyūṭī "used the word as a term of praise for himself and others, and in this sense it has been used up to the present day."[52] Friedmann summarizes al-Suyūṭī's role as consolidator: "al-Suyūṭī also assembled the traditions relevant to the issue, and his works are the chief source for the history of the *mujaddidūn* until the beginning of the tenth century of the Islamic era."[53] While correct in a sense, these assessments risk underrating al-Suyūṭī's contribution to the concept of *tajdīd* in particular and also to the larger picture of Islamic renewal and reform more generally.

[52] Lazarus-Yafeh, "*Tajdīd al-Dīn*," 104.
[53] Friedmann, *Prophecy Continuous*, 98.

The Concept of Genre

One way to think about al-Suyūṭī's role in the sphere of Islamic reform is to examine the way in which his work facilitated the formation of a "*tajdīd* genre." To clarify, by 'genre' I do not mean a literary genre in the restricted sense, but rather a concept of genre as formulated by the semiotician and literary critic, Mikhail Bakhtin.[54] Particularly in his later work on the novel and Dostoevsky, Bakhtin opened up the concept of genre beyond a formal Aristotelian categorization of literary types to encompass what he refers to as "speech genres."[55]

Speech genres, according to Bakhtin, are a means by which a producer of written or spoken discourse organizes and expresses "utterances," which serve as the basic units of any discourse. Examples of speech genres could include lines of dialogue in everyday speech, commentary, scientific analysis, or lyrical genres. A novel, for example, is classified as a complex secondary genre because it is a collection of different interlocking speech genres. Utterances have a sociological aspect in the sense that they are created in a particular social and cultural context and in reference to past and future utterances. Therefore, no utterance can be said to exist in a vacuum but is inherently "dialogic" in response to other utterances.[56]

Bakhtin adds a historical understanding to the concept of genres by emphasizing the fact that they accumulate and build up over time. The eminent translators and interpreters of Bakhtin's thought, Gary Saul Morson and Caryl Emerson, put it this way: "Genres are a residue of past behavior, an accretion that shapes, guides, and constrains future behavior."[57] The process of genre formation occurs naturally but not at random. Genres carry with them potential meanings that the successful artist is able to unlock or exploit in "unforeseeable circumstances."[58] Or, in other words:

[54] Of course, Bakhtin himself was strongly influenced by his predecessors and contemporaries in Russian Formalist literary circles. For a brief discussion of his thought in context and its influence on later theorists, see David Duff, ed., *Modern Genre Theory* (Harlow, U.K.: Pearson Education Limited, 2000), 10–11.

[55] See M.M. Bakhtin, *Speech Genres and Other Late Essays*, edited by Caryl Emerson and Michael Holquist, translated by Vern W. McGee (Austin: University of Texas Press, 1986).

[56] Bakhtin, *Speech Genres*, 69.

[57] Gary Saul Morson and Caryl Emerson, *Mikhail Bakhtin: Creation of a Prosaics* (Stanford: Stanford University Press, 1990), 290.

[58] Morson and Emerson, *Mikhail Bakhtin*, 286.

> Genres provide a specific field for future activity, and such activity is never just an 'application,' 'instantiation,' or repetition of a pattern. Genres carry generalizable resources of particular events; but specific actions or utterances must use those resources to accomplish new purposes in each unrepeatable milieu. Each utterance, each use of genre, demands real work; beginning with the given, something different must be created.[59]

Dostoevsky serves as an example of a great novelist who was able both to tap into the past resources of the genre and to "create potentials for the future."[60] Another example that Bakhtin uses is Shakespeare who, during his own Elizabethan epoch, was not yet the great Shakespeare that we know today. Shakespeare's greatness is not simply a result of "modernization and distortion" by later generations; rather, Shakespeare "has grown because of that which actually has been and continues to be found in his works, but which neither he himself nor his contemporaries could consciously perceive and evaluate in the context of the culture of their epoch."[61]

In order to be considered 'great,' a work has to be able to transcend its original context while still being firmly grounded in the speech genres, forms, plots, and mythologies of the past. These elements constitute the 'bricks' that an artist like Shakespeare uses to construct a great work. Once formed, the work only gains in meaning over time until it is able to break free of its epoch and cross into what Bakhtin calls "great time."[62] Another metaphor that Bakhtin uses is that of a great work as a tree with roots extending into the distant past; after centuries of preparation, for the artist "it is merely a matter of picking the fruit that is ripe after a lengthy and complex process of maturation."[63]

The "Problem of Articulation"

The social historian Robert Wuthnow describes a similar process in his study of the discourse, ideologies, and social structures that brought about

[59] Morson and Emerson, *Mikhail Bakhtin*, 291.
[60] Morson and Emerson, *Mikhail Bakhtin*, 288.
[61] Bakhtin, "Response to a Question from the *Novy Mir* Editorial Staff" in *Speech Genres and Other Late Essays*, 4.
[62] Bakhtin, "Response to a Question," 4.
[63] Bakhtin, "Response to a Question," 4.

such enormous societal transformations as the Protestant Reformation, the Enlightenment, and the development of European socialism. In order to be successful, reformers like Martin Luther, for example, had to shape their discourse in such a way that it would "articulate with its social environment and to disarticulate from this environment at the same time."[64] Wuthnow describes the "enigmatic" and seemingly paradoxical relationship of great works of art and literature (such as Luther's sermons) to their social environment as a "problem of articulation." As he explains, great works "draw resources, insights, and inspiration from that environment: they reflect it, speak to it, and make themselves relevant to it. And yet they also remain autonomous enough from their social environment to acquire a broader, even universal and timeless appeal."[65] In the case of discourse that challenges the status quo, it can even be powerful enough under the right conditions to motivate large numbers of people to form a social movement.[66]

Significance for al-Suyūṭī

Although Bakhtin's genre theory can seem rather obscure and overly complicated in its expression, it offers significant insight and indeed a degree of poignancy to the question of al-Suyūṭī's persona and legacy as a scholar. Perhaps the ultimate irony of al-Suyūṭī's life was that he succeeded as a *mujaddid* in spite of himself. As a prolific scholar and champion of the Sunna who died shortly after the turn of the ninth century, al-Suyūṭī would seem to fulfill at least the bare requirements of the *mujaddid* (as Sartain affirms). However, rather than letting his accomplishments speak for themselves, al-Suyūṭī insisted on making grand claims in such a way that was derogatory and insulting to his fellow scholars. As Sartain describes the conflict:

> It is probable that subsequent generations have derived far greater profit from al-Suyūṭī's many works than from the works of any other scholar who died

[64] Robert Wuthnow, *Communities of Discourse: Ideology and Social Structure in the Reformation, the Enlightenment, and European Socialism* (Cambridge, M.A.: Harvard University Press, 1989), 4.

[65] Wuthnow, *Communities of Discourse*, 3.

[66] Wuthnow, *Communities of Discourse*, 4. For a helpful survey of studies relating to discursive framing processes and their relationship to the formation and operation of social movements, see Robert D. Benford and David A. Snow, "Framing Processes and Social Movements: An Overview and Assessment," *Annual Review of Sociology* 26 (2000): 611–39.

> at the beginning of the tenth century. But he was certainly not recognized as *mujaddid* by his contemporaries, who found his conceit intolerable, even in an age in which self-praise was not unusual.[67]

Although al-Suyūṭī may have failed to convince the majority of his contemporaries of his status as a *mujtahid* and *mujaddid*, his works and conceptualization of *tajdīd* transcended his particular context and became building blocks in the hands of later reformers seeking to articulate their own interpretation of *tajdīd* suitable to their own time periods.

Al-Suyūṭī's ultimate success can be attributed to the fact that his writings inspired the continuation of a "*tajdīd* genre" in reformist Islam. He did this by carefully collecting evidence to support the contention that true *ijtihād* and renewal were still possible in later generations and indeed necessary in order to save the community from intellectual and spiritual torpor. Al-Suyūṭī's works dealing with *ijtihād* and *tajdīd* draw on certain themes that find resonance and continuity in the thought of later reformers. These themes represent the resources of the genre that al-Suyūṭī helps to make available to future generations, even as he strives to promote his personal agenda.[68]

Themes of Reform

In his work on the history of the concepts of *tajdīd* and *iṣlāḥ* in Islamic thought, John Voll argues that though the terms may have changed in meaning over time, "there has been a continuity of mood that lies behind the changing specifics of meaning."[69] Voll identifies some of these continuing themes as including: a return to the Qurʾān and Sunna, an affirmation of the need for *ijtihād* and a rejection of *taqlīd*, and an assertion of the authenticity of the Qurʾān as opposed to the incorporation of non-Islamic practices into the religion.[70]

[67] Sartain, *Jalāl al-Dīn al-Suyūṭī*, 71.

[68] Of course, these themes existed long before al-Suyūṭī. Fazlur Rahman, for instance, traces the reformist impulse back to the early schisms and heresies that plagued Umayyad rule and "generated theological, legal, and spiritual rationales" that "have become so entrenched and permanently settled that they have provided an unexceptionable and unique *framework* for whatever future elaboration, alteration, development, and reform may take place or had been attempted during the last thirteen centuries." See his *Revival and Reform in Islam* (Oxford, U.K.: Oneworld Publications, 2000), 32.

[69] Voll, "Renewal and Reform," 32.

[70] Voll, "Renewal and Reform," 35.

The purpose of reform is therefore not to improve upon the religion itself but to "implement an already existing ideal."[71] Reformers do not assume that the religion is in any way flawed, but they do react to what they see as heretical interpretations within the community or unacceptable innovations that deviate from the ideal behavior of the earlier generations (*salaf*). In order to be effective, these reforms must respond to the particular needs of the society in which they arise, which means that the reformer must be in tune with the demands of the present (and future), even as he or she is thoroughly conversant with the accomplishments and resources of the past.

The Ongoing Need for *Ijtihād*

Al-Suyūṭī's career represents a crucial point of transition in Islamic history, a time both of political unrest and apocalyptic anxiety, as well as a period in which scholars had come to doubt that non-derivative, independent reasoning in keeping with the standard of preceding generations was at all possible. Al-Suyūṭī responds to such skeptics in his short treatise, *Taqrīr al-istinād fī tafsīr al-ijtihād*, and then again in his long treatise, *al-Radd ʿalā man akhlad ilā al-arḍ wa-jahil ann al-ijtihād fī kull ʿaṣr farḍ*, stating adamantly that *ijtihād* is a collective duty in every generation and thus it is not permitted to have a period without a *mujtahid*.[72]

While the discussion in *al-Radd* consists mostly of a lengthy set of quotations from authorities from each of the four schools supporting this opinion, al-Suyūṭī is much more pointed in his *Taqrīr*, saying that if someone were to make the same statement today he would be torn apart by his colleagues; he would be regarded as haughty, and his words would probably be counted as senseless drivel.[73] He goes on to say that the reason for their doubt is that none of them are able to claim the rank of *mujtahid* for themselves, since the best that they can do is become proficient in one field at the most.[74]

[71] Voll, "Renewal and Reform," 34.

[72] See al-Suyūṭī, *Taqrīr al-istinād fī tafsīr al-ijtihād* (Alexandria: Dār al-Daʿwa, 1983), 31. See also al-Suyūṭī, *al-Radd ʿalā man akhlad ilā al-arḍ wa-jahil ann al-ijtihād fī kull ʿaṣr farḍ* (Alexandria: Muʾassasat Shabāb al-Jāmiʿa, 1985), 73.

[73] Al-Suyūṭī, *Taqrīr*, 30. Al-Suyūṭī repeats this claim in his *Tanbiʾa* (73).

[74] Al-Suyūṭī, *Taqrīr*, 30.

Similar to the rank of *mujaddid*, al-Suyūṭī considers it perfectly justifiable to claim the rank of *mujtahid* for oneself. In fact, al-Suyūṭī's self-declaration of *mujtahid* and *mujaddid* status constitutes one of his most important contributions to the *tajdīd* genre. He argues in *al-Radd*, as well as in his *Taqrīr*, that the scholar knows when he has met the conditions of *ijtihād* and is able to extract rulings from the sources using the appropriate tools and methods. The public can only become aware of this, however, if he declares it for himself. If he is known by his associates to be pious and of good character then there is no reason to doubt the honesty of his claim.[75]

In listing the sciences necessary for attaining the rank of *mujtahid*, al-Suyūṭī makes a point of putting arithmetic as a lower priority, really only relevant to the *mujtahid* working on calculating inheritances (he admits elsewhere that arithmetic is his weakest subject).[76] As for logic, al-Suyūṭī states his distaste for the discipline in several different contexts and discounts it completely as a prerequisite for *ijtihād*.[77] Of course, mastery of the sciences of the Qurʾān and Sunna are the number one and number two priorities with legal theory and methodology (*uṣūl al-fiqh*) coming third.[78]

When stating his claims to the rank of *mujtahid*, al-Suyūṭī quickly runs into a terminology problem. Exactly what type of *mujtahid* does he imagine himself to be? Since truly independent *ijtihād* has not existed since the time of the four imams (eponyms of the legal schools), he must settle for the next highest rank, which for al-Suyūṭī is the *mujtahid muṭlaq muntasib*, or the unrestricted *mujtahid* affiliated with one of the schools. This is in contrast to the restricted *mujtahid*, or *mujtahid muqayyad*, who is not qualified to draw directly from the sources of law and must therefore base his rulings on precedent within the school. Al-Suyūṭī objects to what he sees as the common error of equating the independent *mujtahid* (*mujtahid mustaqill*) with the unrestricted or absolute *mujtahid* (*mujtahid muṭlaq*).[79]

[75] Al-Suyūṭī, *Taqrīr*, 51–2 and *al-Radd*, 152–3.

[76] Al-Suyūṭī, *Taqrīr*, 49. Al-Suyūṭī discusses his own struggles with arithmetic in *al-Taḥadduth*, 204. He goes on to disparage arithmetic as a subject and quotes Ibn Taymiyya to the effect that anything that could be accomplished using the terminology of arithmetic could just as easily be done in a more authentically Arabic manner.

[77] Al-Suyūṭī, *Taqrīr*, 50 and *al-Radd*, 151–2.

[78] Al-Suyūṭī, *Taqrīr*, 47–8.

[79] Al-Suyūṭī, *al-Radd*, 98. Sartain refers to the distinction between the two types in *Jalāl al-Dīn al-Suyūṭī*, 64 and Hallaq also notes the confusion surrounding the terms in "Was the Gate of Ijtihād Closed?" 25–7.

Furthermore, al-Suyūṭī states in his *Tanbiʾa* that no one, to his knowledge, has reached the level of unrestricted *ijtihād* at the current time except for him.[80] Although al-Suyūṭī's assertion is couched in terms of a lament decrying the marked decrease in qualified *mujtahid*s, it should be noted that it was not in al-Suyūṭī's interest as an aspiring *mujtahid* and *mujaddid* to open up the practice of *ijtihād* to the less qualified; it is for such people that *taqlīd* exists and is so prevalent. Indeed, al-Suyūṭī comes across as less than tactful when "he states that he has striven to free his contemporaries from the sin of not fulfilling the collective duty (*farḍ kifāyah*) of *ijtihād* by himself discharging this duty on their behalf."[81]

Al-Suyūṭī's arguments are "double-voiced" in the Bakhtinian sense in that his words carry a "twofold direction"—they are "directed both toward the referential object of speech, as in ordinary discourse, and toward *another's discourse*, toward *someone else's speech*."[82] In the case of "hidden polemic," the speaker directs a "polemical blow" at the other's discourse even if not stated explicitly; here "the other's words are treated antagonistically, and this antagonism, no less than the very topic being discussed, is what determines the author's discourse."[83] Al-Suyūṭī's discourse responds to two basic groups of opponents: "one of which denies the possibility of the existence of any *mujtahid*, and the second of which admits the possibility, but attempts to show that al-Suyūṭī is unworthy of the rank."[84]

Al-Suyūṭī reserves his most vituperative remarks for the latter group. For example, in his treatise arguing that the end times will not occur before the turn of the millennium, al-Suyūṭī takes time to set the tone:

> whoever puffs himself up and claims to rival me and to deny my claims to *ijtihād* and peerless scholarship at the turn of this century and asserts that he opposes me and mobilizes others against me is one that, if he and they were to be assembled on a single plateau and I blew on them one breath, they would become like scattered dust.[85]

[80] Al-Suyūṭī, *al-Tanbiʾa*, 67.

[81] Sartain, *Jalāl al-Dīn al-Suyūṭī*, 68.

[82] M.M. Bakhtin, *Problems of Dostoevsky's Poetics*, edited and translated by Caryl Emerson (Minneapolis, Minnesota: University of Minnesota Press, 1984), 185 (emphasis in the original).

[83] Bakhtin, *Dostoevsky's Poetics*, 195.

[84] Sartain, *Jalāl al-Dīn al-Suyūṭī*, 68.

[85] Al-Suyūṭī, *al-Kashf ʿan mujāwazat hādhihi al-umma al-alf* in *al-Ḥāwī li-l-fatāwī*, 2 vols. (Beirut: Dār al-Kutub al-ʿIlmiyya, 2000), 2:81.

Although the treatise is not explicitly about *ijtihād*, it is clear that the same enemies who questioned al-Suyūṭī's claims to be a *mujtahid* and *mujaddid* tried to use the expectation of the apocalypse as further justification for their doubt, thus prompting him to lash out with yet another treatise to prove the point.

Attack by al-Sakhāwī

One of al-Suyūṭī's most famous enemies was the *ḥadīth* scholar and historian, Muḥammad b. ʿAbd al-Raḥmān al-Sakhāwī (d. 902/1497). The fact that al-Sakhāwī's very specific and personal criticisms of al-Suyūṭī in his biographical dictionary *al-Ḍawʾ al-lāmiʿ* have been preserved while other attacks have not makes him one of al-Suyūṭī's more notorious rivals, even though he was by no means alone in his sentiments.[86] Al-Sakhāwī's accusations range from somewhat substantive (he lists titles that al-Suyūṭī was supposed to have "stolen" from Ibn Ḥajar and others) to rather petty (he mentions that even al-Suyūṭī's mother used to complain about him).[87]

When it comes to al-Suyūṭī's claims of *ijtihād*, al-Sakhāwī's rebuttal is more personal than ideological; he quotes al-Suyūṭī's claim to have achieved mastery of the sciences and to have fulfilled the requirements for *ijtihād* only to suggest that his level of accomplishment was not as high as he claimed. The fact that arithmetic is his poorest subject further proves al-Suyūṭī's stupidity, according to al-Sakhāwī, since arithmetic is a science of intelligence.[88] He notes that people rose up against al-Suyūṭī after his claims became known and repeats an accusation that al-Suyūṭī's claims of *ijtihād* were meant to disguise his own errors.[89]

As with Dostoevsky and the novel, *tajdīd* as a generic concept existed before al-Suyūṭī and continued to exist after al-Suyūṭī. What made al-Suyūṭī a successful *mujaddid*, in the end, was that the significance of his works was

[86] Sartain, *Jalāl al-Dīn al-Suyūṭī*, 72–3. Sartain's work contains a detailed analysis of al-Suyūṭī's many disputes, so it is unnecessary to repeat all of them here. Al-Sakhāwī represents just one example of contemporary scholarly opinion of al-Suyūṭī.

[87] Muḥammad b. ʿAbd al-Raḥmān al-Sakhāwī, *al-Ḍawʾ al-lāmiʿ li-ahl al-qarn al-tāsiʿ*, 12 vols. (Cairo: Maktabat al-Qudsī, 1934–1936), 4:66 and 69.

[88] Al-Sakhāwī, *al-Ḍawʾ al-lāmiʿ*, 4:67.

[89] Al-Sakhāwī, *al-Ḍawʾ al-lāmiʿ*, 4:67–8.

not confined to the narrow-minded squabbles of jealous fifteenth-century scholars. Had this been the case, the significance of al-Suyūṭī's works would have died along with him. The next section will look at the ways in which early modern and modern reformers of the eighteenth, nineteenth, and twentieth centuries articulated their own visions of religious renewal and reform in accordance with the needs and realities of their distinct social and intellectual environments. For these reformers, al-Suyūṭī's conceptualizations of *ijtihād* and *tajdīd* as expressed in his works (and those of other exemplary pre-modern scholars such as al-Ghazālī and Ibn Taymiyya) provided the resources from which new examples of the genre could be constructed.

TAJDĪD AFTER AL-SUYŪṬĪ

Al-Suyūṭī did receive support both before and after his death from his students, including Shams al-Dīn al-Dāwūdī, ʿAbd al-Qādir al-Shādhilī, and Ibn Iyās (all of whom wrote complementary biographies of their teacher). Later, they were joined by other biographers such as ʿAbd al-Wahhāb al-Shaʿrānī (d. 973/1565), Najm al-Dīn al-Ghazzī (d. 1061/1651), and Ibn al-ʿImād (d. 1089/1679). Al-Suyūṭī's claims to greatness were not fully vindicated, however, until years later. This vindication came in the form of later scholars who sought to emulate al-Suyūṭī as a polymath and defender of the Sunna and of *ijtihād* as opposed to *taqlīd*—in other words, to draw on the resources of the *tajdīd* genre that al-Suyūṭī had helped to make available to future generations.

Defense by al-Shawkānī

One such defender of *ijtihād* and enemy of *taqlīd* is the Zaydī Yemeni scholar, Muḥammad al-Shawkānī (d. 1255/1839). Hallaq says of Shawkānī that his "writings seem to represent not only the classical Sunnī trend in favor of *ijtihād* but also the highest stage to which the controversy between advocates of *ijtihād* and *taqlīd* had reached."[90] Shawkānī joins a distinguished cadre

[90] Hallaq, "Ijtihād," 32.

of pro-*ijtihād ḥadīth* scholars in Yemen, including Ibn al-Amīr al-Ṣanʿānī (d. 1182/1768) and Murtaḍā al-Zabīdī (d. 1205/1791). Shawkānī aligned himself with the Traditionists of Yemen to argue for the continued practice of *ijtihād* in an age in which *taqlīd* had become the norm.

Bernard Haykel in his work on Shawkānī notes that he "drew inspiration from the great Sunnī-Shāfiʿī scholars of Egypt, such as Ibn Ḥajar al-ʿAsqalānī and Jalāl al-Dīn al-Suyūṭī, as well as Ḥanbalī ones, like Taqī al-Dīn Aḥmad Ibn Taymiyya" and Ibn Qayyim al-Jawziyya.[91] Indeed, Haykel goes on to say: "the argument can be made that Shawkānī modeled himself on them, seeking to emulate the polymathic nature of their works, and perhaps wanted to be considered as having their stature as first-rank scholars and 'renovators.' "[92] While it is clear from his works that Shawkānī considered himself to be a *mujtahid*, his *mujaddid* status was left to his students to argue based on the scholar's legacy, as opposed to any direct claims from Shawkānī to that effect.[93]

Haykel suggests that Shawkānī identified with other scholars who were attacked because of their claims to *ijtihād*. One such scholar was al-Suyūṭī, for whom Shawkānī concocts a stirring defense in his biographical dictionary, *al-Badr al-ṭāliʿ bi-maḥāsin man baʿd al-qarn al-sābiʿ*. In the introduction to the book, Shawkānī states his purpose to counter those who claim that *mujtahids* are not to be found after the 6th/12th century or the 7th/13th century.[94] It is ignorant to claim that God would restrict grace to one era over others, thus depriving some ages of the means to interpret the Qurʾān and Sunna; rather, it is God's intention to preserve the religion, not just in books, but by providing scholars to explain the faith to people in every age and according to every need.[95] Shawkānī hopes to show through the entries in his biographical dictionary of scholars after the 7th/13th century that God has been just as generous to the successors (*khalaf*) as to the predecessors (*salaf*), to the extent that some later scholars were so

[91] Bernard Haykel, *Revival and Reform in Islam: The Legacy of Muḥammad al-Shawkānī* (Cambridge, U.K.: Cambridge University Press, 2003), 77.

[92] Haykel, *Revival and Reform in Islam*, 86–7.

[93] Haykel, *Revival and Reform in Islam*, 83.

[94] Muḥammad al-Shawkānī, *al-Badr al-ṭāliʿ bi-maḥāsin man baʿd al-qarn al-sābiʿ*, 2 vols. (Cairo: Maṭbaʿat al-Saʿāda, 1929), 1:2.

[95] Shawkānī, *al-Badr al-ṭāliʿ*, 2–3.

accomplished in different fields of knowledge that they had few rivals from earlier generations.[96]

Shawkānī begins his biographical entry of al-Suyūṭī with a short description of his studies and praise of his compositions in every accepted field (excluding, presumably, non-accepted fields like logic) that have spread throughout the nations like the flow of rivers.[97] In spite of his achievements, though, al-Suyūṭī did not escape envy and rejection on account of his virtues, one example being al-Sakhāwī whose biography of al-Suyūṭī amounts to abuse and slander.[98] Shawkānī then proceeds to quote extensively from al-Sakhāwī's insulting biography so that he can refute the allegations point by point.

First, Shawkānī insists that al-Suyūṭī's difficulties with arithmetic are not indicative of a lack of intelligence, since arithmetic rarely reveals one's intelligence (Shawkānī's contemporaries being a case in point).[99] Also, it is normal procedure to compile and collect the work of previous scholars without implying that one is passing it off as one's own work. Furthermore, al-Suyūṭī never claimed to have written over three hundred volumes, so it is no surprise that some of his works are no more than a page in length. In short, Shawkānī writes that the state of competition that existed between the two scholars makes al-Sakhāwī's evidence unacceptable.[100]

Shawkānī concludes with a statement that is clearly "double-voiced" in its implications. It is both a comment on al-Suyūṭī's situation as well as an expression of the author's own frustration with those in his age who mock and denigrate scholars like al-Suyūṭī and Ibn Taymiyya for claiming to have attained the level of *ijtihād*.[101] Al-Suyūṭī was vindicated (as Shawkānī hopes to be) because God has raised him up after his death to receive the praise that he deserves but that was denied by his contemporaries, allowing his works to benefit people across the nations.

The Spread of al-Suyūṭī's Works

Even though al-Suyūṭī was no world traveler during his lifetime, he achieved "international" influence through the spread of his works. Al-Suyūṭī boasts

[96] Shawkānī, *al-Badr al-ṭāliʿ*, 3.
[97] Shawkānī, *al-Badr al-ṭāliʿ*, 328.
[98] Shawkānī, *al-Badr al-ṭāliʿ*, 328–9.
[99] Shawkānī, *al-Badr al-ṭāliʿ*, 333.
[100] Shawkānī, *al-Badr al-ṭāliʿ*, 333.
[101] Shawkānī, *al-Badr al-ṭāliʿ*, 334.

in his autobiography that his works made their way to the Maghrib, Yemen, and the Ḥijāz,[102] and even as far as Takrūr in West Africa.[103] In his *Tanbiʾa*, he expands the list to include also the Levant (*al-Shām*), Anatolia (*al-Rūm*), Persia (*al-ʿAjam*), India, Abyssinia, and beyond.[104] Al-Suyūṭī describes how he met with students traveling in caravans from Takrūr who would then transport copies of his works back with them to be studied and copied further by their colleagues. In addition to this direct contact, al-Suyūṭī also carried on an indirect correspondence with scholars and ruling authorities in West Africa and issued fatwas in response to their questions.[105] In another incident, al-Suyūṭī recounts how the sultan of India sent a representative to purchase some of al-Suyūṭī's works and take them back with him. The minister from India even visited al-Suyūṭī in Rawḍa, where the scholar engaged him in intellectual discussion, treated him to a recitation, and wrote out an *ijāza* certificate for him.[106] Accompanying the exchange of works amongst al-Suyūṭī's network of scholars was a flow of ideas, including those themes that characterize the *tajdīd* genre.

Evolution of the *Tajdīd* Genre

Although it is difficult to generalize about *mujaddid*s after al-Suyūṭī in their quite disparate contexts, it is possible to make some observations about how

[102] The biographer Najm al-Dīn al-Ghazzī includes an entry on a public official in Mecca (a certain Ḥasan b. Thābit al-Zamzamī, d. 921/1515) whose scholarly life's work consisted of the study of numerology and the works of Jalāl al-Dīn al-Suyūṭī. See Najm al-Dīn al-Ghazzī, *al-Kawākib al-sāʾira bi-aʿyān al-miʾa al-ʿāshira*, 3 vols. (Beirut: al-Maṭbaʿa al-Amīrkāniyya, 1945), 1:177. I am grateful to Jonathan A.C. Brown for alerting me to this reference.

[103] See Sartain, *Jalāl al-Dīn al-Suyūṭī*, 46-52. For al-Suyūṭī's account of how students copied and transported his works across the Islamic world, see *al-Taḥadduth*, 155–9.

[104] Al-Suyūṭī, *al-Tanbiʾa*, 67.

[105] For interesting details regarding al-Suyūṭī's popularity and influence in Takrūr, see E.M. Sartain, "Jalāl ad-Dīn al-Suyūṭī's Relations with the People of Takrūr," *Journal of Semitic Studies* 16 (1971): 193–8. John Hunwick provides a translation and commentary on questions posed to al-Suyūṭī from a certain Muḥammad b. ʿAlī al-Lamtūnī of Takrūr in "Notes on a Late Fifteenth-Century Document Concerning 'al-Takrūr,'" *African Perspectives: Papers in the History, Politics and Economics of Africa Presented to Thomas Hodgkin*, edited by Christopher Allen and R.W. Johnson (Cambridge, U.K.: Cambridge University Press, 1970), 7–33. Hunwick suggests that al-Lamtūnī may have been a local reformer who sought backing from al-Suyūṭī in his condemnation of corrupt practices, particularly those of the 'establishment' scholars. Hunwick notes that many of the issues that come up in al-Lamtūnī's questions recur in the works of the West African reformer Usumanu dan Fodio three hundred years later.

[106] Al-Suyūṭī, *al-Taḥadduth*, 159.

the *tajdīd* genre changed over time. First, the tradition lost its connection to Egyptian Shāfiʿī scholars to encompass a much greater range of geographical areas across the Islamic world. India became an important center for renewers, beginning with Shaykh Aḥmad Sirhindī (d. 1034/1624) who declared himself the *mujaddid-i alf-i thānī*, or Renewer of the Second Millennium. The terminology is significant because it shows a shift in Sirhindī's thought away from the usual centennial chronology in favor of a millennial one.[107]

While al-Suyūṭī had already hinted at a connection between the need for a *mujaddid* and the arrival of the Mahdī, after the turn of the Islamic millennium, would-be renewers increasingly defined their role in relation to the Mahdī. Al-Suyūṭī's assertion that the Mahdī's coming would not occur for at least another five hundred years or so after the turn of the millennium provided justification for restorers of the faith in the 10th/16th century and beyond. For example, the chronicler of Aḥmad Ibrahīm al-Ghāzī's conquest of Abyssinia in the 10th/16th century cites al-Suyūṭī's opinion that the Islamic nation will outlast one thousand years as license for renewal and propagation of the faith:

> He [the Prophet], may God bless him and grant him salvation, had indicated who would be the restorers for this nation of the authority of religion. Some there will be among them who will renew it by spreading knowledge in faraway countries; others will renew it by striking schismatics and hypocrites with their swords. Others again will renew it by good administration and knowledge born of experience.[108]

In addition to the chronological aspect, it is significant that the Abyssinian chronicler refers to both renewal through scholarship as well as by force of arms. The idea of *jihād* and political uprising as vehicles for religious renewal

[107] In defending Sirhindī's claims as a *mujaddid*, Sirhindī's grandson, ʿAbd al-Aḥad, draws the reader's attention to al-Suyūṭī's *Rasāʾil* as well as al-Munāwī's commentary on al-Suyūṭī's *al-Jāmiʿ al-ṣaghīr*. See Sajida S. Alvi, "The *Mujaddid* and *Tajdīd* Traditions in the Indian Subcontinent: An Historical Overview," *Journal of Turkish Studies* 18 (1994): 4. Alvi emphasizes the Sufi aspects of Shaykh Sirhindī's *mujaddid* status. For more on Sirhindī, see Yohanan Friedmann, *Shaykh Aḥmad Sirhindī: An Outline of his Thought and a Study of his Image in the Eyes of Posterity* (Montreal, McGill University: Institute of Islamic Studies, 1971); and Arthur F. Buehler, *Revealed Grace: The Juristic Sufism of Ahmad Sirhindi (1564–1624)* (Louisville, K.Y.: Fons Vitae, 2011).

[108] Shihāb al-Dīn Aḥmad b. ʿAbd al-Qādir ʿArab Faqīh, *Futūḥ al-Ḥabaša: The Conquest of Abyssinia [16th Century]*, translated by Paul Lester Stenhouse (Hollywood, California: Tsehai Publishers and Distributors, 2003), 4.

represents a new interpretation of the *tajdīd* tradition that occurred after the time of al-Suyūṭī. Although by al-Suyūṭī's time the term *mujaddid* had come to be used as an honorary title of sorts to designate the most outstanding scholar of the age, it was understood that the scholar must benefit the community through his works and the knowledge that students derive from his writings. However, this agency on the part of the reformer did not translate into political action during al-Suyūṭī's era.[109] As Algar explains: "it is a strictly modern (not to say modernist) expansion on the concept of *tajdīd* to have it include political activism as a defining element."[110]

Usumanu dan Fodio (d. 1232/1817) in West Africa, who claimed to be the *mujaddid* of the twelfth Islamic century, also saw himself as the last *mujaddid* before the appearance of the Mahdī[111] and also saw *jihād* through force as part of his reformist mission. The concept of *tajdīd* as it developed in West Africa has a long history extending back to al-Suyūṭī's time. Among the many works of al-Suyūṭī to achieve popularity in West Africa was his *Urjūza*,[112] a poem listing the *mujaddids* through the centuries, which scholars of the Kunta clan extended to include West African *mujaddids* for the tenth and eleventh century AH.[113] In his *Tanbīh al-Ikhwān ʿalā aḥwāl arḍ al-Sūdān*, Dan Fodio quotes in full a letter written by al-Suyūṭī addressing the kings and sultans of Takrūr warning them against injustices and condemning superstitious or un-Islamic practices such as sacrificing slaves in order to cure illness.[114] By arguing that certain kingdoms within the region of central Sudan are outside of the nation of believers and that their practices deviate from true Sharīʿa, Dan Fodio seeks to legitimize taking up arms against them.

[109] Although al-Suyūṭī did not see his reformist mission as explicitly political, he did consider it part of his duty as a righteous scholar to resist worldly gain and especially the corrupting favors of the political authorities. For more on al-Suyūṭī's complex and often fraught relationship with the Mamluk state, see Chapter 1.

[110] Algar, "The Centennial Renewer," 296.

[111] Algar, "The Centennial Renewer," 298.

[112] Al-Suyūṭī's rhyming list of *mujaddids* also appears under the title *Tuḥfat al-muhtadīn bi-akhbār al-mujaddidīn.*

[113] Cl. Gilliot, R.C. Repp, K.A. Nizami, M.B. Hooker, Chang-Kuan Lin, and J.O. Hunwick, "ʿUlamāʾ" in the *Encyclopaedia of Islam*, Second Edition (Brill Online, 2010). The authors note that this flow of learning and ideas went both ways as the works of West African scholars spread to the Arab world and even as far as India.

[114] H.R. Palmer provides a translation of Usumanu dan Fodio's *Tanbīh* in "An Early Fulani Conception of Islam," *Journal of the African Society* 13 (1913–1914): 407–14; and 14 (1914–1915): 53–9 and 185–92.

Continuing Calls for *Ijtihād*

The eighteenth and nineteenth centuries witnessed a proliferation of revivalist movements and ideologies across the Islamic world, from Muḥammad b. ʿAbd al-Wahhāb (d. 1201/1787) in Arabia, to Shāh Walī Allāh (d. 1175/1762) in India, to Usumanu dan Fodio (or ʿUthmān b. Fūdī) in West Africa, and Muḥammad b. ʿAlī al-Sanūsī (d. 1275/1859) in North Africa.[115] While historians tend to agree that a common language of Islamic revival and the continuing need for *ijtihād* as opposed to *taqlīd* seems to characterize these diverse movements, it could be misleading to group them into one ideological category.[116] Of course, a cursory examination of these different movements cannot hope to do justice to their individual significance. Suffice it to say, though, that while revivalist movements tend to draw on a common language or framework of *tajdīd*, they do so in ways suited to their quite separate contexts and in a manner that the fifteenth-century Jalāl al-Dīn al-Suyūṭī could never have imagined. It is in precisely this way that Bakhtin says that a genre operates.

Of interest here is how eighteenth and nineteenth century reformers continue to draw on the semantic and thematic resources of the *tajdīd* genre to support their own projects of reform. For example, Rudolph Peters points out that Shāh Walī Allāh and al-Sanūsī both adopt "lock, stock and barrel" the classification of *mujtahids* championed by al-Nawawī (d. 676/1277),[117] al-Suyūṭī, and other Shāfiʿīs that distinguishes between the absolute

[115] Rudolph Peters examines the opinions of the "fundamentalist" authors Shāh Walī Allāh, Ḥamd b. Nāṣir b. Muʿammar (d. 1810) of Arabia, Muḥammad al-Shawkānī and Muḥammad b. ʿAlī al-Sanūsī on the necessities of *ijtihād* and dangers of *taqlīd* arguing that, while the views of these authors are clearly not identical, a systematic investigation of their writings and the quotations embedded in them could yield valuable insight as to the "continuity of the fundamentalist tradition." See Rudolph Peters, "Idjtihād and Taqlīd in 18th and 19th Century Islam," *Die Welt des Islams* 20: 3–4 (1980): 144.

[116] Ahmad Dallal, for example, cautions against lumping together such distinct figures and intellectual trends in one category on the grounds that "no unifying themes can be identified that warrant grouping these ideologies, and by extension the movements they initiated, under one rubric." See Ahmad Dallal, "The Origins and Objectives of Islamic Revivalist Thought, 1750–1850," *Journal of the American Oriental Society* 113: 3 (1993): 358–9. Certainly, the terms 'Wahhābī' and even '*salafī*' have proven to be particularly problematic in characterizing a wide range of pre-modern and modern Islamic movements.

[117] For an analysis of al-Nawawī's classification of *mujtahids*, see Norman Calder, "Al-Nawawī's Typology of *Muftīs* and its Significance for a General Theory of Islamic Law," *Islamic Law and Society* 3:2 (1996): 137–64.

independent *mujtahid* (*mujtahid muṭlaq mustaqill*) and the absolute *mujtahid* affiliated with one of the legal schools (*mujtahid muṭlaq muntasib*).[118] Shāh Walī Allāh makes this point of distinction in his treatise *al-Inṣāf fī bayān sabab al-ikhtilāf*, quoting as evidence al-Suyūṭī's commentary on al-Shirāzī's *Tanbīh*.[119] Meanwhile, al-Sanūsī explains the difference between the independent and affiliated *mujtahid muṭlaq* in his *Īqāẓ al-wasnān fī l-ʿamal bi-l-ḥadīth wa-l-Qurʾān* including a lengthy quotation from al-Suyūṭī's *Radd*.[120] Peters explains the benefit of this typology to scholars hoping to engage in unrestricted *ijtihād* after the formation of the legal schools: "this theory recognized the possibility that there were still absolute *mudjtahids*, without however compromising the superiority of the founders of the *madhhabs*."[121]

Perhaps the only truly unifying factor in the ideologies of the eighteenth and nineteenth century reformers is that they all see a problem affecting the Islamic community and choose to respond to the problem by drawing on resources from within the Islamic tradition, rather than searching for solutions outside of the tradition. The problem in question was not yet the West or secularism, which would come to loom large in later modernist thought.[122] Rather, the problem could be found in several different arenas: incorrect belief, dangerously innovative or deviant practice, intellectual disagreement and disunity, or even political tyranny and oppression. The same answer in these diverse cases was to return to the sources and to seek a solution in the revival of Islamic ideals. The solution, in turn, could take various forms: intellectual synthesis and reconciliation, purification of the creed through a rejection of all forms of unbelief, as well as social and political action to promote the needs of the community. The concept of *tajdīd* appealed to reformers who saw the need to restore an ideal past at a time when Islamic doctrine and practices had become stagnant and corrupted.

118 Peters, "Idjtihād and Taqlīd," 137.

119 Shāh Walī Allāh al-Dihlawī, *Shāh Walī Allāh's Treatises on Juristic Disagreement and* Taqlīd: al-Inṣāf fī bayān sabab al-ikhtilāf *and* ʿIqd al-jīd fī aḥkām al-ijtihād wa-l-taqlīd, translated by Marcia Hermansen (Louisville, K.Y.: Fons Vitae, 2010), 49–50.

120 Muḥammad b. ʿAlī al-Sanūsī, *Īqāẓ al-wasnān fī l-ʿamal bi-l-ḥadīth wa-l-Qurʾān* (Beirut: Dār al-Kitāb al-Lubnānī, 1968), 62–3. Al-Sanūsī includes al-Suyūṭī in a list of later scholars who claimed the rank of *ijtihād* (74). Later, al-Sanūsī quotes from al-Suyūṭī's *Radd* again saying that the Ḥanbalīs were of the opinion that it was not permitted to have an age devoid of a *mujtahid* (82).

121 Peters, "Idjtihād and Taqlīd," 137.

122 See Dallal, "Origins and Objectives," 359.

Revival of the *Ḥadīth* Sciences

The greatest threat to the integrity of the Islamic community in al-Suyūṭī's view was a decline in scholarship, particularly in the sciences most needed for *ijtihād*, such as the sciences of Qurʾān and *ḥadīth*. Al-Suyūṭī saw it as part of his mission as one of the few remaining *mujtahid*s and as the renewer of his age to save the traditional sciences from the onslaught of ignorance and degradation. Al-Suyūṭī faced this task by doing what he did best—carefully compiling, preserving, and recording knowledge before it could be lost.[123]

A fitting example of al-Suyūṭī's need to preserve knowledge is his vast compendia of Prophetic traditions, *Jāmiʿ al-jawāmiʿ fī l-ḥadīth*. Although unfinished at the time of his death, al-Suyūṭī's *Jāmiʿ al-kabīr* (as it is also known) was intended "to contain every single Prophetic tradition known, with a decision on its reliability."[124] This "mega-collection," as Jonathan Brown calls it, apparently gave rise to the "widespread belief that if a hadith was not in the *Jāmiʿ al-kabīr* it did not exist."[125] The shorter version of al-Suyūṭī's *Jāmiʿ al-jawāmiʿ*, his *Jāmiʿ al-ṣaghīr*, has also proven enormously popular among Muslim scholars, especially those who are not primarily specialists in *ḥadīth* studies.[126] For example, the Moroccan *ḥadīth* expert, ʿAbd Allāh b. al-Ṣiddīq al-Ghumārī (d. 1960) says somewhat derisively of Rashīd Riḍā that his knowledge of *ḥadīth* consisted of looking them up in *al-Jāmiʿ al-ṣaghīr* or in one of the Six Books (*al-kutub al-sitta*).[127]

Al-Suyūṭī's insistence on the primacy of Qurʾān and *ḥadīth* studies as an integral part of his vocation as a *mujtahid* and *mujaddid* of Islam in some ways anticipated an effort on the part of the early modern reformers to revive the study of *ḥadīth* as an important aspect of the *tajdīd* genre. With the rise of the eighteenth-century revivalist movements came a parallel resurgence of interest in *ḥadīth* studies that also extended to diverse areas of the Islamic

[123] Sartain, *Jalāl al-Dīn al-Suyūṭī*, 115. [124] Sartain, *Jalāl al-Dīn al-Suyūṭī*, 107.

[125] Jonathan A.C. Brown, *Hadith: Muhammad's Legacy in the Medieval and Modern World* (Oxford, U.K.: Oneworld Publications, 2009), 59.

[126] Brown, *Hadith*, 59.

[127] ʿAbd Allāh b. al-Ṣiddīq al-Ghumārī, *Sabīl al-tawfīq fī tarjamat ʿAbd Allāh b. al-Ṣiddīq* (Cairo: al-Dār al-Bayḍāʾ li-l-Ṭibāʿa, 1990), 58. Al-Ghumārī's autobiography in many ways echoes al-Suyūṭī's *al-Taḥadduth bi-niʿmat Allāh*, especially the section in which he discusses his own scholarly achievements (53–5). Thanks to Jonathan A.C. Brown for alerting me to this reference and for lending me a copy of *Sabīl al-tawfīq*.

world. Brown notes that this renewed focus on *ḥadīth* served the common interest of the reformers "of bypassing the rigid institutions of the Late Sunni Tradition to revive the pure Islam of the Prophet's time and purge it of later cultural or intellectual impurities."[128] Like the revivalist movements, the locus of *ḥadīth* studies shifted away from Iran, Egypt, and Syria toward the increasingly "dynamic reformist regions of the Hejaz, Yemen, India, and eventually Morocco."[129] Although well after al-Suyūṭī's time, the feeling on the part of the early modern reformers that "the Muslim community had lost its moorings in the legacy of the Prophet" and that it "had been led astray by heretical accretions in theology and worship as well as by chauvinistic loyalty to the schools of law,"[130] is a sentiment that al-Suyūṭī would whole-heartedly endorse.

The Role of Sufism

This renewed drive to promote correct *sunna* and rid the tradition of heretical encroachments meant that later reformers very often had to address the complex role of Sufism and Sufi practices in their ideological endeavors. The increased prominence of Sufi brotherhoods prompted reformers to include issues relating to Sufism as part of the *tajdīd* genre, to varying degrees of intensity. On one level, the issue was to reconcile orthodox Sunni belief with doctrines that had come to be associated with some types of mystical thought, such as monism (*waḥdat al-wujūd*), a belief in the infusion of the divine spirit into the human body (*ḥulūl*), as well as the unity of the divine and human natures (*ittiḥād*).[131] Secondly, reformers were often forced to confront the issue of Sufi ritual in terms of correct and forbidden practice, which involved such questions as visiting tombs, entering into ecstatic trances, seeking saintly intercession, and the like.

Not surprisingly, al-Suyūṭī was uncompromisingly orthodox on issues of belief and imagined the true Sufi to be one who adhered to the primacy of the Sunna and to the rules of Sharīʿa. This approach fits with al-Suyūṭī's idea

[128] Brown, *Hadith*, 242.
[129] Brown, *Hadith*, 242.
[130] Brown, *Hadith*, 241.
[131] See Sartain, *Jalāl al-Dīn al-Suyūṭī*, 36.

of the *mujaddid* as an advocate of *sunna* and an enemy of unlawful innovation. As Sartain notes: "al-Suyūṭī's emphasis on the careful observance of the *sharīʿah*, with his rejection of all the more extreme Ṣūfī doctrines, is very much in keeping with his attitude toward logic and the philosophical sciences."[132] Even so, al-Suyūṭī was known to issue interesting responses to some of the specific concerns of his community, such as his arguments for the Sufi hierarchy of ṣaints and his fatwa allowing the celebration of *mawlids*. He even took sides in the debate about the accusation of heresy regarding Ibn ʿArabī and Ibn al-Fāriḍ, both of whom al-Suyūṭī chooses to defend.[133] While remaining a strong supporter of the Sunna, al-Suyūṭī does not exhibit the same concern over aspects of Sufi ritual that would come to preoccupy someone like Ibn ʿAbd al-Wahhāb a few centuries later.[134]

There appears to be some conceptual overlap between the hierarchy of scholars possessing certain gifts and types of knowledge in Sufism and the tradition of naming a centennial (or millennial) *mujaddid*. It was not unusual for a potential *mujaddid* to receive special guidance through visions or through the symbolic bestowal of a Sufi cloak or robe. In Algar's study of the Turkish renewer, Bediüzzaman Said Nursi (d. 1960), he emphasizes the gift of a cloak as a symbol of continuity between him and another renewer, Mawlānā Khālid, one hundred years earlier.[135] Similar reports surround the appointment of Sirhindī and Shāh Walī Allāh, both of whom were said to have received a cloak as a symbol of their *mujaddid* status.[136] In this fluid environment, it is understandable that titles like *mujaddid* and *mahdī* were often conflated with Sufi-related honorifics like *murshid* and *quṭb*.[137]

[132] Sartain, *Jalāl al-Dīn al-Suyūṭī*, 36.

[133] Sartain, *Jalāl al-Dīn al-Suyūṭī*, 36–7.

[134] Alexander Knysh warns against a simplistic Eurocentric classification of Islamic thought based on the broad categories of "orthodoxy" and "heresy" or "heterodoxy." He points out that an individual's worldview was never monolithic but was more of a patchwork of different ideas, creeds, and doctrines. Furthermore, definitions of "orthodoxy" varied according to region and time period, resulting in a "blend of 'orthodox' ideas" that was often "rather unstable and subject to a drastic change as a result of redressing the political and social balance of powers." See Knysh, "'Orthodoxy' and 'Heresy' in Medieval Islam: An Essay in Reassessment," *The Muslim World* 83:1 (1993): 48–67.

[135] Algar, "The Centennial Renewer," 303.

[136] Algar, "The Centennial Renewer," 300.

[137] Algar, "The Centennial Renewer," 310.

Tajdīd in the Modern World

By the time that modernist reformers like Jamāl al-Dīn al-Afghānī (1838–1897), Muḥammad ʿAbduh (1849-1905), and Rashīd Riḍā (1865–1935) entered the picture, the Muslim world was faced with a new set of problems that demanded a novel type of response from scholars and activists. The main concern for this group of reformers came to be the perceived decline of the Muslim world and rise of the West, resulting in the imposition of Western culture and values (not to mention military, political, and economic force) on Islamic societies. Reformers struggled with a desire to preserve the Islamic identity of their communities by proving that the tradition was compatible with modern scientific innovation and progress. They called for concrete action to improve their societies, such as education and language reform. At the same time, they resisted pressure to adopt all of the practices and ideas of the foreign powers that threatened to undermine religion as a basis for transformation in society.

This section will focus briefly on Rashīd Riḍā as an example primarily because he was more overt than other modernist reformers in appealing to the *mujaddid* tradition as justification and inspiration for his project of religious revival and renewal. For Riḍā, the *tajdīd* framework acts as a kind of template that the individual author can adapt to the purposes of his own context. The framework provides a vital link to the cumulative authority of past tradition while still granting flexibility in its articulation. Like al-Suyūṭī and the writers of the past, Riḍā uses the device of naming *mujaddids* both to confer honor on those whom he sees as his ideological and spiritual mentors as well as to suggest that their legacy must be continued through his own reform efforts and those of others within his circle.

Riḍā's treatment of the *tajdīd* genre in many ways embodies his *salafī* ideals. Bypassing much of the Shāfiʿī-dominated discourse, Riḍā goes back to the *ḥadīth* reports and composes his own list of renewers based on his own ideological priorities.[138] In addition to abandoning the *madhhab* allegiance that

[138] Riḍā's list of *mujaddids* can be found in his journal, *al-Manār* 32:1 (1350/1931): 2–3 and *al-Manār* 18:5 (1333/1915): 328. Both excerpts are reprinted in Ḥusayn b. ʿAbd Allāh al-ʿAmrī, *al-Manār wa-l-Yaman, dirāsa wa-nuṣūṣ* (Damascus: Dār al-Fikr, 1987), 374–5 and 517–19. Similar lists can be found in Muḥammad Rashīd Riḍā, *Tafsīr al-Manār*, 13 vols. (Beirut: Dār al-Maʿrifa, 1973),

characterized much of the medieval discourse on *tajdīd*, Riḍā also drops the chronological requirement that the reformer's death date be close to the turn of the century. Riḍā's list starts with ʿUmar b. ʿAbd al-ʿAzīz as the *mujaddid* for the second century AH but then omits al-Shāfiʿī and names instead Aḥmad b. Ḥanbal as the next renewer. Abū al-Ḥasan al-Ashʿarī is fourth followed by al-Ghazālī. It is after al-Ghazālī that Riḍā's list starts to diverge considerably from the classical Shāfiʿī lists. Riḍā praises the Ẓāhirī jurist Ibn Ḥazm as the *mujaddid* for the sixth century, followed by the Ḥanbalī Ibn Taymiyya and his student, Ibn al-Qayyim.[139]

Riḍā acknowledges the shift in reformist thought after the eighth century AH to diverse regions of the Islamic world by identifying a subset of "regional" *mujaddids* whose renewal efforts were confined to a certain area or people, including the Andalusian Mālikī jurist Abū Isḥāq al-Shāṭibī (d. 790/1388),[140] Shāh Walī Allāh, and Muḥammad Ṣiddīq Khān in India, Muḥammad b. Pīr ʿAlī al-Birkawī (d. 981/1573) in Turkey, Ibn ʿAbd al-Wahhāb in Najd, and finally the Zaydī scholars Ṣāliḥ al-Maqbalī (d. 1108/1696), Ibn Ibrāhīm al-Wazīr (d. 840/1436), and al-Shawkānī (d. 1250/1832) in Yemen. Riḍā singles out Shawkānī's works in *ḥadīth* studies (*al-Nayl al-awṭār fī sharḥ muntaqā al-akhbār*) and *fiqh* (*Irshād al-fuḥūl fī taḥqīq al-ḥaqq min ʿilm al-uṣūl*), and the *ḥadīth* commentary of Ibn Ḥajar al-ʿAsqalānī (d. 852/1448), *al-Fatḥ al-bārī*, as indispensable to scholars in the current age.[141]

7:144–5 as well as in Riḍā's introduction to his *Taʾrīkh al-Ustādh al-Imām al-Shaykh Muḥammad ʿAbduh*, vol. 1, part 1 (Cairo: Dār al-Faḍīla, 2003).

[139] Riḍā's inclusion of Ibn Taymiyya (d. 728/1328) and Ibn Qayyim al-Jawziyya (d. 751/1349) is symptomatic of the regard accorded to these two figures by modern *salafī* reformers. For example, the well-known Islamist thinker Mawlānā Mawdūdī (d. 1979) praises Ibn Taymiyya as a *mujaddid* in *A Short History of the Revivalist Movement in Islam*, translated by Al-Ashʿarī, Second Edition (Lahore: Islamic Publications, 1972), 63–9. Ibn Taymiyya is not included as a possible *mujaddid* in the Shāfiʿī-dominated pre-modern lists as far as I have seen. Al-Suyūṭī does not mention Ibn Taymiyya in his discussion of *tajdīd*, much as he respects him as a fellow *mujtahid*. The evolving reputation of Ibn Taymiyya as well as that of his student, Ibn al-Qayyim, deserves more extensive research.

[140] Al-Shāṭibī's views on the objectives of the law (*maqāṣid al-Sharīʿa*) and on the public good (*maṣlaḥa*) make him particularly appealing to modern reformers like Riḍā. For a detailed analysis of al-Shāṭibī's legal theories, see Wael B. Hallaq, *A History of Islamic Legal Theories: An Introduction to Sunnī* uṣūl al-fiqh (Cambridge, U.K.: Cambridge University Press, 1997), 162–206; and Felicitas Opwis, Maṣlaḥa *and the Purpose of the Law: Islamic Discourse on Legal Change from the 4th/10th to the 8th/14th Century* (Leiden: Brill, 2010), 247–320.

[141] Riḍā, *Tafsīr al-Manār*, 7:145.

Of course, naming scholars that one admires in the form of a list of *mujaddids* and actually using their ideas to construct a project of reform are two very different matters. For instance, in an insightful article dealing with Riḍā's appropriation and "reconstruction" of Shawkānī's opinions regarding the use of legal analogy (*qiyās*), Dallal observes that "there is a basic tension between Riḍā's celebration of these reformers and his own ideas and program of reform. Riḍā's general assertions regarding the standing of his reformers inevitably runs into problems as soon as he proceeds to discuss their ideas in greater detail and specificity."[142] Dallal argues, for example, that Riḍā cast Shawkānī as being more receptive to *qiyās* than he actually was in his writings. Riḍā is no exception to the general rule that the "requisites of renewal" upon which the *mujaddids* are selected "have been defined retrospectively; as such, they are better representations of the perceived needs of the age of the examiner than of the period under examination."[143]

In a speech entitled, *al-Tajdīd wa-l-tajaddud wa-l-mujaddidūn* ("Renewal, Renewing and Renewers"), Riḍā outlines further his interpretation of the *tajdīd* genre.[144] Riḍā distinguishes between true renewal, which involves "excellence in knowledge or wisdom, guidance or virtue, or in revealing unknown truths" and "initiating practices useful to the *umma* in preserving its true nature, developing its wealth, or restoring its glory" and false renewers, whose idea of reform means adopting the trappings of Western civilization in service to a secular idea of 'progress.'[145] A model for this misguided kind of renewal is Ottoman Turkey with its rapid secularization, while Japan represents a country that is able to advance economically, militarily, and politically while preserving its "religion, culture, laws and language, and its national characteristics of dress, good traditions, and values."[146] For Riḍā, the key to real renewal is striking a balance between the old and the new, reaping the benefits of both but rejecting innovations that are at odds with religion.

[142] Ahmad Dallal, "Appropriating the Past: Twentieth-Century Reconstruction of Pre-Modern Islamic Thought," *Islamic Law and Society* 7:3 (2000): 342.

[143] Dallal, "Appropriating the Past," 327.

[144] The speech was published originally in several issues of Riḍā's journal, *al-Manār*. The translation by Emad Eldin Shahin can be found in *Modernist Islam, 1840–1940: A Sourcebook*, edited by Charles Kurzman (New York: Oxford University Press, 2002), 77–85.

[145] Riḍā, "Renewal," 79. [146] Riḍā, "Renewal," 78.

Riḍā quotes the famous *mujaddid* tradition twice during the course of the speech, saying that al-Suyūṭī testified to the correctness of the report in his *ḥadīth* collection, *al-Jāmiʿ al-ṣaghīr*.[147] However, it is clear that Riḍa's interpretation of the *tajdīd* concept differs in some key ways from that of the medieval scholars. First, *tajdīd* is not confined to religious renewal, but also entails social, political, scientific, and civic reforms. Additionally, while Riḍā speaks of the Islamic *umma*, he also takes into account the reality of the modern nation-state and its concerns, issues that did not occupy the medieval scholars as part of their project of *tajdīd*. It is significant that Riḍā opens up the field of *tajdīd* to encompass multiple reform efforts by people in different occupations, such as scientists and legislators. While the original wording of the tradition does allow for multiple renewers in a centennial cycle, Riḍā does not try to argue this point exegetically but assumes it to be the case, much as the medieval renewers tended to assume that the *mujaddid* had to be a religious scholar (and even a *mujtahid*).[148]

CONCLUSION

In order for the *tajdīd* genre to survive, it had to be adaptable and responsive to the needs of different ages and generations. As Bakhtin would put it, a great work:

> cannot live in future centuries without having somehow absorbed past centuries as well. If it had belonged *entirely* to today (that is, were a product only of its own time) and not a continuation of the past or essentially related to the past, it could not live in the future. Everything that belongs only to the present dies along with the present.[149]

Al-Suyūṭī's career marks an important transition in the history of the debate in Islamic scholarship surrounding the concepts of *ijtihād* and *tajdīd*. Hallaq

[147] Riḍā, "Renewal," 81.

[148] Riḍā's idea of multiple *mujaddids* in different occupations is not entirely without historical precedent. Al-Suyūṭī cites several authorities who allow for more than one *mujaddid* per cycle and includes a long quotation from Ibn al-Athīr to the effect that legal scholars are not the only ones that can benefit the religion; political leaders, *muḥaddithūn*, Qurʾān reciters, preachers, and ascetics are all benefactors in their own ways. See al-Suyūṭī, *al-Tanbiʾa*, 54–5.

[149] Bakhtin, *Speech Genres and Other Late Essays*, 4.

observes that al-Suyūṭī "can be seen as the last major Sunnī *mujtahid* in a nine-century chain of *mujtahids*" since after his lifetime fewer and fewer jurists were in a position to claim the level of *ijtihād*.[150] It was certainly the case that by al-Suyūṭī's time the golden age of classical *ijtihād* was coming to an end, a deterioration of which al-Suyūṭī and his contemporaries were well aware.

However, while al-Suyūṭī does mark the end of one era, he also anticipates the beginning of another. Al-Suyūṭī's claims of *mujtahid* and *mujaddid* status could easily have died with the dismissal and mockery of rivals like al-Sakhāwī, but they did not do so. Instead, al-Suyūṭī's formulation of the *mujaddid* tradition became an important point of reference for future generations as they sought to mold the *tajdīd* framework to suit their own purposes, while his works continue to stand as testament to his relevance and reputation.

Al-Suyūṭī's ability to distill the ideas of past scholars into a format that was adaptable by later scholars as diverse as al-Shawkānī, Dan Fodio, and Riḍā in their own efforts to encourage *ijtihād* and religious revival ensured that his thought not only survived but even took on a life of its own. Premodern and modern reformers could use the legitimacy of the tradition as established by al-Suyūṭī and others as a starting point for their own projects of renewal, reinterpreting the tradition to meet the various needs of their specific circumstances. It is fitting that with the survival of the *tajdīd* genre, al-Suyūṭī was at last able to find the personal vindication and regeneration that so eluded him during his own lifetime.

[150] Hallaq, "Ijtihād," 29.

4

Authority by Aggregation and Abstraction: The Pragmatics of Communication in al-Suyūṭī's Book on Legal Precepts

INTRODUCTION

In recent years, a resurgence of interest in the genre of Islamic legal scholarship known as *qawāʿid* has put this field and its related subfields at the center of new and vital work in jurisprudence (*fiqh*). The study of legal precepts[1] and their application to cases in the substantive law within the framework of the legal schools has gained prominence as a key part of the curricula within Islamic institutions of higher learning and knowledge of these precepts is incumbent on the aspiring jurist.[2] One observer notes what amounts to an "explosion" of works on legal precepts in Arabic and other Near Eastern languages in the last few decades.[3] Western critical scholarship has yet to catch up with this trend, leaving a sizeable gap for future scholars to fill in our understanding of legal precepts in both classical and modern Arabic literature.

[1] Legal precepts are short pithy statements (or questions) that sum up areas of the law. These statements perform a number of discourse functions for the jurist, which will be explored in this chapter. Legal precepts are sometimes also referred to as 'rules' or 'principles' or 'maxims.' In this chapter, I refer to precepts and maxims interchangeably, but avoid rules and principles to escape confusion between the different Arabic terms.

[2] Mohammad Hashim Kamali, "Legal Maxims and Other Genres of Literature in Islamic Jurisprudence," *Arab Law Quarterly* 20:1 (2006): 78. See also Khaleel Mohammed, "The Islamic Law Maxims," *Islamic Studies* 44:2 (2005): 191.

[3] Intisar A. Rabb, *Doubt's Benefit: Legal Maxims in Islamic Law, 7th–16th Centuries*, Ph.D. Diss. (Princeton University, 2009), 18. For a list of such works, see her extensive and very helpful appendix, 481–3. For another list of modern works on *qawāʿid* and related genres, see Wolfhart Heinrichs, "*Qawāʿid* as a Genre of Legal Literature," in *Studies in Islamic Legal Theory*, edited by Bernard G. Weiss (Leiden: Brill, 2002), 383–4.

Historical Development of Legal Precepts

Scholars differ on the question of when legal maxims first appeared in Islamic legal writing. Heinrichs suggests that jurists as early as the 4th/10th century had begun to identify general rules (then termed *uṣūl* rather than *qawāʿid*) in works of substantive law (*furūʿ*).[4] It was not until the 7th/13th century, though, that the *qawāʿid* literature reached its zenith, a period which lasted through to the 10th/16th century. Jurists in each of the legal schools (*madhāhib*) worked to derive general principles that would help both to consolidate school doctrine and procedure and to aid the *mujtahid* within the *madhhab* seeking to apply the opinion of the school to new rulings. Scholars worked to identify the similarities (*ashbāh*) uniting cases and the differences (*furūq*) that produce different rulings in cases that appear similar. For the Mālikī school, Shihāb al-Dīn al-Qarāfī (d. 684/1285) did much to advance the *qawāʿid* genre during this earlier period, as did Ibn ʿAbd al-Salām (d. 660/1262) for the Shāfiʿīs.[5] The 8th/14th century saw the rise of important works in *qawāʿid* under the title *al-Ashbāh wa-l-naẓāʾir*, including works by the Shāfiʿīs Tāj al-Dīn al-Subkī (d. 771/1370) and Ibn al-Wakīl (d. 716/1317), a trend that continued with al-Suyūṭī (d. 911/1505) and the Ḥanafī Ibn Nujaym (d. 970/1563).[6]

For the Shāfiʿī school of law, Jalāl al-Dīn al-Suyūṭī's *al-Ashbāh wa-l-naẓāʾir fī l-qawāʿid al-fiqhiyya* remains one of the core pre-modern works in the field. Together with his fatwas, al-Suyūṭī's work in the area of *qawāʿid* constitutes a major part of his legacy as a legal scholar. Not only is his book still coming out in new editions today, it is also in regular use as a textbook for students in Islamic institutions of higher learning, training to become the next generation of muftis and legal scholars. Therefore, any study of al-Suyūṭī's legal discourse would be remiss without a discussion of his work on legal precepts as one of the author's primary contributions to Islamic legal thought.

The renewal of interest in legal precepts by teachers and researchers of Islamic law in the last few decades can be attributed to a number of factors.

[4] W.P. Heinrichs, "Ḳawāʿid Fiḳhiyya," *Encyclopaedia of Islam*, Second Edition (Brill Online, 2010).
[5] Rabb, *Doubt's Benefit*, 459.
[6] Heinrichs, "Ḳawāʿid Fiḳhiyya."

Put simply, legal precepts are useful to the jurist striving to interpret God's law in context. With the waning importance of Islamic law as part of state legal systems, modern jurists struggle to maintain relevance and to achieve a delicate balance between preserving the spirit of the law as it has developed over the centuries, while still allowing it to change and adapt to contemporary circumstances. Legal precepts therefore represent a powerful tool for jurists seeking to tap into the essence of substantive *fiqh* and to extract from it principles universal enough to meet the demands of the current day.

While some precepts do make direct reference in their wording to statements from the Qurʾān and *ḥadīth*, they can be described as "extratextual" in the sense that they are removed from the textual sources to some extent.[7] Rather, precepts are formulated *by* jurists *for* jurists and their relevance lies in how they are used in legal discourse. Jurists derive precepts inductively from the body of the substantive law (unlike the deductive process of establishing a *ratio legis*, or *ʿilla*, for rulings based on an interpretation of the sources that is normally associated with legal theory methodology, *uṣūl al-fiqh*).[8] Therefore, precepts are constructed by jurists for a purpose and in a particular context. Indeed, separated from their context, legal precepts become meaningless abstractions of doubtful utility.

Pragmatic Theory

For modern linguistic theory, legal precepts fit comfortably within the area known as pragmatics. Pragmatics is, roughly speaking, the study of speech acts in context. A speech act is an utterance produced by a speaker with a particular intention. This branch of linguistics assumes that utterances (units of discourse) are produced within a certain context and reflect the pragmatic goals of the speaker. It also assumes that contextual factors contribute to how a hearer infers meaning from an utterance outside of the semantic content of the utterance.

[7] Rabb, *Doubt's Benefit*, 3.
[8] Wolfhart Heinrichs, "Structuring the Law: Remarks on the *Furūq* Literature," in *Studies in Honour of Clifford Edmund Bosworth*, edited by Ian Richard Netton (Leiden: Brill, 2000), 335.

The field of pragmatics expanded considerably in the late 1960s with the work of the philosopher H.P. Grice, who examined the unspoken rules that govern conversation. Grice's theory hinges on the idea that conversation is a "cooperative and purposive process" in which participants contribute according to agreed upon standards of quantity, quality, relation, and manner.[9] Any flouting of these conversational maxims results in an aberration (or, as Grice would say, an "implicature") that demands an explanation.[10] Very often, the apparent contradiction is resolved through knowledge external to the conversation itself. For instance, a statement that is clearly untrue (and thus flouting the maxim of quality) could be intended sarcastically. However, the listener would interpret the statement in such a manner only if he or she knew something about the personality and intentions of the speaker.

Grice's maxims are useful in understanding how legal precepts work in terms of the specific discourse functions that they fulfill for the jurist. Legislative speech is similar to conversation in that it conforms to certain guidelines and accords to a set of assumptions and expectations. Legal language in general and maxims in particular have attracted attention by scholars seeking to justify the use of such devices pragmatically. M.B.W. Sinclair, for example, looks at statutes in light of Grice's conventions to construct a set of pragmatic rules that apply specifically to statutory interpretation. As Sinclair explains, his work offers a theory of pragmatics that is "based on the assumption that legislatures act in a context, for a purpose, and within the requirements imposed by communication."[11] Building on Sinclair's article, Geoffrey Miller puts forward a further interpretation of legal maxims using Grice's conversational constraints as a model. Miller expands his analysis to include examples of maxims not just from American law, but also from the

[9] M.B.W Sinclair, "Law and Language: The Role of Pragmatics in Statutory Interpretation," *University of Pittsburgh Law Review* 46 (1984–1985): 377. I will discuss Grice's maxims in more detail in a later section.

[10] Mohamed M. Yunis Ali discusses the debate amongst medieval Sunni legal scholars in regards to deriving a meaning for a given utterance based on information that exists outside of the explicit meaning of the utterance. Specifically, the debate concerned the use of congruent implicature (*mafhūm al-muwāfaqa*), counter implicature (*mafhūm al-mukhālafa*), and the principle of relevance (*al-munāsaba*) to derive legal rulings. See Ali, *Medieval Islamic Pragmatics: Sunni Legal Theorists' Models of Textual Communication* (Richmond, Surrey: Curzon Press, 2000), 187–224.

[11] Sinclair, "Law and Language," 375.

early Hindu, Christian, and Jewish traditions.[12] However, Miller makes no mention of Islamic law and its highly developed system of legal precepts.

A Pragmatic Interpretation of Legal Precepts

This chapter makes an initial foray into a pragmatic interpretation of Islamic legal precepts in light of al-Suyūṭī's work in this field. Legal precepts perform specific discourse functions both in terms of their form and content. As such, they can be considered within the framework of pragmatic speech acts that fulfill objectives for the speaker within a certain context. This chapter considers how the form and content of Islamic legal precepts contribute to their function. Keeping in mind Grice's maxims of conversation, I will examine the assumptions and expectations behind the operation of legal precepts as they derive meaning from context.

Also, the chapter offers an analysis of one precept, *al-ʿāda muḥakkama* ("custom should be made to serve as an arbiter"), as an example of a concept that demands knowledge of context as an essential part of its function. Although the analysis focuses on al-Suyūṭī's *al-Ashbāh wa-l-naẓāʾir*, it necessarily draws on other pre-modern and modern works within the *qawāʿid* genre as well. I will investigate how al-Suyūṭī uses custom (within the framework of legal precepts) pragmatically both to resolve contradictions in the law and to interpret speech acts such as contracts and oaths. I suggest that al-Suyūṭī employs contradictory arguments to the strategic benefit of his own legal school. Finally, I argue that this effort by the jurist to negotiate a preferable outcome based on the realities of the context does, in fact, constitute a form of *ijtihād* within the bounds of the legal school. Al-Suyūṭī's own authority as a *mujtahid* is thereby strengthened due to his ability to consolidate, organize, and manipulate a vast corpus of substantive law.

FORM

Legal precepts bear some similarity to proverbs in terms of their formal structure. Like proverbs, maxims tend to be "pithy full sentences embedded

[12] Geoffrey P. Miller, "Pragmatics and the Maxims of Interpretation," *Wisconsin Law Review* (1990): 1183–91.

in discourse."[13] Also, like proverbs, they display certain formal features that play a role in their function as pragmatic speech acts.[14] Lelia Gándara explains in the case of proverbs that they often contain qualities like lexical or morphological archaism, binary rhythmic structure ("penny wise, pound foolish"), rhyme, assonance, alliteration, or repetition.[15] Examples of such formal features in Islamic legal maxims include *al-tābiʿ tābiʿ* ("the attachment follows") as well as the famous *ḥadīth* and legal precept, *lā ḍarar wa-lā ḍirār* ("no harm or retaliatory harm will be imposed"), which uses two words from the same root. The root and pattern structure of the Arabic language as well as its propensity for assonance and parallel syntactic constructions facilitates the formation of catchy or memorable phrases.

Another common format for Arabic maxims is a binary opposition that indicates two options. One example of such a maxim is the general directive championed by the prominent jurist, ʿIzz al-Dīn b. ʿAbd al-Salām (d. 660/1262): *jalb al-maṣāliḥ wa-darʾ al-mafāsid* ("attaining benefits and averting harms"), where the verbal nouns *jalb* and *darʾ* are in opposition and the broken plurals *maṣāliḥ* and *mafāsid* are also in opposition. Often, an opposition is put forward where one side of the equation is indicated as clearly preferable to the other and is thus given priority in the determination of a legal ruling. For instance, the precept *iʿmāl al-kalām awlā min ihmālihi* ("acting on a statement is better than omitting it") puts two verbal nouns of the same pattern (*iʿmāl* and *ihmāl*) in opposition, where the former is preferable to the latter.

These formal features of assonance, repetition, and binary rhythmic structure yield the clear advantage of rendering the maxim simple to memorize and to repeat. As Gándara points out, the memorable nature of proverbs and maxims adds to their illocutionary force, "so much so that any proverbs used in the development of an argument are likely to be among the most

[13] Lelia Gándara, "'They That Sow the Wind . . .': Proverbs and Sayings in Argumentation," *Discourse and Society* 15: 2–3 (2004): 346.

[14] Although maxims and proverbs share some formal features and discourse functions, they also differ in other aspects. Proverbs, as Gándara observes, tend to represent popular usage, whereas maxims tend to be more formal ("They That Sow the Wind," 348). Thus, a politician, for example, might insert a proverb into his or her speech in order to appear connected to the populace, while maxims tend to be confined to legal and educational discourse.

[15] Gándara, "They That Sow the Wind," 346.

easily recollected items."[16] Therefore, this discussion leads me to identify the first discourse function of Islamic legal precepts in terms of form: *legal precepts aid memorization.*

This feature of legal precepts also adds to their convenience as a teaching tool. The importance of memorization in the traditional Islamic studies curriculum is well known and was certainly one of the main factors driving the collection of *ḥadīth* and the preservation of poetry (even from pre-Islamic times). It seems, though, that the late medieval era, particularly the 7th/13th–9th/15th centuries, marked a subtle change in the kind of material that was memorized for the purpose of teaching. This period, for instance, saw a rise in popularity of verse grammars, of which the *Alfiyya* of Ibn Mālik (d. 672/1273) is a prime example. Ibn Mālik's work attempts to compress the essence of classical Arabic grammar into one thousand lines of verse. The *Alfiyya* quickly became a standard of the Islamic studies curriculum and continued to be a required text for generations of students as late as the nineteenth century.[17] Like legal precepts, verse grammars sought to consolidate vast amounts of information and theoretical discussion into pithy memorable phrases. However, with the educational reforms of the nineteenth century, classical works like the *Alfiyya* were gradually phased out in favor of more modern grammar textbooks, whereas legal precepts have gained prominence as a mainstay of *fiqh* instruction in Islamic institutions such as Egypt's al-Azhar.

In addition to their distinctive syntactic structure, legal precepts are also characterized by their brevity and abstraction. This formal feature of legal maxims has both positive and negative implications for their pragmatic function. The trenchant literary style of legal precepts and their "abstract and synoptic character" imbue them with a degree of inherent objectivity.[18] In other words, *legal precepts represent general truths.* As Gándara notes, this trait makes proverbs and maxims difficult to refute rhetorically, except with other proverbs.[19] It also adds to their continuity, since, as Kamali observes,

[16] Gándara, "They That Sow the Wind," 349.

[17] Monique Cardinal, "Islamic Legal Theory Curriculum: Are the Classics Taught Today?" *Islamic Law and Society* 12:2 (2005): 261.

[18] Kamali, "Legal Maxims," 99–100.

[19] Gándara, "They That Sow the Wind," 348.

it "gives them a degree of versatility and timelessness that is not hampered by burdensome detail."[20]

However, it is easy to overestimate the truth value of legal precepts. In the context of the Islamic legal tradition, for instance, jurists tend to agree that maxims do not have the same authoritative level of certainty as other sources of law and can thus be considered only a probable indicator for a ruling that is non-binding to the jurist.[21] While legal precepts may be presented as general, they are not universal in the sense that they allow for exceptions and particularization.[22] Legal precepts may contribute to the formation of rulings, but they are not rulings in themselves. In this way, they are actually similar to the principles of pragmatics (such as Grice's maxims), which, as Sinclair explains: "are not rules that bind their subjects as do, say, the rules of chemistry or mathematics. They are not invalidated by individual counter-examples, and they can even conflict with one another."[23]

It is also this sense of abstraction that has caused some to question the scope and relevance of legal maxims, particularly in the Western legal tradition.[24] Indeed, both Sinclair and Miller frame their articles as responses to attacks on legal maxims by Karl Llewellyn and others. Llewellyn argues that maxims are indeterminate as canons of construction, since for every maxim there is a counter-maxim supporting a contradictory interpretation.[25] The implication is that, because maxims are so general and abstract, a judge can effectively use maxims as "mere conclusory explanations appended after

[20] Kamali, "Legal Maxims," 99.

[21] This is not always the case, however. Pre-modern jurists engaged in a lively debate about whether or not indicators based on inductive reasoning could yield certain knowledge. For example, Opwis shows how the Ḥanafī jurist, Najm al-Dīn al-Ṭūfī (d. 716/1316), gives preponderance to the precept of *lā ḍarar wa-lā ḍirār* ("no harm or retaliatory harm will be imposed") and its corollary, the injunction to safeguard the public good (*maṣlaḥa*), thus elevating the concept to the level of certainty as an indicator of legal rulings. See Felicitas M. M. Opwis, *Maṣlaḥa and the Purpose of the Law: Islamic Discourse on Legal Change from the 4th/10th to 8th/14th Century* (Boston, M.A.: Brill Academic Publishers, 2010), 209–16.

[22] Mohammed, "The Islamic Law Maxims," 193.

[23] Sinclair, "Law and Language," 382.

[24] Khaleel Mohammed points out that the fact that most legal maxims in the Western tradition are in Latin also makes them less accessible to contemporary jurists. See Mohammed, "The Islamic Law Maxims," 207.

[25] Rabb, *Doubt's Benefit*, 4. See also Karl N. Llewellyn, "Remarks on the Theory of Appellate Decision and the Rules or Canons about how Statutes are to be Construed," *Vanderbilt Law Review* 3 (1950): 395–406.

the fact to justify results reached on other grounds."[26] When applied in an arbitrary manner or "diverted from their original function of standards for the decision of controversies," maxims can become "vague high-sounding generalities, of no practical import, and may even serve to darken counsel and to retard the working out of a sound principle."[27] These criticisms are a good reminder that precepts divorced from their context lose much of their meaning.

CONTENT

Taking a step back from the level of form, legal precepts also perform a number of important discourse functions on the broader level of content. Most of these functions are tied to the fact that "legal maxims represent a late development in the history of Islamic jurisprudence."[28] Although writing on precepts has roots as early as the 4th/10th century, they did not become prevalent in Islamic legal literature until roughly two hundred years later, or not till after the 6th/12th century.[29] The rise of precepts corresponds to a larger transition in legal thought from an era in which school doctrine was under formation to one in which consolidation and systematization were the primary goals. Therefore, legal precepts seek to manage an already existing vast corpus of Islamic jurisprudence. In other words, *legal precepts consolidate information.*

Sherman Jackson describes this function of legal maxims in terms of "legal scaffolding," where "rather than abandon existing rules in favor of new interpretations from the sources, needed adjustments are sought through new divisions, classifications, distinctions, exceptions and expanding or restricting the scope of existing rules."[30] Jackson emphasizes, however, that this process does not constitute a mere rehashing of previous thinking but leaves room for skill and positive innovation on the part of the jurist. In

[26] Miller, "Pragmatics and the Maxims of Interpretation," 1180.

[27] Roscoe Pound, "The Maxims of Equity I: of Maxims Generally," *Harvard Law Review* 34:8 (June, 1921): 815.

[28] Kamali, "Legal Maxims," 77. [29] Rabb, *Doubt's Benefit*, 459.

[30] Sherman A. Jackson, *Islamic Law and the State: The Constitutional Jurisprudence of Shihāb al-Dīn al-Qarāfī* (Leiden: E.J. Brill, 1996), 97.

fact, he uses the development of the *qawāʿid* genres in Islamic jurisprudence to argue that following precedent (*taqlīd*) does not necessarily indicate a "decline to a more primitive stage of development," but rather, "it is in this very process of legal scaffolding that a legal tradition reaches the height of innovative acumen."[31]

The discourse function of legal precepts and their role in the development of Islamic jurisprudence does not end with consolidation. Even more importantly, *legal precepts provide a bridge between the substance of the law and the purposes of the law.* Roscoe Pound explains that in an advanced legal tradition a transition takes place in which jurists move from considering just the substance of the law as a body of rules and individual legal opinions to take on the spirit or intent behind the law.[32] As the product of conscious reflection and inductive reasoning on the part of the jurist, legal precepts help to "bridge the gap between customary moral rules and ethical principles."[33]

The close relationship between legal precepts and the purposes of the law (*maqāṣid al-Sharīʿa*) is key to understanding their significance not only during the age of consolidation in Islamic law, but also their renewed popularity in modern scholarship. Kamali notes that the "renewed interest in legal maxims is also informed by a parallel revival of interest, among teachers and researchers of Sharīʿa, in the *maqāṣid al-Sharīʿa*, goals and objectives of Islamic law." For modern scholars, it is often the case that since "legal maxims bear close affinity to the *maqāṣid*, they tend to provide an efficient entry into the understanding of the *maqāṣid al-Sharīʿa*."[34]

This link between the substance of the law as it was forged by generations of jurists and the purposes and objectives behind the law is crucial both in establishing continuity with past precedent and in facilitating new legislation. Even in an age of *taqlīd*, jurists worked tirelessly to solidify the doctrine of the legal school (*madhhab*) and to extract greater theories and principles from the sources to guide current and future decisions. *Qawāʿid* and its various subgenres such as *ashbāh wa-naẓāʾir* (the study of the similarities binding cases) and *furūq* (the study of the differences producing separate outcomes

[31] Jackson, *Islamic Law and the State*, 99.
[32] Pound, "The Maxims of Equity," 813.
[33] Pound, "The Maxims of Equity," 810.
[34] Kamali, "Legal Maxims," 78. Heinrichs also points out the overlap between the *qawāʿid* and *maqāṣid* genres. See "*Qawāʿid* as a Genre of Legal Literature," 376.

in similar cases) represents an area in which the jurist can still practice independent reasoning (*ijtihād*) in the post-formative period. As Heinrichs explains: "As opposed to full *ijtihād* which goes beyond the confines of the *madhāhib*, it is the structuring of the *furūʿ* within a certain *madhhab* that the latter-day jurist tries to achieve."[35]

Legal precepts help the jurist to extract new rulings by acting as a kind of shortcut for the jurist, allowing him to examine groups of cases arranged around a common *ʿilla* (or to establish the *ʿilla* himself) without forcing him first to sift through vast amounts of raw data to determine the commonalities and differences before coming to a decision. It is this function of legal precepts that prompts the Ḥanafī jurist, Ibn Nujaym (d. 970/1563) to declare that the jurist can "rise to the level of *ijtihād* through them, if only as a jurisprudent (*wa-law fī l-fatwā*) [within the *madhhab*]."[36]

Indeed, during the 6th/12th and 7th/13th centuries when works on legal precepts began to emerge in larger numbers, *ijtihād* within the *madhhab* was effectively the only form of *ijtihād* available. As Jackson sums up the situation:

> Meanwhile, the appearance, between the 6th/12th and 7th/13th century, of works on legal precepts or so-called *qawāʿid* mark the beginning of an era during which, in treating unprecedented cases, judges and jurists retain access to the sources of law only through the lenses of their *mujtahid*-Imāms and other recognized ancient authorities. All of this stood as a confirmation of a new order, according to which not only was the judicial function restricted to choosing rules already deduced, but legal opinions themselves came ultimately to be judged not on the basis of their intrinsic quality but by whether or not they carried the endorsement of the *madhhab* as a whole.[37]

Interestingly, legal precepts as a tool for the jurist in forming new rulings may be losing some of their *taqlīd*-laden characteristics in the modern era. Kamali points out that, as in the case of the *maqāṣid*, modern jurists are increasingly turning to the *qawāʿid* to meet the demands of *ijtihād*. He asserts that legal maxims are not as burdened by the legacy of *taqlīd* as other areas

[35] Heinrichs, "Structuring the Law," 339.
[36] Zayn al-ʿĀbidīn b. Nujaym, *al-Ashbāh wa-l-naẓāʾir ʿalā madhhab Abū Ḥanīfa al-Nuʿmān* (Beirut: Dār al-Kutub al-ʿIlmiyya, 1985), 15.
[37] Jackson, *Islamic Law and the State*, 79.

of *fiqh* literature and "can thus be more readily utilised as aids in the renewal of *fiqh* and contemporary *ijtihād* (independent reasoning)."[38]

To summarize from the previous sections on form and content, legal precepts perform a number of key discourse functions for the jurist. In pragmatic terms, these functions serve to bolster the use of legal precepts on the dual fronts of continuity and applicability and are rooted in both the form and content of the maxims themselves. The five functions that have been identified above are the following:

1. Legal precepts aid memorization.
2. Legal precepts represent general truths.
3. Legal precepts consolidate information.
4. Legal precepts provide a bridge between the substance of the law and the purposes of the law.
5. Legal precepts help the jurist to extract new rulings.

Naturally, the pragmatic significance of legal precepts is not confined to these five functions but includes others as well. These and other functions will be explored in more detail in the final section of this chapter that looks more closely at precepts dealing with customary law.

LEGAL PRECEPTS AND PRAGMATICS

Before turning to customary law as an example of the discourse functions of legal precepts, it will be helpful first to clarify some aspects of pragmatic theory. This section examines the ways in which legal discourse resembles conversation and to what extent conversational constraints such as Grice's maxims can be applied to legal precepts. As noted previously, legal precepts are, on the whole, constructed by jurists for other jurists and are thus limited in scope to the professional practice of jurisprudence. Therefore, as

[38] Kamali, "Legal Maxims," 78. I look at how jurists in contemporary Egypt teach al-Suyūṭī's *Ashbāh* and engage in *ijtihād* by applying precepts to the extraction of legal rulings in Chapter 5.

Sinclair points out: "legislative discourse more closely approaches the idealized conversation than does ordinary social discourse."[39]

This last point raises the question of who is the speaker in legislative discourse. Sinclair refers to legislatures as the speaker and to statutes as the speech acts that the legislatures produce. Of course, he acknowledges that legislatures do not speak "in the literal sense," but rather, they "speak through their statutes."[40] He also argues that the conversation is "one-sided" since the addressee of the legislative utterance is not usually present and able to respond.[41] For Islamic law, it is harder to speak about legislatures issuing statutes since, prior to the modern era, "*fiqh* was mainly developed by private jurists who were not acting on behalf of governments and institutions that might have exerted a unifying influence."[42] Indeed, Kamali suggests that legal maxims helped to provide some continuity and a "set of general guidelines in an otherwise diverse discipline that combined an impressive variety of schools and influences into its fold."[43]

Even if we consider the jurist to be the speaker, when it comes to the *qawāʿid* literature, the matter is not without complication. All jurisprudence is necessarily cumulative in that each statement by a jurist draws on the opinions of previous jurists and incorporates their combined learning into the formation of a new ruling. This cumulative effect is particularly pronounced in the case of legal precepts, which "are essentially broad-based rules or tests deduced from the aggregate opinions of the early Imāms."[44] So, while al-Suyūṭī is the author of *al-Ashbāh wa-l-naẓāʾir*, his discussion of legal precepts encapsulates the thinking of his predecessors, particularly those authorities within his own legal school. One might even go further and say that legal precepts not only epitomize the views of earlier jurists, they also exemplify the larger social context in which they are produced. Legal precepts, like proverbs, "reflect a culture's evaluative attitudes towards certain facts or events; they are impregnated with value

[39] Sinclair, "Law and Language," 385.
[40] Sinclair, "Law and Language," 375.
[41] Sinclair, "Law and Language," 386.
[42] Kamali, "Legal Maxims," 93.
[43] Kamali, "Legal Maxims," 93.
[44] Jackson, *Islamic Law and the State*, 92.

judgements and legitimise behavior, attitudes or points of view."[45] Thus, legal precepts represent a collective voice to which new interpretations are constantly being added. In the ongoing conversation that is jurisprudence, no one has the last word.

Grice's Maxims

Grice's conversational maxims are rooted in what he calls the "cooperative principle," namely: "make your conversational contribution such as is required, at the stage at which it occurs, by the accepted purpose or direction of the talk exchange in which you are engaged."[46] In other words, one assumes that a conversational utterance is purposive, relevant, and timely. Broken down further, Grice's maxims[47] are as follows:

Maxims of Quantity:

1. Make your contribution sufficiently informative.
2. Do not make your contribution excessively informative.

Maxims of Quality:

1. Do not say anything false.
2. Do not say anything for which you lack sufficient evidence.
3. Do not say anything meaningless.
4. Do not say anything self-contradictory.

Maxim of Relevance:

1. Do not say anything irrelevant.

Maxims of Manner:

1. Avoid obscurity.
2. Avoid ambiguity.
3. Be brief.
4. Be orderly.

[45] Gándara, "They That Sow the Wind," 347.

[46] Sinclair, "Law and Language," 377.

[47] I have used Miller's phrasing of the maxims from Grice's notes. See Geoffrey Miller, "Pragmatics and the Maxims of Interpretation," 1226–7.

According to Grice, if one conforms to the maxims, then one is acting "felicitously" and, if one flouts one or more of the maxims, it results in a conversational "implicature" that requires other information in order to interpret its meaning. Either way, the theory of pragmatics assumes that the speaker chose a particular wording at a certain juncture in order to fulfill a purpose. As far as legal discourse is concerned, Sinclair notes that in order to use Grice's maxims as a framework for understanding "canons of construction" or legal precepts: "we must assume legislative compliance, that is, that the legislature did act felicitously, saying as much as it could, as clearly as it could, to further its purposes as best it could."[48] This assumption does not rule out the possibility that a statute could be composed in a manner that is deliberately obscure in order to create an implicature that necessitates interpretation as well as added effort on the part of the jurist. In fact, as this discussion will show, it is in these instances of implicature in legal discourse that change is most likely to occur.

Ejusdem Generis

Sinclair and Miller point to several canons of construction in American statutory law that lend themselves to interpretation using pragmatic theory. In keeping with the nature of pragmatic principles as well as legal precepts in allowing for exceptions and contradictions, the two authors explain some of the same canons in different ways. One such canon is the rule of *ejusdem generis*, which holds that "general terms in a list take their meaning from specific terms."[49] Thus, the task for the court or jurist is to determine what sort of items are akin to those listed in the statute.

For example, for a statute barring "cats, dogs, and other animals" from a public park, the kinship rule helps to determine which specific references are included under the general term "animal."[50] Miller analyzes the application of *ejusdem generis* in terms of the cost and benefit of providing

[48] Sinclair, "Law and Language," 420.
[49] Miller, "Pragmatics and the Maxims of Interpretation," 1199.
[50] Miller, "Pragmatics and the Maxims of Interpretation," 1200.

more general or specific information. Grice's maxim of quantity requires the speaker (or statute) to offer just as much information as necessary, no more, no less. Any extra or lacking information results in an implicature that the jurist must try to explain if the statute is to be properly enacted and applied to other cases that arise. Miller assumes, according to the cooperative principle, that the statute uses the more general term "animals" rather than "pets" in order to cover cases that would not be included under the more specific term (such as a canine model used to film a dog food commercial). As he explains: "the benefits of greater specificity must be weighed against the costs; in many cases the cooperative purposes of the communication would be best served by a more general term even if it is slightly less precise."[51]

Sinclair approaches the *ejusdem generis* maxim from a slightly different angle, though still using the rubric of Grice's conversational constraints. For him, determination of the "criterion of similarity" binding items in a list falls under Grice's first maxim of quality adapted to suit statutory legislation: "do not enact a provision that can be shown not to further the legislative purpose."[52] Therefore, for Sinclair, the purpose of the legislation is the deciding factor in determining kinship. As he puts it: "Only if the item in question can be shown to further the legislative purpose in the same way as do the items listed should it be held to come under the statutory provision."[53]

Expressio Unius est Exclusio Alterius

A second canon of construction common to both Sinclair and Miller's pragmatic approach to statutory law is *expressio unius est exclusio alterius* ("to express one thing is to exclude others").[54] Again, Miller interprets this canon as reflecting Grice's maxim of quantity, where one is expected to provide as

[51] Miller, "Pragmatics and the Maxims of Interpretation," 1202.

[52] Sinclair, "Law and Language," 397. [53] Sinclair, "Law and Language," 412.

[54] This maxim closely resembles the concept in Islamic jurisprudence of *mafhūm al-mukhālafa*, or "divergent meaning." As Kamali explains, it is generally assumed that "a legal text never implies its opposite meaning" without "a separate text to validate it." In order to be accepted, the divergent meaning must be in harmony with the pronounced meaning contained in the words of the text. See Mohammad Hashim Kamali, *Principles of Islamic Jurisprudence*, Third Edition (Cambridge, U.K.: The Islamic Texts Society, 2003), 175–85.

much information as is required and no more. One example he uses is of a statute ruling "that no one under eighteen may operate a motor vehicle on a public street."[55] Using *expressio unius*, one might assume that, since the ruling specifies "on a public street," a person who is under eighteen is allowed to operate a motor vehicle in a location other than a public street, such as driving a tractor in a field. Miller explains that, since "the legislature is obviously capable of stating other areas in which the statute applies, the fact that it did not do so gives rise to the implicature that it did not intend the statute to apply in settings other than in those expressly mentioned."[56]

This premise also applies to other rules that attempt to maintain a status quo and make it difficult for governing bodies or courts to interfere with existing statutes. For example, the plain meaning rule "expresses the principle that where the statute is narrowly and tightly drawn, the courts have considerably less interpretive flexibility than when the statute is phrased in vague or general terms."[57] Generally speaking, the more specific the statute, the harder it is to extend or change.

Sinclair also interprets *expressio unius* from the standpoint of Grice's maxim of quantity. He responds to the criticism that this rule can lead to logical fallacies. For instance, if one were to say that "some swans are white," it is incorrect to deduce that "some swans are not white." If "all swans are white" is true, then "some swans are white" is also true, but "some swans are not white" is false. Therefore, if a speaker who is assumed to be acting felicitously makes the statement that "some swans are white" he violates the maxim of quantity by not providing as much information as he could, thus creating a pragmatic implicature. As Sinclair observes, the implicature can be resolved by considering the context: one concludes that the speaker believes that some swans are not white. As he puts it: the "pragmatic implicature comes not just from the truth conditions of the words used but from the context of their use and the social conventions governing conversation."[58]

[55] Miller, "Pragmatics and the Maxims of Interpretation," 1196.
[56] Miller, "Pragmatics and the Maxims of Interpretation," 1196.
[57] Miller, "Pragmatics and the Maxims of Interpretation," 1199.
[58] Sinclair, "Law and Language," 415.

Islamic Maxims of Interpretation

For Islamic legal precepts, the closest equivalent to Sinclair and Miller's canons of construction are the maxims of interpretation that some jurists refer to as *qawāʿid uṣūliyya*. These canons of interpretation or "hermeneutic principles" guide the jurist in extracting rulings from the sources of law.[59] Like the canons of construction described by Sinclair and Miller, these precepts often concern the language itself, thus helping the jurist to interpret ambiguous statements, for example, based on linguistic expression as well as the pragmatic intent behind the statements. A precept like *al-amr li-l-wujūb* ("the imperative produces obligation"), for instance, derives legal action from the use of the grammatical imperative. Heinrichs notes that some later sources distinguish between *qawāʿid uṣūliyya* and *qawāʿid fiqhiyya*, which are general rules derived from substantive legal rulings that usually encompass several specific sub-categories.[60] Earlier sources tend to blend the two together and, indeed, there is a large degree of conceptual overlap between different types of *qawāʿid* that may perform several different functions.[61]

Like *expressio unius*, many of the precepts in Islamic law set a baseline or default condition that makes it more difficult for the legislature or jurist to change the framework already in place. Such precepts usually identify a "norm" or *aṣl* under the assumption that anything contrary to the norm will require further justification by the jurist using textual (or contextual) evidence to resolve the implicature. One such maxim is *al-aṣl baqāʾ mā kāna ʿalā mā kāna* ("the norm is maintaining the status quo") and an example would be the missing person who is presumed to be alive unless evidence emerges to prove the contrary.[62] Another application of this precept is a wife's continued right to maintenance as long as she remains married to her husband.[63]

[59] Wolfhart Heinrichs, "*Qawāʿid* as a Genre of Legal Literature," 372.

[60] Heinrichs, "*Qawāʿid* as a Genre of Legal Literature," 372. See also Heinrichs, "Structuring the Law," 335–6.

[61] Rabb recognizes the overlap between interpretative and substantive maxims by including a separate category of combined "interpretive-substantive maxims." See *Doubt's Benefit*, 12.

[62] ʿIzzat ʿUbayd al-Daʿās, *al-Qawāʿid al-fiqhiyya* (Beirut: Dār al-Tirmidhī, 1989), 17.

[63] Kamali, "Legal Maxims," 84. This question and that of the wife's right to remarry if her husband has been missing for an extended period fall under the disputed, post-formative legal concept of *istiṣḥāb al-ḥāl*, or the presumption of continuity. Jurists from different legal schools often differed on such issues. For example, a majority of Ḥanafī jurists were of the

Even more general are the maxims *al-aṣl fī l-ashyāʾ al-ibāḥa* ("the norm regarding things is permissibility") and *al-aṣl barāʾat al-dhimma* ("the norm is non-liability"), which assume that a given action is permitted unless otherwise specified and a given person is not liable unless proven guilty. The first maxim applies, for instance, when one is unsure whether or not a certain type of animal (like a giraffe) is lawful to eat. The default position is that it is permissible unless it can be proven to fall into a category of foods that are expressly forbidden.[64] The second maxim is similar to the idea that a defendant is presumed to be innocent unless more than one witness can attest to his guilt.[65] The same is true with a disputed loan—the burden of proof falls on the accuser rather than on the one accused.[66]

In each of these cases, a baseline or default is established that conforms to the legal interpretation of Grice's maxim of quantity: the law as it stands is assumed to be sufficiently informative. Therefore, any change to the status quo requires extra work on the part of the court or jurist to prove that the law extends to a case not already covered in the language of the statute. Also illustrative of this idea is the much debated maxim *lā yunsab li-l-sākit qawl* ("a statement shall not be ascribed to one who is silent"). In most cases, silence should not be interpreted as equivalent to a statement such as denial or assent. For example, if a house is not intended for rent and the owner is silent on the matter, the silence is not to be interpreted as a demand for

opinion that the wife cannot remarry because the missing husband is presumed to be alive until evidence of his death is produced, whereas Shāfiʿīs allowed the wife to remarry after four years and even allowed the missing person's heirs to claim their inheritance. See Mohammad Abdeljaber, "*Istiṣḥāb al-ḥāl*," *The Oxford Encyclopedia of Islam and Law, Oxford Islamic Studies Online*, accessed July 24, 2015, http://www.oxfordislamicstudies.com.proxy.wm.edu/article/opr/t349/e0093?_hi=0&_pos=2.

[64] Jalāl al-Dīn al-Suyūṭī, *al-Ashbāh wa-l-naẓāʾir fī l-qawāʿid al-fiqhiyya* (Cairo: al-Maktab al-Thaqāfī li-l-Nashr wa-l-Tawzīʿ, 2007), 95.

[65] Al-Suyūṭī, *al-Ashbāh wa-l-naẓāʾir*, 85.

[66] Al-Daʿās, *al-Qawāʿid al-fiqhiyya*, 21. The norms listed above are similar to rebuttable presumptions common in civil law, where the burden of proof rests on the accuser wishing to disprove the presumption. The presumption of innocence until proven guilty is the most widely known of these presumptions in civil law. Another example is the presumption of paternity in which a child born in the context of a marital relationship is presumed to be the child of the husband unless proven otherwise. This presumption resembles the Islamic legal maxim of *al-walad li-l-firāsh* ("the child belongs to the [marital] bed"), where paternity of a child is based on the marital status of the child's mother. Interestingly, the example regarding a missing person comes up in the context of rebuttable presumptions as well, where the missing person is presumed dead after seven years have passed.

rent in a contractual obligation, and the owner has no right to demand rent retroactively.[67]

However, there are some notable exceptions to this precept that have rather significant implications. In a situation where a statement is required and no such statement is made, it is possible to attribute tacit denial or assent to the one who is silent. If a defendant is asked to respond to charges against him and remains silent, his silence is taken to indicate denial of the charges and the burden of proof falls to the accuser.[68] Also, if a young virgin is asked by her guardian to respond to a marriage proposal, her silence is equivalent to approval of the marriage contract.[69] Al-Suyūṭī specifies that this is not the case with a non-virgin widow or divorcée whose silence is never to be taken as acceptance of a marriage proposal.[70] The case of the virgin versus the non-virgin from whom a statement is required in response to a marital contract would seem to be contradictory and an apparent flouting of the maxim of quality ("Do not say anything self-contradictory"). The resulting implicature would need to be explained using information external to that which is already available from the text.[71] While al-Suyūṭī offers no such explanation, he does seem to acknowledge that many of the exceptions to *lā yunsab li-l-sākit qawl* are either weak or contested.[72]

In addition to these substantive and procedural issues of jurisprudence, Grice's maxims are also relevant to the *qawāʿid uṣūliyya*, the interpretive principles that aid the jurist in drawing legal implications from different kinds of speech acts. Grice's maxims of quality and manner are instructive, for example, when the literal meaning of an oral or written statement comes into question. The interpretive maxim *al-aṣl fī l-kalām al-ḥaqīqa* ("the default meaning for a statement is its literal meaning") assumes that a statement is true and not contradictory or absurd according to its literal meaning. Consequently, if the literal meaning of the statement renders it impossible

[67] Al-Daʿās, *al-Qawāʿid al-fiqhiyya*, 23.
[68] Al-Daʿās, *al-Qawāʿid al-fiqhiyya*, 24.
[69] Al-Daʿās, *al-Qawāʿid al-fiqhiyya*, 24. See also al-Suyūṭī, *al-Ashbāh wa-l-naẓāʾir*, 188.
[70] Al-Suyūṭī, *al-Ashbāh wa-l-naẓāʾir*, 188.
[71] The implicature could be resolved, for example, if one assumes that more weight is given to the opinion of the experienced woman who has had legal intercourse as opposed to that of the inexperienced virgin.
[72] Al-Suyūṭī, *al-Ashbāh wa-l-naẓāʾir*, 188.

or absurd, then the implicature can be resolved by taking into account a metaphorical or non-literal meaning.

If a man sets up an endowment for his 'children,' for example, the literal interpretation would preclude grandchildren from the endowment. However, if the man does not have any immediate children, then the non-literal meaning of the word 'children' is understood to include grandchildren as well.[73] Similarly, if someone swears not to eat from a certain tree, he is understood to mean that he will not eat the fruit from the tree, since eating the bark or leaves would not make sense, even though the literal meaning would allow such an interpretation.[74] In both cases, violation of the maxim of quality ("Do not say anything false") and the maxim of manner ("avoid ambiguity") is resolved by resorting to the metaphorical or non-literal meaning.

PRAGMATICS AND CUSTOMARY LAW

This section singles out customary law (*ʿurf*) as an example of the pragmatic function of legal maxims for two main reasons, one historical and the other conceptual. Like the literature on *qawāʿid*, Western critical scholarship on *ʿurf* is extremely sparse.[75] However, it is possible to piece together the major developments that led customary law to shift from its status as less than a formal source of law to assume a more prominent role in Islamic jurisprudence as a source in its own right. It is significant in my view that growing acceptance by jurists of custom as a source of law reached a new height around the late medieval and early modern period, or in other words, during and after al-Suyūṭī's lifetime.

[73] Al-Suyūṭī, *al-Ashbāh wa-l-naẓāʾir*, 97–8. See also al-Daʿās, *al-Qawāʿid al-fiqhiyya*, 65–6.

[74] Al-Suyūṭī, *al-Ashbāh wa-l-naẓāʾir*, 98; see also al-Daʿās, *al-Qawāʿid al-fiqhiyya*, 66; see also Jamāl al-Dīn ʿAbd al-Raḥīm al-Isnawī (d. 772/1370), *al-Tamhīd fī takhrīj al-furūʿ ʿalā al-uṣūl* (Beirut: Muʾassasat al-Risāla, 1980), 196.

[75] Two helpful contributions are Gideon Libson's article, "On the Development of Custom as a Source of Law in Islamic Law: *al-rujūʿu ilā al-ʿurfi aḥadu al-qawāʿidi al-khamsi allatī yatabannā ʿalayhā al-fiqhu*," *Islamic Law and Society* 4:2 (1997): 131–55 as well as Ayman Shabana, *Custom in Islamic Law and Legal Theory: The Development of the Concepts of* ʿUrf *and* ʿĀdah *in the Islamic Legal Tradition* (New York: Palgrave Macmillan, 2010). For a useful study in Arabic, see al-Sayyid Ṣāliḥ ʿAwaḍ, *Athar al-ʿurf fī l-tashrīʿ al-islāmī* (Cairo: Dār al-Kitāb al-Jāmiʿī, 1981).

In addition to being closely related in terms of historical development, legal precepts and custom share a number of conceptual similarities that offer an intriguing area of study. Ayman Shabana describes the relationship between legal precepts and custom as interdependent and of mutual benefit. He notes that custom, though rooted in the Qurʾān and Sunna, was mostly derived by jurists inductively from normative behavior and then made subject to further classification and abstraction by later generations of scholars. As he puts it:

> Through the abstraction process, custom was incorporated into legal theory as one of the inductive secondary sources of law. Together with this development, custom was concurrently incorporated within the genre of legal maxims. Following these two parallel processes, substantive law was able to reinvigorate legal theory while being constantly shaped by it.[76]

The conceptual similarities between legal maxims and customary law are even more striking from the standpoint of pragmatic theory. Like *qawāʿid*, custom as it was abstracted and formulated by jurists became a useful discursive tool fulfilling a variety of pragmatic functions. First, custom, much like legal maxims, is helpful in resolving contradictions in the substantive law by drawing in extra-textual information. In this way, custom provides a crucial link between the theory of jurisprudence and its context. By bringing context into the equation, custom allows the law to grow and adapt to changing circumstances. This function became especially important in the post-formative era where much of the methodology and substance of the law was already in place and jurists were looking for new ways to apply the tradition and maintain its relevance in society.

In addition to helping to resolve contradictions in the law, custom is useful in the interpretation of speech acts. Speech acts, as discussed by theorists of pragmatics, are utterances that are not only informative but also "performative"; they are used to *do* things instead of just to say things.[77] Examples of speech acts would include marital vows or a statement declaring war. In these cases, as Levinson explains, the words themselves are

[76] Shabana, *Custom in Islamic Law*, 11.
[77] Stephen C. Levinson, *Pragmatics* (Cambridge, U.K.: Cambridge University Press, 1983), 228.

"performative" because they are by convention linked to institutional procedures.[78]

In the context of Islamic law, the declaration of divorce is a classic situation in which words fulfill a purpose with clear legal consequences for the speaker and addressee. Thus, it is often crucial for the jurist to be able to judge in cases of doubt or ambiguity whether the linguistic form of the utterance matches the intentions of the speaker and to resolve any discrepancies that might arise. Custom very often provides the vital link between the words themselves and the context in which they were produced. The same is true for other oaths or contracts where custom supplies the key clue as to how the speaker's words should be interpreted and given legal import. For this reason, many of the standard examples that jurists like al-Suyūṭī use to demonstrate the authority of custom involve the interpretation of oaths and contracts (such as endowment deeds, sales, hiring services, and other financial transactions).

Custom also relies on a framework of expectations and assumptions regarding acceptable social behavior and practice. *ʿUrf* is usually defined as "recurring practices that are acceptable to people of sound nature."[79] This definition implies that not every practice that recurs can be considered worthy of consideration in law-making and that a distinction must be made between what amounts to 'bad' *ʿurf* and 'good' *ʿurf*. For instance, pre-Islamic practices such as usury and disinheriting female relatives, while widely practiced, are deemed not in conformity with the principles of Sharīʿa.[80]

As one modern expert on customary law, Aḥmad Fahmī Abū Sunna, warns, basing the authority of custom solely on human judgment (or even on the judgment of most Muslims as implied by the *ḥadīth* 'what the Muslims deem to be good is good in the eyes of God') is problematic, since humans are capable of error.[81] The difficulty is compounded by the fact that rulings based on social custom are subject to "changes of conditions of time and

[78] Levinson, *Pragmatics*, 230.
[79] Kamali, *Principles of Islamic Jurisprudence*, 369. See Ibn Nujaym, *al-Ashbāh wa-l-naẓāʾir*, 93.
[80] Kamali, *Principles of Islamic Jurisprudence*, 378.
[81] Aḥmad Fahmī Abū Sunna, *Qāʿidatān fiqhiyyatān* (Cairo: Dār al-Baṣāʾir, 2004), 20. Although both al-Suyūṭī and Ibn Nujaym cite this tradition as the textual proof for the authority of custom, they indicate that it is not Prophetic in origin but is attributed to the Companion ʿAbd Allāh b. Masʿūd.

place."[82] Nevertheless, in spite of these problems, later jurists in particular were unable to deny the importance of custom in shaping social practice and behavior and were challenged to come up with guidelines reconciling social realities and the purposes of the law. The *qawāʿid* genre provided a convenient framework for such discussions.

The next section examines how custom is used pragmatically by jurists like al-Suyūṭī to resolve contradictions in the law, to interpret speech acts such as oaths and contracts, and to reconcile social realities and the purposes of the law in reference to the overarching legal maxim, *al-ʿāda muḥakkama*, or "custom should be made to serve as an arbiter." Used as a template for this discussion is the chapter on custom in al-Suyūṭī's major *qawāʿid* work, *al-Ashbāh wa-l-naẓāʾir*. The analysis follows roughly the same layout as al-Suyūṭī's (with some adaptations), using many similar headings and emphasizing examples that feature prominently in al-Suyūṭī's work in order to reflect better the intentions of the author.

Introducing the Concept

Like Tāj al-Dīn al-Subkī (d. 771/1370) in his earlier *Ashbāh* work, al-Suyūṭī examines *al-ʿāda muḥakkama* as one of the five major precepts that are general enough that each one encompasses several sub-maxims.[83] The fact that this maxim is included as one of the five universal maxims points to its growing significance by al-Suyūṭī's time. Al-Subkī's section on custom is a relatively terse list of cases and does not include any of the linguistic interpretation that was later subsumed under the custom precept. Another prominent Shāfiʿī jurist, al-Zarkashī (d. 794/1392), includes a similar list of cases in which *ʿurf* can be applied, as do al-Suyūṭī and Ibn Nujaym.[84]

Each item in the list, such as assigning weights and measures to commodities where there is no clear text indicating its value during the Prophet's time or obtaining tacit approval to collect ripened fruit that has fallen to

[82] Kamali, *Principles of Islamic Jurisprudence*, 380.
[83] In al-Subkī's work, this precept appears under the heading *al-rujūʿ ilā al-ʿāda* ("recourse to custom"). See Tāj al-Dīn al-Subkī, *al-Ashbāh wa-l-naẓāʾir* (Beirut: Dār al-Kutub al-ʿIlmiyya, 1991), 50.
[84] Muḥammad b. Bahādur al-Zarkashī, *al-Manthūr fī l-qawāʿid*, 2 vols. (Beirut: Dār al-Kutub al-ʿIlmiyya, 2000), 1:96. See also al-Suyūṭī, *al-Ashbāh*, 127 and Ibn Nujaym, *al-Ashbāh*, 93–4.

the ground from privately owned trees, encapsulates a whole legal discussion on its own. Al-Suyūṭī makes it clear that by lumping the various topics together he wants the reader to see just how many issues can be attributed to *ʿāda* and *ʿurf*.[85] As he says: "Know that recourse is given to consideration of *ʿāda* and *ʿurf* in *fiqh* in regards to countless issues."[86] Ibn Nujaym echoes al-Suyūṭī's sentiment and takes it a step further, adding the clause: "to the extent that they made it a source [*ḥattā jaʿalū dhālik aṣlan*]."[87] Libson highlights this impulse on the part of the later jurists (particularly those from the sixteenth century onwards) to "collect all the legal rulings relating to custom" in what amounted to "recognition of custom as a formal source of law, as stated explicitly by Ibn Nujaym."[88]

Having established the relevance of custom to a broad range of legal issues, al-Suyūṭī goes on to investigate areas in which a contradiction or discrepancy has given rise to a dispute amongst legal scholars. In the absence of a clear text indicating a particular ruling, the jurist draws on contextual factors to resolve the contradiction. In each case, the jurist engages in a complex negotiation of meaning in which the semantic content of a statement is weighed against a framework of expectations and assumptions located outside of the literal meaning of the words themselves. For this reason, writes Ibn Nujaym, jurists often included custom in *uṣūl* works in cases where literal meaning is abandoned on the basis of an inferential indicator and custom.[89]

Contradictions Between General and Specific *ʿUrf*

Jurists tend to classify custom as either general (*ʿurf ʿāmm*) or specific (*ʿurf khāṣṣ*). A general custom is one that is predominant in most places, whereas

[85] Jurists tend to use the terms *ʿāda* and *ʿurf* interchangeably in relation to customary practice. Some scholars differentiate between the two by saying that *ʿāda* can be used to refer to the personal practice or habit of an individual, whereas *ʿurf* can only refer to the collective practice of a group of people. See Kamali, *Principles of Islamic Jurisprudence*, 367.

[86] Al-Suyūṭī, *al-Ashbāh*, 127. Translations are mine unless otherwise indicated.

[87] Ibn Nujaym, *al-Ashbāh*, 93.

[88] Libson, "On the Development of Custom," 142.

[89] Ibn Nujaym, *al-Ashbāh*, 93. The maxim, *al-ḥaqīqa tatruk bi-dalālat al-ʿāda* ("literal meaning is abandoned on the basis of an indicator of custom") is sometimes listed as a sub-maxim of the custom precept. See, for example, al-Daʿās, *al-Qawāʿid al-fiqhiyya*, 51.

a specific custom pertains only to a particular locality or to the technical terminology of a certain profession.[90] Normally, a general *ʿurf* would take precedence over a specific one. However, the issue arose as to whether under certain conditions a particular custom could act as a general one in the absence of a clear statement to the contrary. Al-Suyūṭī cites two rather interesting examples, both in relation to endowed institutions.

The first example is taken from the Shāfiʿī jurist Ibn al-Ṣalāḥ (d. 643/1245) concerning vacation days for teachers in schools that are financed through religious endowments (*awqāf*). As al-Suyūṭī reports:

> When asked about this issue, Ibn al-Ṣalāḥ answered that the vacation time that falls during the months of Ramaḍān and half of Shaʿbān does not prevent [the teacher] from earning his wages, since there is no text from the founder stipulating that one work during the period in question, but any vacation time that occurs before these two [months] does prevent [the teacher from earning his wages] because there is no continuous custom to support it, nor does it occur with certainty in a majority of schools or locales. If a prior custom does occur in some regions and is prevalent and not contradictory, then a dispute arises in those regions as to whether a specific custom can act in place of a general custom. The evident [opinion] is that it does act as such for that group of people.[91]

The issue described by Ibn al-Ṣalāḥ and cited by al-Suyūṭī evokes the earlier discussion surrounding the legal maxim, *expressio unius est exclusio alterius* ("to express one thing is to exclude others"). In guessing the intentions of the endower, the jurist assumes that if the endower did not wish for salaried employees to collect their wages during certain specified vacation times, then he would have included such a stipulation in the original deed. Assuming that the endower was acting felicitously, one would expect his statement to provide sufficient information (according to Grice's maxim of quantity).

By Ibn al-Ṣalāḥ's time, though, people had clearly become accustomed to taking vacation days during certain months of the year and expected to continue to collect a salary during that time. Therefore, it became incumbent on the jurist to prove that the new practice was in accord with the intent of the endower, thus cancelling out any implicatures that would arise from a violation of the maxim of quantity. In this case, *ʿurf* provides the needed

90 See Kamali, *Principles of Islamic Jurisprudence*, 377.
91 Al-Suyūṭī, *al-Ashbāh*, 129.

justification and resolves the potential implicature. Also, since general custom tends to carry more weight than specific custom by virtue of being more prevalent, it is convenient to say that the specific custom acts in the same way as the general one for certain groups of people in some contexts (though this argument is disputed).

Effectively, Ibn al-Ṣalāḥ's opinion opens the door for customs established after the time of the endowment—even those that vary according to region—to prevail in the absence of a direct statement against them. The problem is that relying on a later custom to interpret the original intention of the founder also allows for abuse and exploitation of the system as *waqf* rules grew more lax. Indeed, al-Suyūṭī himself observes in one of his fatwas on the issue of scholarly stipends that if one looks at the opinions of Ibn al-Ṣalāḥ and al-Nawawī regarding *waqf*, one will find them exceptionally strict, whereas the opinions of later scholars like al-Subkī and al-Bulqīnī are much more lenient and accommodating.[92] By al-Suyūṭī's time, practices that had been frowned upon by earlier jurists (such as appointing deputies to endowed positions and holding multiple posts in different institutions) had become commonplace, thus ramping up the pressure on jurists to justify such practices. Customary law presented an appealing option for making these kinds of arguments.

A remark by Ibn Nujaym in his corresponding discussion of the vacation issue is quite revealing of the corruption that had crept into the *waqf* system by the sixteenth century. He asserts that teachers, like judges, should be allowed to collect their salaries during vacation days since it is necessary to rest on occasion. He goes on to say: "However, the convention of scholars in our day is to take such a long vacation that their days off outnumber their teaching days."[93] Ibn Nujaym continues:

> Some teachers even claim precedence in compensation since teaching is a religious rite, citing *al-Ḥāwī al-qudsī*, in spite of the fact that *al-Ḥāwī al-qudsī* refers only to teachers in the *madrasa*, not to any teacher. Teachers in mosques (like in Egypt) are excluded, the difference being that the school would fail without the teacher, but the mosque would not shut down if the teacher were absent.[94]

[92] Al-Suyūṭī, *al-Inṣāf fī tamyīz al-awqāf* in *al-Ḥāwī li-l-fatāwī*, 2 vols. (Beirut: Dār al-Kutub al-ʿIlmiyya, 2000), 1:151. See Chapter 1 for a detailed discussion of this fatwa.

[93] Ibn Nujaym, *al-Ashbāh*, 96.

[94] Ibn Nujaym, *al-Ashbāh*, 96. The reference is to *al-Ḥāwī al-qudsī fī furūʿ al-fiqh al-Ḥanafī* by Aḥmad b. Muḥammad al-Ghaznawī (d. 593/1196–1197).

As it turns out, al-Suyūṭī was, among his many professional appointments, a teacher of *ḥadīth* in the Shaykhūniyya *madrasa*, which becomes obvious from his second example. This example pertains to endowed schools in which *ḥadīth* is one of the subjects stipulated by the founder. Again, the problem is one of insufficient specificity, since it is not clear what the endower intends by the study of *ḥadīth*. Does he mean the technical terminology of *ḥadīth* criticism as laid out in works like the *Mukhtaṣar*[95] of Ibn al-Ṣalāḥ, or the analysis of topics relating to the content of traditions? Al-Suyūṭī indicates that the latter approach constitutes the current custom, as he observed in the stipulations of the founder of the Shaykhūniyya *madrasa*.[96] Al-Suyūṭī then cites the opinion of the great *ḥadīth* scholar and teacher of Ibn Ḥajar, Abū Faḍl al-ʿIrāqī, to the effect that the founder's stipulations should be followed, even if the stipulations and teaching methodology vary from one region to the next (Syria is different from Egypt, for example).

The implication is that, if the intentions of the founder in regards to *ḥadīth* methodology are unknown, then specific custom steps in to resolve the dispute. The example is striking because it represents a rare occasion in which al-Suyūṭī speaks from direct experience rather than just relating examples already formulated by earlier scholars. Al-Suyūṭī demonstrates the task on the part of the jurist to reconcile the intention of the founder (as inferred from the text) with social practice as he witnessed it in context.

Contradictions Between Customary Usage and *Sharʿī* Usage[97]

In the next two sections, al-Suyūṭī launches into an analysis of contradictions arising from the linguistic interpretation of speech acts, especially various oaths and contractual agreements. The first scenario is one in which linguistic expressions as they appear in the Qurʾān conflict with how people would normally understand those terms. If one swears not to eat meat, for

[95] The reference is to Ibn al-Ṣalāḥ's well known manual of the science of *ḥadīth* criticism, *Muqaddima Ibn al-Ṣalāḥ fī ʿulūm al-ḥadīth*.

[96] Al-Suyūṭī, *al-Ashbāh*, 130.

[97] Normally, a ruling would be based on how a particular term is used in the Qurʾān or Sunna (or its *sharʿī* usage). The example of oaths presents an interesting exception to that rule, allowing more authority to be attributed to customary usage in many cases.

example, eating fish will not break the oath, even if the Qurʾān uses the word 'meat' (*laḥm*) to refer to fish, since fish is not conventionally classified as meat.[98] This logic flies in the face of the notion that *sharʿī* usage should always outrank the authority of custom. Jurists try to evade this difficulty by arguing that if the speech act concerns a legal provision (*ḥukm*), such as prayer or fasting, the *sharʿī* usage overrules the customary usage. If one swears not to pray, for instance, it is interpreted to mean ritual prayer as required by divine law with the appropriate prostrations, not any invocation commonly referred to as 'prayer.'[99]

Contradictions Between Custom and Language

The second set of examples involves conflicts in how certain terms are used by convention and their literal meanings. Jurists dispute in the case of oaths, for example, whether customary usage or literal connotation should take precedence in how the oath is enforced. Here, al-Suyūṭī cites a number of standard examples repeated from earlier *fiqh* works such as Ibn al-Wakīl's *al-Ashbāh wa-l-naẓāʾir* and al-Zarkashī's *al-Manthūr fī l-qawāʿid*. If one swears not to eat 'bread,' for instance, eating rice bread will break the oath since it still falls under the linguistic definition of 'bread' as baked goods (even if one comes from a region where people are not accustomed to rice bread).[100] However, if one swears not to eat 'heads' or 'eggs' the oath is not broken by consuming fish or locust eggs nor by the heads of birds or fish, since these are not customarily included in those categories.[101]

Ibn al-Wakīl acknowledges the difference of opinion amongst jurists and comes down in favor of the customary usage specific to the region in which the oath is made.[102] Therefore, as Ibn Nujaym later clarifies, 'heads' in Egypt

[98] Al-Suyūṭī, *al-Ashbāh*, 130. [99] Al-Suyūṭī, *al-Ashbāh*, 130.

[100] Al-Suyūṭī, *al-Ashbāh*, 131. On this point, al-Suyūṭī seems to be at odds with the general consensus. Ibn Nujaym favors the opposite opinion, which is that one breaks the oath only by eating the kind of bread prevalent in the particular region where the oath is made. So, for Cairo one commits perjury only by eating wheat bread, in Ṭabaristān rice bread, and in Zabīd corn or millet bread. He adds that one does not break the oath with donuts, except by intention. See *al-Ashbāh*, 97–8.

[101] Al-Suyūṭī, *al-Ashbāh*, 131.

[102] Muḥammad b. ʿUmar b. al-Wakīl, *al-Ashbāh wa-l-naẓāʾir*, 2 vols. (Riyadh: Maktabat al-Rushd, 1993), 2:84.

are understood to refer only to sheep heads that are sold in the market.[103] For al-Zarkashī, the deciding factor is whether or not a certain group is accustomed to selling the heads separately or not. So, if it is the custom in a certain region to sell fish heads separately, then the oath is broken by eating them in that region.[104]

While these examples seem to contain numerous contradictions even in themselves, some unifying concerns stand out as guiding the jurist's reasoning in these and similar cases. First, the issue is one of pragmatic interpretation because it takes into account the communicative goals of the speaker within a certain context. Unless the hearer can interpret what the speaker means when he swears not to eat 'meat' or 'heads' or 'eggs' or to ride an 'animal' or to enter a 'house,' the maxims of manner ("avoid obscurity" and "avoid ambiguity") and relevance ("do not say anything irrelevant") remain violated and the resulting implicatures unresolved. As these examples show, the jurist will usually resort to customary usage, where the conventional sense of a term is given priority in interpretation over an unconventional sense. The customary usage is determined by context, either because it is the understanding of people in a certain region, or the technical terminology of a certain trade or profession.

As Miller explains in relation to Western statutory law: "For the most part the maxim that words in a statute should be interpreted according to their ordinary usage does not give rise to implicatures, simply because the maxim is not flouted."[105] So, as al-Zarkashī observes in relation to the heads issue:

> If someone swears not to eat heads, he breaks the oath with that which is sold separately, such as [the heads of] sheep and cows, not the heads of birds and fish, because custom does not apply the word 'heads' (meaning those which are normally eaten either fried or boiled) to them; custom and language do not conflict in this case, rather, they agree on the lack of designation.[106]

However, if the same oath were to be made in a region in which people are accustomed to referring to the heads of birds and fish sold individually as 'heads,' then the speaker flouts the maxim of manner and an implicature is

[103] Ibn Nujaym, *al-Ashbāh*, 98. [104] Al-Zarkashī, *al-Manthūr*, 2:117.
[105] Miller, "Pragmatics and the Maxims of Interpretation," 1222.
[106] Al-Zarkashī, *al-Manthūr*, 2:116.

created. In that case, the hearer looks for a way to ascertain the speaker's intention based on context.

Another way to assess the intentions of the speaker from context is to adopt a process of interpretation based on the principle of relevance. Dan Sperber and Deirdre Wilson argue in favor of such an approach in their revision and expansion of Grice's inferential model of communication. Consider, for example, the utterance, 'the child left the straw in the glass.' According to Sperber and Wilson: "At a purely linguistic level, there is no reason to assume that the *cereal-stalk* sense of 'straw' is less accessible than the *drinking-tube* sense; no reason, then, why one interpretation should be preferred. The selection manifestly involves contextual factors."[107] In this case, the hearer searches for an interpretation that matches his or her expectations of relevance. The theory assumes that the speaker is communicating cooperatively to convey a particular thought and has left enough clues that the hearer will be able to infer the speaker's intended meaning as efficiently as possible.

Contradictions Between Earlier and Later Meanings

The final set of examples involves words in contracts whose connotations have changed over time. Is the new association considered a particularization of the previous one? Al-Suyūṭī writes that for contracts in which the meaning of words is attributed to custom, the later association would normally take precedence over the previous one.[108] This idea is consistent with Ibn al-Ṣalāḥ's vacation issue mentioned earlier, where endowments made after it had become customary to take certain months off take precedence over endowments preceding that custom. Therefore, the prevailing custom for teachers to take vacation time during the months of Shaʿbān and Ramaḍān is the interpretation that must be upheld and any previous associations are not supported.

Al-Suyūṭī's argument changes when it comes to the second endowment issue. Here, the jurist takes a stance that is inconsistent with the previous

[107] Dan Sperber and Deirdre Wilson, *Relevance: Communication and Cognition*, Second Edition, (Oxford: Blackwell Publishers Ltd, 1995), 186.
[108] Al-Suyūṭī, *al-Ashbāh*, 133.

vacation example (thus creating an implicature). This discussion takes up a sizeable portion of al-Suyūṭī's chapter on customary law, indicating that the issue was both close to his heart and that it required extra justification. For the Shāfiʿī jurist, like al-Zarkashī and al-Suyūṭī, a problem arises when the rule regarding earlier and later word associations extends to cases in which a later interpretation would decrease the power held by their legal school. In such instances, it was in the interest of Shāfiʿīs like al-Suyūṭī to uphold a previous association and to maintain the status quo.

So, in the case of old endowment deeds that specify that the supervision of the *waqf* should be assigned to 'the judge' (*al-ḥākim*), there was no doubt that this term referred to the head Shāfiʿī judge (supported by deputies from the other legal schools). Then, in 663/1265, the sultan al-Ẓāhir Baybars established a new judicial system with four chief judges, one from each of the legal schools. Thus, al-Zarkashī concludes:

> for endowments made before this new custom came into effect, the supervisory role was confined solely to the Shāfiʿī judge and no one else. As for assigning supervision after that, the matter is disputed due to a contradiction between the linguistic expression (*al-lafẓ*) and the custom, since the word 'judge' (*ḥākim*) was not normally understood to refer to anyone other than the Shāfiʿī judge, especially since he was already the one connected to the supervision of public endowments.[109]

Al-Suyūṭī repeats the problem as stated by al-Zarkashī and adds evidence from a fatwa[110] by Taqī al-Dīn al-Subkī (d. 756/1355), who affirms that even after the imposition of the three additional judges, the Shāfiʿī judge did not relinquish any of the supervisory roles already assigned to him. When that judge passed away, the new Shāfiʿī judge assumed all of the responsibilities of his predecessor with the other three continuing to act as his deputies, not his replacements.[111] Furthermore, says al-Suyūṭī, the intention of the endower is to promote the interests of the endowment and several judges competing over supervision of the *waqf* leads to harm because of the difference of opinion. Therefore, the supervisory role should belong only to one person,

[109] Al-Zarkashī, *al-Manthūr*, 2:121.
[110] The fatwa can be found in Taqī al-Dīn al-Subkī, *Fatāwā al-Subkī*, 2 vols. (Cairo: Maktabat al-Qudsī, 1937), 2:21–6.
[111] Al-Suyūṭī, *al-Ashbāh*, 134–5.

that person being the most important (i.e., the Shāfiʿī judge).[112] Similarly, if someone makes an endowment for the upkeep of the *ḥaram* in Mecca and stipulates that the endowment be administrated by 'the judge,' the preferred option is that the supervision be entrusted to the judge of the region in which the endowment was made, not the judge where the *ḥaram* is located.[113]

The Ḥanafī jurist Ibn Nujaym has yet another take on the *waqf* issue. He omits the reference to al-Ẓāhir Baybars and the four chief judges entirely and instead formulates the question as the following:

> An endower stipulates that the supervision of the endowment belong to 'the judge' (*al-ḥākim*), who at that time was Shāfiʿī but is now Ḥanafī with no judges other than him (except as deputies). Is the supervision his because he is 'the judge' or not because it is a later [interpretation] and thus the previous one does not apply?[114]

Ibn Nujaym compares the situation to a governor who swears an oath, where the oath is cancelled upon the resignation of the governor and is not carried over to his successor. Presumably, then, the supervision of the *waqf* also would not transfer to the successor of the Shāfiʿī judge.

The example is interesting because it shows two divergent attempts on the part of the Shāfiʿī and Ḥanafī jurists to force a reconciliation between the law and changing circumstances. It also shows al-Suyūṭī using two different arguments in matters relating to endowments in order to achieve a pragmatic goal. The determining factor for al-Suyūṭī is that the earlier custom of Shāfiʿī dominance in the judiciary was more favorable than the shift to the four judge system and later ascendance of the Ḥanafī school preferred by the Mamluks and Ottoman Turks. Thus, supported by al-Subkī, al-Suyūṭī argues that the supervision of endowments established before the shift should remain in the hands of the Shāfiʿī judge, who is still 'the judge' stipulated by the endower regardless of changes in the organization of the judiciary. Even though al-Suyūṭī shows a reluctance to acknowledge

[112] Al-Suyūṭī, *al-Ashbāh*, 135.

[113] Al-Suyūṭī, *al-Ashbāh*, 135–6. An analogous situation is a case where an orphan and his source of funding are in two different places. Is the orphan's maintenance supervised by the judge of the region where the orphan is located or by the judge of the region where his money is kept? See Ibn Nujaym, *al-Ashbāh*, 102.

[114] Ibn Nujaym, *al-Ashbāh*, 102.

the implicature presented by al-Zarkashī where the original wording of the deed conflicts with changed reality, he still devotes a substantial section of the chapter to the issue (indicating that the matter is far from clear).

The dispute was not confined to semantics, but involved a considerable amount of power and money as well. The person in charge of the disbursement of endowment funds could manipulate the salaries of employees and even give priority to some employees over others if he so wished.[115] The control of public endowments and the large reserves of money associated with them was crucial both to the function of the Mamluk state and to the ever increasing numbers of employees, scholars, and welfare recipients who depended on endowment stipends. Meanwhile, as endowments shifted in favor of the Ḥanafī school, it was in the interests of Ḥanafī jurists like Ibn Nujaym to highlight the disconnect between the old association of 'the judge' (*al-ḥākim*) with the Shāfiʿī judge and the new desire of Ḥanafīs to assume control.

Implications for the Jurist

Al-Suyūṭī's chapter on customary law raises several important questions that have a bearing on how jurists use *ʿurf*, particularly during the post-formative period of Islamic law. It is telling that the same criticisms that have been leveled against legal maxims also apply to the use of custom. For instance, Llewellyn's charge that jurists can pick and choose maxims based on a desired outcome could just as easily be said of al-Suyūṭī's use of customary law. However, it is the very fickleness of custom that allows it to adapt to new situations and contexts, thus making it a valuable tool for the *mujtahid* in the post-formative era. In his treatise on *ʿurf*, Ibn ʿĀbidīn (d. 1252/1836) gets to the heart of the matter:

> many rulings vary according to different time periods due to changes in people's practice as new needs arise to the extent that some rulings, if kept in place, would actually cause harm to people and would contradict precepts of

[115] In fact, al-Suyūṭī was the supervisor in charge of managing the funds of the Baybarsiyya Sufi lodge, an institution with an endowment dating back to 706/1306. The residents of the lodge took issue with al-Suyūṭī's performance as supervisor, causing uproar and leading to al-Suyūṭī's eventual dismissal from the position. See Chapter 1 for an analysis of this incident and of al-Suyūṭī's opinions regarding the disbursement of endowment funds from the state Treasury.

> Sharīʿa designed to promote ease and deter corruption. For this reason, many scholars within the school [*al-madhhab*] departed from the statements of an [earlier] *mujtahid* in several instances where the statements were based on the situation at the time of the *mujtahid*, knowing that if he were around during their time he would rule as they did, taking [his opinion] from the principles of the *madhhab*.[116]

The process of interpretation that Ibn ʿĀbidīn describes is one in which the *mujtahid* quite deliberately breaks with precedent to promote a preferred outcome based on the needs of people within a particular context. At the same time, Ibn ʿĀbidīn specifies that this effort is done not through personal whim but rather in accordance with the precept that the purpose of the Law is to promote ease over difficulty and corruption. Also, the preferred opinion is expected to come from within the bounds of the legal school.

Thus, al-Suyūṭī's flouting of the maxim of quality ("do not say anything self-contradictory") in the two scenarios involving endowments alerts the reader to the possibility that more is being implied in the text than the words themselves suggest. From clues in the context, one infers that al-Suyūṭī has opted for the interpretation that most benefits his own legal school by preserving the authority of the Shāfiʿī chief judge. For al-Suyūṭī, the ability to decide when a later customary interpretation supersedes an earlier one and when it does not is not purely academic but translates into real authority and power on the part of the jurist. Al-Suyūṭī demonstrates in his pragmatic use of legal precepts his skill as an interpreter of the law and as a master consolidator of knowledge. His careful use of customary law in particular to interpret the intentions of a speaker in context represents the work of a true *mujtahid* according to the expectations of the era.

CONCLUSION

This chapter intends to show that jurists use legal precepts pragmatically in order to achieve a purpose within a certain context. The first section examined how the form and content of legal maxims contribute to their

[116] Muḥammad Amīn b. ʿĀbidīn, *Majmūʿat rasāʾil Ibn ʿĀbidīn*, 2 vols. (Beirut: Muʾassasat Fuʾād al-Baʿīnū li-l-Tajlīd, 1978), 2:125; also cited in al-Daʿās, *al-Qawāʿid al-fiqhiyya*, 57.

rhetorical function as an important part of a mature and developed legal discourse. By the 7th/13th–9th/15th centuries, jurists were looking for ways to consolidate a vast corpus of substantive law and to distill from it core principles, which could in turn be adapted to guide the formation of new rulings in changing circumstances. Legal precepts provide a useful vehicle for such an endeavor. The second part of the chapter illustrated the link between legal precepts and customary law. Jurists resort to custom to resolve contradictions (or implicatures) between the linguistic form of a speech act (such as an oath, deed, or contract) and the intended meaning of the speaker. They also draw on contextual factors to reconcile the purposes of the law (as inferred from substantive *fiqh*) with social practice as they observe it in the world.

With his work on legal precepts, al-Suyūṭī proves himself as a late medieval jurist extraordinaire. Rather than just claiming greatness and titles, al-Suyūṭī engages in the actual business of jurisprudence in the manner that the later scholars did best: consolidation, systematization, and reformulation of the tradition. In his application of the precept, *al-ʿāda muḥakkama* ("custom should be made to serve as an arbiter"), al-Suyūṭī goes beyond strictly formulaic arguments to address issues that were of vital importance to those within Mamluk society who administrated or benefited from endowments (a group that includes al-Suyūṭī himself). He suggests that, while later custom replaces prior interpretations in the case of teachers claiming leave from their duties, the authority of the chief Shāfiʿī judge over the administration of public endowments should be preserved regardless of subsequent changes in the judicial system to allow for multiple chief justices. Al-Suyūṭī shows (through pragmatic implicature) the ability of the *mujtahid* to select an opinion with the aim of reinforcing the authority of his legal school and, by so doing, ultimately strengthens his own authority as a jurist as well.

5

Authority by Allusion: The Legacy of al-Suyūṭī in Contemporary Egypt

INTRODUCTION

Al-Azhar, Egypt's thousand-year-old institution of higher learning, is on the move. Two keen observers of Egyptian politics, Nathan Brown and Ahmed Morsy, wrote in November of 2013, just a few months after the July 3 overthrow of President Muḥammad Mursī: "The current moment is one of tremendous opportunity for al-Azhar. The institution seems to be on the brink of achieving more autonomy and influence than it has ever had in the modern era."[1] This statement may seem surprising at first given the common perception that Egypt's state-sponsored religious institutions had been co-opted by the former Mubārak regime to the point where traditionally educated scholars associated with al-Azhar had lost much of their relevance. In the critical period between the mass demonstrations that prompted Mubārak's resignation in February of 2011 and those that preceded the removal of Mursī by Egypt's military leaders in July of 2013, al-Azhar was engaged in a two-front struggle—one political and the other ideological.

Politically speaking, Brown and Morsy affirm that al-Azhar's leadership under Shaykh al-Azhar Aḥmad al-Ṭayyib and former state Mufti Shaykh ʿAlī Gumʿa (and current state Mufti Shaykh Shawqī ʿAllām) has been largely successful in pursuing its political goals, lobbying for greater autonomy while continuing to claim a role in the process of drafting a new constitution.[2] The

[1] Ahmed Morsy and Nathan J. Brown, "Egypt's al-Azhar Steps Forward," Carnegie Endowment for International Peace, accessed July 18, 2014, http://carnegieendowment.org/2013/11/07/egypt-s-al-azhar-steps-forward/gt0b?reloadFlag=1#.

[2] On the role of al-Azhar's leadership in the drafting and enforcement of the 2012 Constitution, see Gianluca P. Parolin, "Shall We Ask Al-Azhar? Maybe Not: Lessons from the Ṣukūk Bill Incident," *Middle East Law and Governance* 7 (2015): 212–35.

The Legal Thought of Jalāl al-Dīn al-Suyūṭī: Authority and Legacy. Rebecca Skreslet Hernandez.

reinstatement of the Council of Senior Scholars by the Supreme Council of the Armed Forces (SCAF) interim government in early 2012 was seen as a victory for al-Ṭayyib, particularly since he was given the power to appoint the members of the Council, who in turn have the responsibility of electing the Shaykh al-Azhar and nominating the state Mufti. Al-Azhar's leadership has also been successful, following the removal of Mursī, in coordinating more closely with the Ministry of Religious Endowments to begin efforts to regulate mosques, preachers, and even sermons (though the feasibility of enforcing such regulation is disputed).[3] In spite of these political gains, al-Ṭayyib's calls for national dialogue have not resulted in any major steps toward reconciliation between the main factions of the liberal secularists, the *fulūl* (old guard of the Mubārak regime), the Muslim Brotherhood, and the Salafīs (represented mainly by the Nūr Party). In addition, al-Azhar University itself continues to be unsettled by divisions and political polarization amongst its faculty and students. Furthermore, although al-Azhar has succeeded in securing a greater degree of autonomy for itself, it is still financially dependent on the state.

The ideological battle in which the leadership of al-Azhar is engaged has emerged as a result of the state religious institutions representing just one voice (with its own internal divisions) in a "cacophony" of competing voices.[4] Government ministries, courts, universities, research institutes, and independent activists and intellectuals all claim some say in the vital questions of what role Islamic law should have in the state and who should hold the authority to interpret and enforce laws based on Sharīʿa.[5] Rather than weakening al-Azhar, it seems that increased competition and contention has been invigorating for the institution in the sense that senior members of al-Azhar associated with the office of the Shaykh al-Azhar and Dār al-Iftāʾ have launched a campaign to consolidate and promote the message of these

[3] Brown and Morsy, "Al-Azhar Steps Forward."

[4] Nathan J. Brown expands on the cacophony idea in "Egypt: Cacophony and Consensus in the Twenty-first Century," in *Sharīʿa Politics: Islamic Law and Society in the Modern World*, edited by Robert W. Hefner (Bloomington: Indiana University Press, 2011), 94–120.

[5] Nathan J. Brown outlines the role of some of the major actors in these debates in post-revolutionary Egypt (particularly those of al-Azhar and the Muslim Brotherhood) in "Contention in Religion and State in Postrevolutionary Egypt," *Social Research* 79:2 (Summer 2012): 531–50.

institutions through a variety of media outlets. The launching of al-Azhar's own satellite channel, for example, was cast as a direct challenge to Salafī preachers who regularly issue what are seen as rogue or illegitimate fatwas on their own satellite networks.[6]

It is through this ideological aspect rather than the political one that al-Azhar's leadership hopes to portray itself as the conscience of Egypt with the authority to preserve and interpret the traditions that make up the rich heritage of Muslims in the modern world. In a time of fragmented religious authority, it is this connection to their historical and intellectual heritage that al-Azhar's scholars claim as their most valuable asset and that they say differentiates them most noticeably from the competition. Within the context of legal authority, Rachel Scott explains that "tradition" refers not to "a fixed body of law that is outdated and incapable of change, but to a methodological approach to the interpretation of the core Islamic religious texts derived from the founders of the four schools of law."[7] Muhammad Qasim Zaman affirms that it is this aspect of the identity and authority of the *ʿulamāʾ* that makes them most relevant and worthy of study.[8]

The Azharī methodology or *manhaj* is fashioned as a moderate, centrist (*wasaṭī*) interpretation of Islam that stands as a buffer between extreme secular and extreme *salafī* approaches.[9] The appeal of Azharī scholars to

[6] Shaykh ʿAlī Gumʿa quoted in "A Talk with Egypt Grand Mufti Dr. Ali Gomaa," *Asharq Alawsat* (English), February 25, 2013, accessed July 24, 2014, http://www.aawsat.net/2013/02/article55293289.

[7] Rachel M. Scott, "What Might the Muslim Brotherhood do with al-Azhar? Religious Authority in Egypt," *Die Welt des Islams* 52 (2012): 141.

[8] As Zaman puts it: "What makes the ʿulama of the modern world worth studying is not merely that they have continued to lay claim to and self-consciously represent a millennium-old tradition of Islamic learning, however. Their larger claim on our attention lies in the ways in which they have mobilized this tradition to define issues of religious identity and authority in the public sphere and to articulate changing roles for themselves in contemporary Muslim politics. The ʿulama's tradition is not a mere inheritance from the past, even though they often argue that that is precisely what it is. It is a tradition that has to be constantly imagined, reconstructed, argued over, defended, and modified." See Muhammad Qasim Zaman, *The Ulama in Contemporary Islam: Custodians of Change* (Princeton, N.J.: Princeton University Press, 2002), 10.

[9] As this analysis will show, the term '*manhaj*' is itself a potent term that contains an implied reference to an opposing methodology. Salafīs claim to represent the true *manhaj*, which comprises more than just a literal interpretation of Qurʾān and *ḥadīth* texts but covers areas of doctrine (*ʿaqīda*) and conduct (*sulūk*) as well. Jonathan Brown explains that the broader reform movement that spawned modern Salafism permeates the thinking of a wide spectrum of Muslims, including members of the Muslim Brotherhood, the Salafī political

wasaṭī rhetoric reflects the rise of a larger centrist trend in Egyptian political discourse since the 1990s that has included members of the Muslim Brotherhood, a subset of independent Islamist intellectuals, and members of the religious establishment.[10] The *wasaṭī* approach sponsored by the Shaykh al-Azhar, by Dār al-Iftāʾ, and by the Council of Senior Scholars is promoted as being representative of the views of the majority of Sunni Muslims and boils down to three essential elements: theology/creed (*ʿaqīda*) according to Ashʿarī doctrine, legal interpretation (*sharīʿa*) according to the four Sunni legal schools (*madhāhib*), and conduct (*sulūk*) according to the principles of Islamic mysticism (*taṣawwuf*).[11]

What may not be obvious at first is how these three descriptive elements of the Azharī *manhaj* translate into a methodology. In answering this question, first it is necessary to emphasize (as I have done throughout this study of al-Suyūṭī's legal writing), that very often positive assertions of principles such as the three listed above contain an implied condemnation of alternative approaches.[12] As simple as it may seem at the outset, the way in which the Azharī *manhaj* is framed is "double-voiced" in that it strikes a "polemical

parties, and the faculty and students of universities like al-Azhar. Modern Salafism is not confined to a single group or nationality but, broadly speaking, denotes a shared rejection of "the byzantine complexities of Islamic law and theology as well as the superstitions of popular Sufism." See Jonathan Brown, *Salafis and Sufis in Egypt* (Carnegie Endowment for International Peace, 2011), 4. On Salafī self-representation, see Adis Duderija, "Constructing the Religious Self and the Other: Neo-traditional Salafi Manhaj," *Islam and Christian-Muslim Relations* 21:1 (2010): 75–93.

[10] On centrist ideology in Egypt, see Sagi Polka, "The Centrist Stream in Egypt and its Role in the Public Discourse Surrounding the Shaping of the Country's Cultural Identity," *Middle Eastern Studies* 39:3 (2003): 39–64, DOI: 10.1080/00263200412331301667; and Raymond William Baker, *Islam Without Fear: Egypt and the New Islamists* (Cambridge, M.A.: Harvard University Press, 2003). On the initiative to form a Wasaṭ political party, see Carrie Rosefsky Wickham, *Mobilizing Islam: Religion, Activism, and Political Change in Egypt* (New York: Columbia University Press, 2002), especially 218–20; and Carrie Rosefsky Wickham, *The Muslim Brotherhood: Evolution of an Islamist Movement* (Princeton, N.J.: Princeton University Press, 2013), especially 81–95.

[11] Senior scholars associated with al-Azhar and Dār al-Iftāʾ have articulated these three essential elements of the Azharī *manhaj* in a number of contexts, including in statements to the press and in sermons to the public. Two examples include statements by Shaykh ʿAmr al-Wardānī quoted in *al-Waṭan*, February 26, 2013, accessed July 23, 2014, https://www.elwatannews.com/news/details/138154; and a Friday sermon by Shaykh Muḥammad Wisām Khiḍr entitled "In Defense of al-Azhar's Centrism" (*al-difāʿ ʿan wasaṭiyyat al-Azhar*), March 8, 2013, accessed July 23, 2014, https://www.youtube.com/watch?v=SwNp7hLEUOA.

[12] As Stephen Greenblatt observes in his study of Renaissance figures, "self-fashioning is achieved in relation to something perceived as alien, strange, or hostile," *Renaissance Self-Fashioning: From More to Shakespeare* (Chicago: University of Chicago Press, 1980), 9.

blow"[13] at an antithetical approach that is characterized as irrational, superficial, and irresponsible in its interpretation of texts, neglectful of centuries of legal tradition, and callous (almost to the point of being inhuman) in its harsh condemnation of other Muslims as apostates based on flimsy pretexts.

In their efforts to promote a centrist methodology and to discredit what is portrayed as an antithetical approach espoused by extreme Salafīs, Azharī scholars have focused on what they do best—interpreting the texts that make up the rich cultural and intellectual heritage of Muslims, particularly in the context of Islamic jurisprudence. Although it may seem that they are doing what they have always done, the difference is that in a time of crisis the task takes on a greater sense of urgency and the stakes seem higher than ever before. While challenges to the authority of the traditionally educated *ʿulamāʾ* are certainly nothing new, the response has been more systematic and media-savvy than in the past. Not only do we see Azharī scholars arguing for a methodology, but we see them actually putting it into practice. It is this new-found unity and clarity of purpose that has led analysts like Brown and Morsy to suggest that religion will no doubt continue to play a central role in public life in Egypt, but "the vision of Islam is emerging as more coherent and more susceptible to guidance by al-Azhar's senior leadership."[14]

It is in this crucial period between 2011 and 2013 that we see al-Azhar scholars taking full advantage of the lifting of some of the restrictions of the Mubārak era to disseminate their message to a wider audience, including making use of social media (Facebook and Twitter accounts), posting videos to al-Azhar YouTube channels, publishing editorials in newspapers, and hosting programs on satellite television.[15] The older structures (such as the issuing of fatwas both to private individuals and in response to current affairs affecting the nation, delivering sermons in mosques, and lecturing

[13] Bakhtin elaborates on the idea of discourse containing "hidden polemic" against another person's discourse in *Discourse in Dostoevsky's Poetics*, edited and translated by Caryl Emerson (Minneapolis: University of Minnesota Press, 1984), 195.

[14] Brown and Morsy, "Al-Azhar Steps Forward."

[15] Dār al-Iftāʾ has also sponsored a number of educational "caravans" in recent years to rural parts of Egypt and abroad to spread *wasaṭī* ideology. For example, in September of 2014, a group led by four scholars from Dār al-Iftāʾ traveled to West Africa with the mission to 'correct' the image of Islam in that region and to combat extremist ideologies. See Aḥmad al-Buḥayrī, *al-Maṣrī al-Yawm*, September 6, 2014, accessed July 1, 2015, http://www.almasryalyoum.com/news/details/517204.

to students and members of the public through traditional study circles at al-Azhar mosque, for example) have not been abandoned in favor of new methods, but transformed and adapted to new technologies such that they are able to reach larger numbers of people—within Egypt and beyond—than ever before.[16]

Al-Azhar's leading scholars are adamant in the assertion that not only is the legal tradition in the form of classical jurisprudence still essential knowledge for Muslims today, but that such knowledge can only truly be gained from studying the great works of that tradition under the guidance of trained experts (i.e., themselves). Given the importance of the Shāfiʿī *madhhab* in Egypt, it is not surprising that the works of the great Shāfiʿī scholars are frequently the topic of lectures and seminars, including those of al-Ghazālī (d. 505/1111), al-Nawawī (d. 676/1277), al-Isnawī (d. 772/1370), Ibn Ḥajar al-ʿAsqalānī (852/1449), and al-Suyūṭī (d. 911/1505).

As far as the influence of al-Suyūṭī in contemporary Egypt is concerned, it is significant that between 2011 and 2013, three senior scholars from Dār al-Iftāʾ, Shaykh ʿAlī Gumʿa (former state Mufti), Shaykh Muḥammad Wisām Khiḍr (Director of the Written Fatwa Committee), and Shaykh ʿAmr al-Wardānī (Director of Fatwas and Training) all published multi-part commentaries on al-Azhar sponsored YouTube channels analyzing al-Suyūṭī's book on legal precepts, *al-Ashbāh wa-l-naẓāʾir fī l-qawāʿid al-fiqhiyya*. Although al-Suyūṭī's book was considered an advanced text in the Shāfiʿī legal curriculum at al-Azhar prior to the 2011 revolution, it seems clear that a special effort has been made to make the teaching of this text available to a wider audience within the last few years via new media outreach.[17] All three of

[16] Thomas Pierret comments in relation to the religious scholars of modern Syria that "The rapid growth of a literate population wishing to study the Quran, the hadith, and fiqh has brought new customers to the old networks of religious scholarship, thus entailing the latter's development to an extent unprecedented in history. To this was added the now familiar phenomenon of sheikhs who have exploited the potential of mass media (newspapers, essays, tapes, radio, and television, Internet) to reach an even wider audience. Social change was thus transformed from a threat into an opportunity," *Religion and the State in Syria: The Sunni Ulama from Coup to Revolution* (New York: Cambridge University Press, 2013), 6.

[17] In a twelve-minute biographical segment on al-Suyūṭī in the series "Stories of the Righteous," Shaykh ʿAlī Gumʿa asserts that al-Suyūṭī's *al-Ashbāh wa-l-naẓāʾir* is a "copious incomparable book" taught to post-graduate students at al-Azhar as the best book of its kind, even exceeding similar works by Taqī al-Dīn al-Subkī, Ibn al-Wakīl, Ibn Nujaym, and Ibn ʿĀbidīn in terms of format and composition ("Imām Galāl al-Dīn al-Suyūṭī," accessed July 24, 2014,

the series are recorded lectures presented to students in study circles at the al-Azhar mosque. The students include muftis-in-training, other students at al-Azhar, and members of the general public and are predominantly (but not exclusively) men. The segments currently available on YouTube cover al-Suyūṭī's introduction in which he lays out the content, organization, and methodology of the book as well as the beginning of the first chapter explaining the precept *al-umūr bi-maqāṣidihā* ("matters shall be judged according to their objectives").

Each scholar approaches the material in his own style and highlights different aspects of al-Suyūṭī's work depending on his particular didactic and pragmatic goals. In each case, I will argue, the discourse is "double-voiced" to refer to another discourse external to the text on which the commentary is based. This other discourse concerns the authority of the commentator himself and of the institution that he represents. In the case of Muḥammad Wisām, al-Suyūṭī's discussion of *qawāʿid* is used explicitly and directly as a platform to argue for the correctness of the Azharī *manhaj* against the misguided extreme *salafī* approach, while for the others the reference is made in a more subtle fashion. This chapter examines how the medieval jurist makes an appropriate ally in a struggle for authority in the modern era. Critical attention is given to each of the elements that Azharī scholars have highlighted as essential to their identity as Sunni jurists (Ashʿarī doctrine, *madhhab*-based jurisprudence, and Sufi conduct) to understand how al-Suyūṭī's legacy appeals to all three of these aspects.

In my analysis of the contemporary commentaries, the aim is to demonstrate how each of the three scholars employs the discursive strategy of "authority by allusion"—that is, when an "echo" is created between the primary text (al-Suyūṭī) and an external, absent text (defense of the Azharī methodology and critique of rival approaches). In this sense,

https://www.youtube.com/watch?v=zyYmhKlJScc&list=PL41247C8F13901AE7&index=2). The Arabic-language series, posted on Gumʿa's English YouTube channel, is described by the following statement: "This series is dedicated to narrating the stories of the Muslim scholars who contributed to the process of Islamic legislation through their intellectual discernment and religious scholarship with a unique ability to comprehend the vast ocean of Islamic knowledge and deduct the legal maxims on which all juristic issues are based." Besides al-Suyūṭī, other jurists featured in the series include the eponyms of the Sunni and Shiʿi legal schools, the Prophet's wife ʿĀʾisha, Abū Ḥāmid al-Ghazālī, al-Nawawī, and Ibn Ḥajar al-ʿAsqalānī.

allusion is more than a literary device and instead constitutes a pragmatic use of language on the part of the producers of the discourse. A pragmatic theory of communication assumes that communication is effective when the recipients are able to determine the relevance of the utterance with a limited amount of effort.[18] Pragmatic allusion works, for example, when the cognitive environments of the speaker and recipients are aligned such that the recipients are able to recognize from the speech itself and from contextual clues that an allusion is being made. In this light, I will revisit the pragmatic functions of legal precepts discussed in Chapter 4 to see how they are re-contextualized in a particular time and place, that of post-revolutionary Egypt.

EVOLUTION OF AN "ORTHODOX" SUNNI IDEOLOGY

The effort to define a centrist Sunni orthodoxy in the Islamic tradition has very deep roots. Historian Jonathan Berkey traces the "recentering" and "homogenization" of learning and authority in the pre-modern Muslim world back to what he terms the Middle Period (roughly the era following the decline of the ʿAbbasid empire after about 950 CE up until the end of the Mamluk regime after about 1500).[19] A Sunni consensus emerged gradually during this time that defined itself in opposition to both internal threats (mostly various forms of Shiʿism) and external threats (such as invasions by Mongols and Crusaders).

Indeed, the role of the Crusades and Counter-Crusades on the part of Muslim rulers in defining a sense of Sunni orthodoxy and communal ideology should not be underestimated. Recent scholarship[20] examines a few key examples of scholars who provided the necessary textual evidence from Qurʾān and *ḥadīth* as well as the emotion-stirring propaganda to support the

[18] The key work on Relevance Theory in pragmatics is Dan Sperber and Deirdre Wilson's *Relevance: Communication and Cognition* (Oxford, U.K.: Blackwell Publishers Ltd, 1995). I discuss Relevance Theory in relation to Islamic legal precepts in Chapter 4.

[19] Jonathan P. Berkey, *The Formation of Islam: Religion and Society in the Near East, 600–1800* (New York: Cambridge University Press, 2003), 189.

[20] For a foundational study on polemical literature by Muslim scholars during the time of the Crusades, see Emmanuel Sivan, *L'Islam et la Croisade: Idéologie et Propagande dans les Réactions*

military campaigns (portrayed in terms of *jihād*) of their political patrons. The *Kitāb al-Jihād* of ʿAlī b. Ṭāhir al-Sulamī (d. 1106) stands out as a work intended to inspire its readers (and listeners when read aloud) to unite and fight the foreign invaders following the fall of Jerusalem to the crusaders during the First Crusade.[21] A second Damascene scholar, Abū al-Qāsim ʿAlī b. ʿAsākir (d. 1176), promoted *jihād* ideology in a number of works written after the Second Crusade to promote the interests of his patron, the Turkish war-lord Nūr al-Dīn (r. 1146–1174).[22] Carole Hillenbrand argues that it was during Nūr al-Dīn's reign that the military and religious aspects of the Counter-Crusade really came together in the works of Muslim authors, marking a turning point in the evolution of Sunni revivalist ideology.[23]

The ideological campaign that began with the Saljuks, continued under the Ayyubids, and reached a peak by the fourteenth-century Mamluk era was, for the most part, successful in promoting four Sunni legal schools (*madhāhib*) and two theological orientations (the Ashʿarī and Māturīdī schools) as acceptable, normative, and fully compatible with each other.[24]

Musulmanes aux Croisades (Paris: Adrien Maisonneuve, 1968). A selection of more recent works by Carole Hillenbrand, Niall Christie, Suleiman A. Mourad, James E. Lindsay, and Yasser Tabbaa are noted below.

[21] Niall Christie has written extensively on al-Sulamī's works. See, for example, Niall Christie, "Jerusalem in the *Kitab al-Jihad* of ʿAli ibn Tahir al-Sulami," *Medieval Encounters* 13 (2007): 209–21; and Niall Christie, "Motivating Listeners in the *Kitab al-Jihad* of ʿAli ibn Tahir al-Sulami (d. 1106)," *Crusades* 6 (2007): 1–14.

[22] Nikita Elisséeff's exhaustive three-volume study of Syrian society during the reign of Sultan Nūr al-Dīn includes a discussion of the Sunni revival and the growth of institutions (*madrasas*, mosques, *ḥadīth* study centers) used to promote his ideological campaign. See Nikita Elisséeff, *Nūr al-Dīn: Un Grand Prince Musulman de Syrie au Temps des Croisades (511–569/1118–1174)*, 3 vols. (Damascus: Institut Français de Damas, 1967), especially 3:750–79. Suleiman A. Mourad and James E. Lindsay discuss in detail the ideological works of Ibn ʿAsākir in response to the Crusades. See, for example, "A Muslim Response to the Second Crusade: Ibn ʿAsākir of Damascus as Propagandist of Jihad," in *The Second Crusade: Holy War on the Periphery of Latin Christendom*, edited by Jason T. Roche and Janus Møller Jensen (Turnhout, Belgium: Brepols, 2015), 91–111; and "Rescuing Syria from the Infidels: The Contribution of Ibn ʿAsākir to the Jihad Campaign of Sultan Nur al-Din," *Crusades* 6 (2007): 37–55. Mourad and Lindsay outline three aspects to Nūr al-Dīn's religious agenda that are reflected in the works of Ibn ʿAsākir: "first, the promotion of Islam against its enemies (for example, the Franks); second, the promotion of Sunnism against Shiʿism (that is, the two major sectarian divisions within Islam); and third, the promotion of Ashʿarism against Ḥanbalism (which were the two main theological divisions at the time within Sunni Islam in Damascus" ("Ibn ʿAsākir of Damascus as Propagandist of Jihad," 99). The contributions of Ibn ʿAsākir to pro-Ashʿarī polemics are discussed below.

[23] Carole Hillenbrand, *The Crusades: Islamic Perspectives* (New York: Routledge, 2000), 131.

[24] Jeffry R. Halverson, *Theology and Creed in Sunni Islam: The Muslim Brotherhood, Ashʿarism, and Political Sunnism* (New York: Palgrave Macmillan, 2010), 13.

The decision by Sultan Baybars to replace the Shāfiʿī chief *qāḍī* with chief judges from each of the four Sunni *madhhabs* also speaks to the push toward Sunni solidarity and conformity that culminated under Mamluk rule.

Of course, it is worth noting that efforts to promote a certain ideology[25] and to suppress others do not occur abstractly but are tied to the work of people (scholars and members of the political elite) and of institutions that are subject, in turn, to the socioeconomic conditions present in the societies in which such efforts are produced. In his compelling study of religious ideology and politics during the time of the Saljuks, Omid Safi explores how the Saljuks sought to "identify, demarcate, and defend orthodoxy" by waging an ideological battle against forces deemed heretical (the Ismāʿīlīs) and by cultivating the work of compliant scholars and Sufis through patronage of key institutions involved in the transmission of knowledge (*madrasas* and *khānqāhs*).[26]

The political, social, ideological, and economic functions of institutions in the medieval Muslim world did not end with the Saljuks in Baghdad and Khurāsān; rather, they found new expression in the art and architecture of areas that became key to the larger Sunni revival, including Syria and Egypt. Yasser Tabbaa shows, for example, how broad concepts associated with the Sunni revival such as "urbanism, patronage, institutional development, and sectarian rivalry" are manifested in the specific socio-historical context surrounding the construction of buildings in the city of Aleppo during

[25] I follow Naṣr Ḥāmid Abū Zayd's lead in referring to the "ideology" of pre-modern and modern scholars as a way to encapsulate the whole worldview of the scholar along with his role as an active agent in society. Abū Zayd points out, for example, that the very term *ahl al-sunna wa-l-jamāʿa* has an ideological tone to it because it implies an opposition (i.e., those deemed to be outside of the consensus of the community). See Naṣr Ḥāmid Abū Zayd, *al-Imām al-Shāfiʿī wa-taʾsīs al-aydiyūlūjiyya al-wasaṭiyya* (Cairo: Maktabat Madbūlī, 1996).

[26] Omid Safi, *The Politics of Knowledge in Premodern Islam: Negotiating Ideology and Religious Inquiry* (Chapel Hill: University of North Carolina Press, 2006), xxv. In his influential article on the Ashʿarī bid to infiltrate and eventually dominate the Sunni legal schools, George Makdisi explains that the *madrasa* system after the eleventh century was used as a "recruiting center for orthodoxy" in which different schools and jurists competed for power, financial backing, and influence. See his "Ashʿarī and the Ashʿarites in Islamic Religious History I," *Studia Islamica* 17 (1962): 45–6. On the ideological use of institutions such as *madrasas* and *khānqāhs* in the Sunni restoration project during the Ayyubid and Mamluk periods in Egypt, see also Gary La Viere Leiser, *The Restoration of Sunnism in Egypt: Madrasas and Mudarrisūn, 495–647/1101–1249*, Ph.D. Diss. (University of Pennsylvania, 1976); Robert Hunter Moore, *The Role of the* Madrasah *in the Structure of Islamic Legal Education in Mamluk Egypt (1250–1517)*, Ph.D. Diss. (Emory University, 2010); and Nathan Hofer, *The Popularisation of Sufism in Ayyubid and Mamluk Egypt, 1173–1325* (Edinburgh: Edinburgh University Press, 2015).

the Ayyubid period.[27] The "construction" examined in Tabbaa's study is not limited to architectural features but includes constructed paradigms of power and piety as well. Tabbaa's work offers an intriguing glimpse of ways in which the ideological power struggles within the Muslim world (between Sunni and Shiʿi regimes, for example) at the time of the Sunni revival of the Middle Period played out in parallel transformations in the realm of architecture and visual culture, thus allowing him to draw connections between the form, context, and meaning of medieval Islamic calligraphy, public inscriptions, vegetal and geometric ornamentation, and *muqarnas* vaulting.[28]

In a similar vein, the analysis of al-Suyūṭī's fatwas on scholarly stipends in Chapter 1 of this study seeks to expose the delicate power relations behind legal discourse pertaining to the function of endowed institutions. By the late Mamluk period, scholars like al-Suyūṭī had come to rely on the financial sustenance that accompanied prestigious appointments and teaching positions in such institutions founded by members of the political elites, even as they tried to maintain a degree of independence and moral authority free from the corruption and worldly interests of those elites.

Promotion of Ashʿarī Theology and Rationalism

The Sunni solidarity movement of the Mamluk era was remarkably successful in suppressing alternate or dissenting versions of Islamic faith and practice. As Jeffry Halverson explains:

> The notion of the equality and full orthodoxy of the four Sunni *madhāhib*, initiated by their predecessors, the Ayyubids (and perhaps the Zangids), was officially sanctioned under Mamluk rule, with conformist Sunni solidarity against nonbelievers (e.g., Crusaders), Shiʿism, Muʿtazilism, and the philosophers (*falāsifah*), dominating intellectual life.[29]

[27] Yasser Tabbaa, *Constructions of Power and Piety in Medieval Aleppo* (University Park, P.A.: The Pennsylvania State University Press, 1997), 2. On the propaganda value of structures and inscriptions from the reign of Nūr al-Dīn, see further Carole Hillenbrand, *The Crusades: Islamic Perspectives*, 122–32.

[28] Yasser Tabbaa, *The Transformation of Islamic Art during the Sunni Revival* (Seattle, W.A.: University of Washington Press, 2001).

[29] Halverson, *Theology and Creed in Sunni Islam*, 13–14.

Halverson even suggests that the staunchly Ashʿarī scholar, Tāj al-Dīn al-Subkī (d. 771/1370), deliberately obscured the differences between the Ashʿarī and Māturīdī theological schools "in the name of Sunni solidarity."[30] Ironically, this blurred distinction between theologies may have served to stifle theological disputation and intellectual thought more than it helped to strengthen it, which in turn may have led to a "creedal collapse" and the decline of *kalām* by the fifteenth century CE.[31]

George Makdisi argues that the ideological campaign waged by the Ashʿarīs between the eleventh and fourteenth centuries aimed to portray their school of thought as occupying a sensible middle ground between the extreme rationalism of the Muʿtazilī theologians and the extreme traditionalism of the Ḥanbalī (and some Shāfiʿī) *ahl al-ḥadīth*. In fact, through a careful analysis of two key works of Ashʿarī "propaganda" by the twelfth-century Ibn ʿAsākir and the fourteenth-century Tāj al-Dīn al-Subkī, Makdisi suggests that this ideological middle road actually had two branches: one that accommodated the use of rationalist *kalām* and one that remained harshly critical of it. Both of these paths were attributed to the school's eponym, Abū al-Ḥasan al-Ashʿarī (d. 324/936), and both were touted as "equally Ashʿarite, equally orthodox."[32]

In making a case for the suitability of Ashʿarī theology for the Shāfiʿī legal school, Ibn ʿAsākir and Ibn al-Subkī worked to demarcate a legitimate role for *kalām* in Ashʿarī thought and to refute the anti-theological traditionalism of scholars within their own school. They also had to explain statements condemning *kalām* attributed to key scholars within the Shāfiʿī school, including al-Ghazālī and even Shāfiʿī himself. Makdisi argues that Ibn al-Subkī, as a jurist and *ḥadīth* scholar, is particularly effective in portraying Ashʿarī as someone who defended and upheld the beliefs of the *salaf* using reason and rational proofs. Similarly, Ibn al-Subkī achieves the difficult rhetorical task of defining a new identity for the Shāfiʿī school as one that, reflective of the thought of Ashʿarī himself, is a "school composed of traditionalists and

[30] Halverson, *Theology and Creed in Sunni Islam*, 14.

[31] Halverson, *Theology and Creed in Sunni Islam*, 54. Other factors that Halverson includes as contributing to the decline of *kalām* by the fifteenth century include: the persistent influence of anti-theological Atharī thought, the blurred boundaries between *kalām* and philosophy (*falsafa*), and the increasing influence of Sufism (*Theology and Creed in Sunni Islam*, 45).

[32] Makdisi, "Ashʿarī and the Ashʿarites," 52.

rationalists, a broad-minded school, inclusive of all the religious sciences, especially *kalām*, leader among the orthodox schools of law."[33]

In spite of these successes, Ashʿarī rationalism continued to attract opponents among some traditionalists, both within the Shāfiʿī school and beyond. Pro-rationalist and anti-rationalist strains were still active during al-Suyūṭī's lifetime and both continued to find adherents after his death in 1505 CE. Much like Ashʿarī himself or even al-Ghazālī, one can find in al-Suyūṭī's thought conflicting attitudes toward *kalām* that make use of both anti-theological and pro-Ashʿarī sources. In his *Ṣawn al-manṭiq wa-l-kalām ʿan fann al-manṭiq wa-l-kalām*, al-Suyūṭī compiles statements against the study of *kalām* and logic by prominent scholars over the centuries (including al-Ghazālī). In the introduction to this work, al-Suyūṭī claims that his purpose in writing it is to show his familiarity with debates surrounding the study of Greek-inspired sciences such as logic, philosophy, and *kalām* in order to counter any perceived deficiency on his part as a self-proclaimed *mujtahid* as well as to defend a controversial fatwa condemning logic by a fellow Shāfiʿī traditionalist, Ibn al-Ṣalāḥ (d. 643/1245).[34] To further prove his knowledge of the debates surrounding the study of logic, al-Suyūṭī wrote an abridgement of Ibn Taymiyya's *Naṣīḥat dhawī al-īmān fī radd ʿalā manṭiq al-Yūnān* ("Advice of those with faith against the logic of the Greeks").[35]

In a fatwa written late in al-Suyūṭī's career, the author once again forbids the study of logic, listing prominent scholars from each of the four Sunnī legal schools who, he says, have written on this subject in the past (implying that they represent a consensus of opinion in this regard). In my discussion of this fatwa in Chapter 2 of this study, I have argued that al-Suyūṭī's stance in the logic debate is tied to personal attacks on his own qualifications and is indicative of the continued influence of parallel trends in Islamic thought in the fifteenth century CE—one tolerant of sciences of logic and *kalām* as necessary tools, and the other suspicious of such disciplines as dangerous innovations that could lead the unsuspecting believer into heresy. Even

[33] Makdisi, "Ashʿarī and the Ashʿarites," 60.

[34] Al-Suyūṭī, *Ṣawn al-manṭiq wa-l-kalām ʿan fann al-manṭiq wa-l-kalām* (Cairo: Maktabat al-Khānjī, 1947), 1–3.

[35] Al-Suyūṭī's abridgement, entitled *Jahd al-qarīḥa fī tajrīd al-Naṣīḥa*, has been edited and translated by Wael Hallaq as *Ibn Taymiyya against the Greek Logicians* (Oxford, U.K.: Clarendon Press, 1993).

al-Suyūṭī's passionate defense of al-Ghazālī as a Shāfiʿī master-jurist in the logic fatwa could be seen as part of al-Suyūṭī's own discursive attempt to situate himself as next in a long line of jurists who have attained not just the rank of *mujtahid*, but who can also be considered renewers of the faith sent by God to lead believers back to correct practice (*sunna*) and away from unlawful innovation (*bidʿa*).

Al-Suyūṭī's articulation of the concept of religious renewal (*tajdīd*) relies heavily on the work of pro-Ashʿarī polemicists of the Shāfiʿī legal school, including Ibn ʿAsākir, Tāj al-Dīn al-Subkī, and Badr al-Dīn al-Ahdal (d. 403/1013). As I have suggested in Chapter 3 of this study, it is not too great an exaggeration to say that efforts by scholars after the 5th/11th century to identify at least one *mujaddid* for every century has direct ties with the Sunni solidarity movement in general and with the Ashʿarī–Shāfiʿī integration project in particular. By relying on the lists of possible *mujaddids* compiled by these earlier scholars, al-Suyūṭī affirms indirectly their pro-Ashʿarī and pro-Shāfiʿī agenda as well. While this stance may seem to be at odds with his rejection of logic and *kalām* elsewhere in his writing, it is understandable if viewed within the context of Makdisi's theory of two middle roads within orthodox Ashʿarī Shāfiʿī thought, one that accommodates rationalism and logical proofs and one that might appeal to *salafī* traditionalists.

The struggle to establish Ashʿarī doctrine as the "official" doctrine of orthodox Sunni Islam in opposition to alternate interpretations that raged during the time of Ibn ʿAsākir, al-Ghazālī, and Ibn al-Subkī can still be felt today, though the terms of the debate have changed. Contemporary Sunni scholars who identify Ashʿarī rationalism as being an important element of their doctrine (*ʿaqīda*) and legal methodology (*sharīʿa*) still define their position in terms of a middle ground between extremes, only the extremes have shifted to include secular liberalism on one side and what has been termed Atharī, "neo-Salafī," Wahhābī, or even "neo-fundamentalist" literalism on the other side. In contrast to these two extremes, "moderate" Islamists affiliated with the Muslim Brotherhood and al-Azhar as well as establishment religious scholars promote Ashʿarism as a reasonable approach that allows the use of logic in matters of *ʿaqīda* and *sharīʿa*, that represents the majority of Sunni Muslims, and that rejects radical *takfīrī* elements that seek to condemn other Muslims as apostates and use violence to intimidate innocent people.

In a 2010 meeting of the International Association of al-Azhar alumni titled "Imām Abū al-Ḥasan al-Ashʿarī: Imām of the Adherents to the Sunna and the Community (*ahl al-sunna wa-l-jamāʿa*)," Shaykh Aḥmad al-Ṭayyib asserts that "The current realities are similar to those of the time of Imām al-Ashʿarī as the nation is divided and segregated and radical groups have permeated our societies," and goes on to conclude that "the Islamic nation needs an approach similar to that of al-Ashʿarī, who emphasized moderation and tolerance."[36] In a symposium honoring the late Shaykh Muḥammad al-Ghazālī (d. 1996), Shaykh Yūsuf al-Qaraḍāwī praises his mentor as a fellow Azharī scholar who, in spite of persecution by the state as a result of his affiliation with the Muslim Brotherhood, never ceased to defend Islam and to condemn all forms of oppression. Al-Qaraḍāwī devotes a sizeable portion of his remarks to explaining and defending al-Ghazālī's Ashʿarī sensibilities, including his use of logical proofs in matters of faith and as a tool for textual criticism (after the Qurʾān, of course).

Al-Qaraḍāwī prefaces his remarks on Muḥammad al-Ghazālī's Ashʿarī sensibilities in his speech with the following statement:

> Azharī knowledge has certain characteristics. Al-Azhar, like most religious schools and universities, follows the Ashʿarī school of *ʿaqīda*. I know that our Salafī brethren do not like this, but I would like to say that the whole Muslim *umma* follows the Ashʿarī school. So, has the whole *umma* gone astray?[37]

Al-Qaraḍāwī then goes on to discuss two aspects of al-Ghazālī's thought that suggest that he wrote with "a Salafī spirit and an Ashʿarī breath." First, al-Ghazālī recognized that logic and texts are both essential tools for proving matters of doctrine and that the two can and should work hand-in-hand. A second point emphasized by al-Ghazālī is that *ḥadīth* reports that have a

[36] Ahmed el-Beheri, "Azhar sheikh warns West against double standards," *Egypt Independent* (May 9, 2010), accessed December 30, 2014, http://www.egyptindependent.com/news/azhar-sheikh-warns-west-against-double-standards.

[37] Shaykh Yūsuf al-Qaraḍāwī, "Al-Ghazaly—The Man of Daʿwa," accessed January 23, 2015, http://www.ikhwanweb.com/article.php?id=801. It is important to note that Shaykh Yūsuf al-Qaraḍāwī and Shaykh Aḥmad al-Ṭayyib have been at odds since the 2013 overthrow of Mursī. In December of 2013, al-Qaraḍāwī announced his resignation from al-Azhar's Council of Senior Scholars, denouncing the Shaykh al-Azhar for supporting a "military coup" and for not speaking out against the massacre of Egyptian civilians earlier that year. See "Islamic scholar El-Qaradawi announces resignation from Al-Azhar clerical committee," *Al-Ahram* Online, December 2, 2013, accessed July 16, 2015, http://english.ahram.org.eg/NewsContent/1/64/88116/Egypt/Politics-/Islamic-scholar-ElQaradawi-announces-resignation-f.aspx.

single chain of transmission should be considered "doubtful and never absolute," so logic, reason, and "common sense" can be used as tools with which to interpret revealed texts that are unclear or to judge the acceptability of *āḥād ḥadīth* (even those that have been considered authentic by virtue of their inclusion in canonical *ḥadīth* collections).

It is significant that al-Qaraḍāwī chooses to focus on legal reasoning and textual (especially *ḥadīth*) criticism as two areas that illustrate the Ashʿarī orientation of the late Muḥammad al-Ghazālī, because it is precisely these methodological aspects that the major Azharī commentators featured in this chapter choose to highlight in their approach to al-Suyūṭī's *Ashbāh.* In all three commentaries, the scholars agree that one of the factors that makes al-Suyūṭī's work superior in the *qawāʿid* genre is that, for every one of the universal maxims, the fifteenth-century author provides textual evidence for the precepts from Qurʾān, Sunna, or both.

The next three sections look at each of the three commentaries beginning with the former Grand Mufti of Egypt, Shaykh ʿAlī Gumʿa, since he is the most senior of the three and acts as a mentor to the two younger scholars. The two younger scholars are both senior administrators in Dār al-Iftāʾ, and both can be seen attending the study sessions of Shaykh ʿAlī in the videos. Chronologically, Shaykh ʿAlī and Shaykh ʿAmr al-Wardānī's series overlap, while Shaykh Muḥammad Wisām's series was posted shortly thereafter. In terms of the volume of material under analysis, Shaykh ʿAlī Gumʿa's series on al-Suyūṭī's *Ashbāh* runs approximately eight hours. Shaykh ʿAmr al-Wardānī's is the longest at approximately fifteen hours, and Shaykh Muḥammad Wisām's sessions reach about eight hours in length. I have not seen any critical analysis of these commentaries up to this point, so part of my goal in this section is to outline some of the main features of each scholar's approach and to provide a starting point for future analysis.

As it will become clear in this analysis, each scholar employs a different rhetorical and pedagogical style to his commentary on the same material (al-Suyūṭī's Introduction and first chapter of his *Ashbāh*). As pragmatic discourse, the commentaries function on many different levels. Each scholar chooses to focus on different themes as well as methodological and linguistic aspects of al-Suyūṭī's text. In so doing, the authority of the fifteenth-century author is reconstructed in a contemporary context. This discursive effort on the part of the three commentators has the added pragmatic effect of reinforcing the authority of the speakers themselves.

SHAYKH ʿALĪ GUMʿA

Shaykh ʿAlī Gumʿa was appointed Grand Mufti of Egypt by President Mubārak in 2003 and stepped down from his position in 2013. Even before Mubārak was forced to resign from power following massive pro-democracy protests in early 2011, Shaykh ʿAlī was embroiled in controversy and locked in an ideological battle with several hard-line Salafī scholars and preachers.[38] In the tumultuous months in which the country was under the control of the Supreme Council of the Armed Forces (SCAF) and then by Muḥammad Mursī's Freedom and Justice Party (FJP), protests against al-Azhar's leadership escalated. In April of 2011, Salafī opposition to Shaykh ʿAlī Gumʿa converged in protests at al-Azhar University and in the city of Kafr al-Shaykh. Amani Maged reports that the trigger for these incidents was controversial statements by the Grand Mufti describing the full face veil (*niqāb*) as dangerous innovation (*bidʿa*) and condemning the destruction of Sufi shrines by Salafī activists. Insulting comments by Shaykh Abū Isḥāq al-Ḥuwaynī and Shaykh Khālid ʿAbd Allāh prompted the Grand Mufti to file a libel suit.[39]

Tensions erupted once again in April of 2012 when members of the FJP denounced the Grand Mufti's visit to Jerusalem as a treasonous violation of the unwritten ban against Egyptian officials visiting Israel (since such a move might be perceived as an attempt to normalize relations with the Jewish state).[40] Following this incident, pro-Muslim Brotherhood preacher Ṣafwat Ḥigāzī led protests outside of Dār al-Iftāʾ calling for the Grand

[38] Prior to the 2011 Revolution, the Salafīs in Egypt were kept under harsh repression by the state and thus found expression more as a popular social movement than as an organized political force. Like the Muslim Brotherhood, independent Salafī preachers and activists took advantage of the political vacuum and initial weakness of the religious establishment to become vocal participants in political debates.

[39] Amani Maged, "Salafis vs. Sufis," *Al-Ahram Weekly On-line*, Issue No. 1071 (November 3–9, 2011), accessed June 10, 2015, http://weekly.ahram.org.eg/2011/1071/eg4.htm.

[40] "Egypt's Grand Mufti visit to Jerusalem sparks uproar among political forces," *Ahram Online*, April 19, 2012, accessed June 10, 2015, http://english.ahram.org.eg/NewsContent/1/64/39622/Egypt/Politics-/Egypts-Grand-Mufti-visit-to-Jerusalem-sparks-uproa.aspx.

Mufti and other holdovers from the Mubārak regime to be removed from office.[41] As Mursī's first year as President wore on, polarization continued to increase both within the ranks of al-Azhar itself as well as in the Egyptian population in general. Even after Shaykh ʿAlī Gumʿa was replaced by Shaykh Shawqī ʿAllām in February of 2013, scandals continued to break out putting al-Azhar's leadership on the defensive. For example, an alleged mass poisoning of students in al-Azhar University dormitories prompted more protests during the spring of 2013.

In late June of 2013, more waves of demonstrations broke out expressing anger against Mursī and calling for expedited presidential elections. On July 3, Minister of Defense ʿAbd al-Fattāḥ al-Sīsī announced on national television that Mursī would be removed from office, the constitution suspended, and an interim government installed. In August, the interim government authorized the violent clearing of two squares in Cairo occupied by pro-Mursī demonstrators, leading to hundreds of deaths and mass arrests. Shortly after the crackdown, videos were posted on YouTube of Shaykh ʿAlī Gumʿa and two other influential religious leaders that appeared to give the security forces moral justification for killing "dissidents." While the videos could be interpreted as authorizing the armed forces to kill terrorists carrying out attacks in Northern Sinai, the timing seemed to correspond with the violent suppression of pro-Mursī demonstrations.[42] In any case, the support of al-Azhar's leadership for the removal of Mursī and for the military was not ambiguous. This clear political involvement on the part of the religious establishment was especially jarring to some observers who recalled Shaykh ʿAlī's earlier calls for restraint during the 2011 uprising, urging protesters to return home so as not to provoke chaos and bloodshed.[43]

[41] Haitham Zaki, "Safwat Hegazy: Down with military's mufti," *Egypt Independent*, April 22, 2012, accessed June 10, 2015, http://www.egyptindependent.com/node/790726. Ḥigāzī was imprisoned in August of 2013 along with other Muslim Brotherhood leaders.

[42] David D. Kirkpatrick and Mayy El Sheikh, "Egypt Military Enlists Religion to Quell Ranks," *The New York Times*, August 25, 2013, accessed June 11, 2015, http://www.nytimes.com/2013/08/26/world/middleeast/egypt.html?_r=0.

[43] Gihan Shahine, "Alarming Messages," *Al-Ahram Weekly*, Issue No. 1162, August 29, 2013, accessed June 11, 2015, http://weekly.ahram.org.eg/News/3898/17/Alarming-messages.aspx. The fact that this decree was disregarded and even scorned by many Egyptians complicates the issue of Shaykh ʿAlī Gumʿa's authority and power as a jurist. Clearly, possessing the ability to make legal arguments is not sufficient for one's legal opinions to be recognized as authoritative. State support and popular sentiment play a role in one's ability to bring power into

Given this highly charged political backdrop, it is all the more remarkable that three senior figures at Dār al-Iftāʾ all chose to give multi-part lectures to study circles in the Azhar mosque on al-Suyūṭī's *Ashbāh* between 2011 and 2013. As the fate of the nation was hanging in the balance, Shaykh ʿAlī and two of his protégés turned to an Egyptian "orthodox" exemplar of late Sunni jurisprudence whose personal struggles act as a model with which to combat ideological enemies and whose work provides fertile material with which to instill correct principles and methodology in the minds of today's students. The first session in Shaykh ʿAlī's six-part series is dated May 27, 2012, during the most contentious period of his tenure as Grand Mufti. Although Shaykh ʿAlī studiously avoids overt political references in his commentary on al-Suyūṭī's *Ashbāh*, the act of convening such a study circle amidst turmoil and uncertainty about the future of the institutions that he represents sends a message of its own. The message being communicated is that the cumulative knowledge of the great medieval scholars remains relevant to Muslims today and that it is the traditionally trained *ʿulamāʾ* who are uniquely qualified to make this heritage accessible to a new audience. Indeed, the nation of Egypt is relying on these centrist scholars to hold the middle ground and to fend off rising extremism.

In the introductory statements to his commentary on *al-Ashbāh wa-l-naẓāʾir*, Shaykh ʿAlī Gumʿa asserts that al-Suyūṭī is among the most masterful scholars in the field of *qawāʿid*, especially within the Shāfiʿī school. His *Ashbāh* is more useful to students than earlier works of the same type, including those of Ibn al-Wakīl (whose book is unfinished) and Ibn al-Subkī, whose writing is quite difficult to read.[44] Shaykh ʿAlī goes on to say that if one compares al-Suyūṭī's work to that of Ibn al-Subkī, one would find the difference between the two to be considerable. This points to the fact that al-Suyūṭī put extra effort into laying out the differences of opinion behind each principle and sub-principle. When the difference of opinion is strong in regards to a certain piece of evidence, al-Suyūṭī explains the relative strengths and weaknesses of each argument (much like al-Nawawī in his

being. I am grateful to my anonymous reviewer for providing insightful and intriguing comments on this issue.

[44] Shaykh ʿAlī Gumʿa, commentary on *al-Ashbāh wa-l-naẓāʾir*, Part 1, accessed May 19, 2015, https://www.youtube.com/watch?v=PEFPHAXigyw.

famous *Minhāj* [*al-ṭālibīn*]).[45] Every time al-Suyūṭī judges a piece of evidence to be the most sound, it speaks to the knowledge and thought process of the author.

Shaykh ʿAlī emphasizes several times in the first segment of his commentary (which runs close to two hours) that the study of legal precepts takes hard work and determination. In fact, al-Suyūṭī says as much in his Introduction when he observes that the study of likenesses and similarities in jurisprudence (*al-ashbāh wa-l-naẓāʾir*) is not perfected through wishful thinking, but can only be realized if one puts one's nose to the grindstone, even cutting oneself off from one's family if necessary.[46] A theme that comes up repeatedly in the commentary is that the medieval scholars, such as al-Suyūṭī, were able to produce such a large number of influential works in different fields because they were blessed by God and because they took the time to study with the best teachers and to develop their skills properly. For example, Shaykh ʿAlī makes a point of mentioning that al-Suyūṭī authored a comprehensive book on grammar when he was only seventeen. He also draws a contrast between those who understand that becoming proficient in jurisprudence takes real learning under the supervision of a teacher and the "take out" approach where people study for a few months and then call themselves legal scholars.[47]

The implication seems to be that today's students are lazy in comparison to scholars like al-Suyūṭī. Indeed, Shaykh ʿAlī chides his audience at several

[45] Ibid. Shaykh Muḥammad Wisām compares al-Suyūṭī's *Ashbāh* to another work by al-Nawawī, his *Riyāḍ al-ṣāliḥīn*. He suggests that God chose to distinguish these two works from the multitude of similar compositions on account of their superior structure. The widespread popularity of the book is a direct reflection of the devotion of the author to his scholarship, as well as of the purity of his intention in writing it and of his closeness to God (commentary on *al-Ashbāh wa-l-naẓāʾir*, Part 14, accessed May 19, 2015, https://www.youtube.com/watch?v=cuVE4yWfM1M). In an earlier segment, he compares al-Suyūṭī's *Ashbāh* to al-Ghazālī's *Mustaṣfā min ʿilm al-uṣūl*, saying that while neither author invented the field, they excelled in extracting and compiling its main principles, and that this intellectual accomplishment speaks to the piety and blessedness of the author (commentary on *al-Ashbāh wa-l-naẓāʾir*, Part 2, accessed May 19, 2015, https://www.youtube.com/watch?v=rLSIDEjahsw).

[46] Jalāl al-Dīn al-Suyūṭī, *al-Ashbāh wa-l-naẓāʾir fī l-qawāʿid al-fiqhiyya* (Cairo: al-Maktab al-Thaqāfī li-l-Nashr wa-l-Tawzīʿ, 2007), 21.

[47] Shaykh ʿAlī Gumʿa, commentary on *al-Ashbāh wa-l-naẓāʾir*, Part 1, accessed June 12, 2015, https://www.youtube.com/watch?v=PEFPHAXigyw. The term "take away" (*tēk ʾawēh*) in colloquial Egyptian usage refers to "take out" or delivered fast food, which here has the connotation of knowledge attained in a hasty fashion without expending the effort needed in order to gain true understanding. I am grateful to my anonymous reviewer for helping to explain this point.

points for not responding correctly to grammar questions that he poses to them during the lecture. The desired balance is a mix of being able to repeat the correct answer and real comprehension of the material. A large percentage of the first session and of subsequent sessions as well is taken up by detailed grammatical explanations. He spends about twenty minutes during the third session quizzing the students on the rules regarding hollow verbs, for example. The lectures follow a traditional format in which a member of the study circle reads al-Suyūṭī's text aloud in segments while the other students follow along in their textbooks and the shaykh interjects comments and answers occasional questions. The fact that the mufti spends so much time discussing rules of Arabic grammar that his audience should already be familiar with from secondary school suggests that he believes that the students are in need of a reminder and that grammatically correct language use is quickly becoming a lost art. For example, he observes that newspapers frequently misuse the term 'chaos' (*fawḍā*) ignoring the rule that the word must be placed after a noun thus acting like an adjective.[48] Again, the implication seems to be that people must be reminded of the rules of the language before they are forgotten entirely.[49]

Of course, grammar does have a practical application in jurisprudence and is therefore not purely a question of abstract rules. One of the areas in which legal precepts are most helpful to the jurist is the interpretation of unclear language. In the case of speech acts like oaths, for example, it is often necessary to look for contextual clues in order to determine the intention of the speaker if the words carry many possible meanings.[50] In his list of issues in jurisprudence in which intention plays a key role, al-Suyūṭī brings up a somewhat complicated example involving the distribution of wages for a particular commission. Shaykh ʿAlī uses the wage (*juʿāla*) example as a way to illustrate a methodology of reasoning through an issue and applying both grammatical and legal analysis to find an answer. To illustrate his

[48] Shaykh ʿAlī Gumʿa, commentary on *al-Ashbāh wa-l-naẓāʾir*, Part 1, accessed June 12, 2015, https://www.youtube.com/watch?v=PEFPHAXigyw.

[49] The idea that the intellectual heritage is slipping away and must be preserved by qualified scholars is very much in keeping with al-Suyūṭī's own outlook, especially his desire to amass large numbers of *ḥadīths* so that they are not lost through negligence.

[50] I discuss the role of legal precepts in interpretation in Chapter 4, including the role of custom in providing contextual information for the meaning of a given utterance, all of which has an effect on its legal application.

interpretive approach to the thought of al-Suyūṭī, I will attempt to trace Shaykh ʿAlī's argument as it develops over three sessions of his commentary as briefly as possible.

Although the reference in al-Suyūṭī's text is a bit opaque, he seems to say that when a wage is promised by an employer (person A) to a certain individual (person B) and that person partners with someone else in fulfilling the assigned task (person C), the partner (person C) gets the full wage if the intention of person B was to appoint the partner to do the task in his place. If person C was hired with the assumption that he is actually working for the person who commissioned the job originally (person A), then person C gets a share in the wage, but if that is not the case, and person C is just a volunteer who comes along, then he does not share in the wage.[51] Shaykh ʿAlī gives the example of someone who has lost his child and commissions someone in the neighborhood to go looking for the child, promising him ten pounds if the child is found. That person then brings other people along with him in the search for the missing child. Do those additional people receive a share of the wage (*al-juʿāla*) or not?[52]

Returning to the *juʿāla* issue in the fourth session of his commentary, Shaykh ʿAlī outlines a five-step approach to finding a legal ruling in a particular case. The mufti must first get a comprehensive picture of the issue including the real context in which the issue emerged. The process of describing the issue, *taṣwīr*, is followed by situating the issue, or *takyīf*, in which the mufti determines where the issue fits within the scheme of jurisprudence. The ruling (*ḥukm*) is then presented followed by providing textual evidence (*tadlīl*) for the ruling as well as the reasoning behind the ruling (*taʿlīl*). These five steps act as a kind of code or key to analyzing how a ruling is derived in regards to a certain issue. Such keys to understanding are not always written down but come from the experience of one's teachers.[53]

Engaging in steps one and two (*taṣwīr* and *takyīf*) for the remuneration example, Shaykh ʿAlī looks closely at al-Suyūṭī's phrasing of the issue to explain that it is significant in this case that the wage is to be paid to a

[51] Al-Suyūṭī, *al-Ashbāh*, 39.

[52] Shaykh ʿAlī Gumʿa, commentary on *al-Ashbāh wa-l-naẓāʾir*, Part 3, accessed June 15, 2015, https://www.youtube.com/watch?v=pqp-HgHg1R8.

[53] Shaykh ʿAlī Gumʿa, commentary on *al-Ashbāh wa-l-naẓāʾir*, Part 4, accessed June 15, 2015, https://www.youtube.com/watch?v=ECxFOhbB6NY.

certain individual, not just to whoever is willing to do the task. In other words, it is not the same as saying that ten pounds will be given to whoever finds the missing child, but rather, person A has commissioned person B in particular with the task. Shaykh ʿAlī demonstrates the type of questions the jurist should ask himself while reading the text by trying out two different possible interpretations. The phrase "if he intended to appoint him in his place" could be read to mean if the original employer (A) intended to appoint C in place of B, or it could mean if B intended to appoint C in his place (along the lines of a sub-contract, perhaps). So, which scenario makes more sense in the context? In further discussion with the audience, it becomes clear that the phrase appears two ways in different editions of the text, so both scenarios are possible.

It is clear from this discussion that it is very easy to read (or to misread) classical texts in various ways. So what does the interpreter do to resolve the confusion? He or she must go back to the books of jurisprudence and look at the rules regarding wages. As Shaykh ʿAlī explains, *al-Ashbāh* is not a book of *fiqh*. It is a book that refers to points of substantive law (*furūʿ al-fiqh*). The only problem is that when one goes back and looks at the *fiqh* books, one still finds that both scenarios are possible. The truly learned person admits in such a case that he is unsure of the correct answer, whereas the ignorant person insists that he understands even when he really does not.[54] Shaykh ʿAlī adds a postscript to the *juʿāla* issue at the beginning of the fifth session in which he asks one of the shaykhs in attendance to read from one of the well-known commentaries on al-Nawawī's *Minhāj al-ṭālibīn*, the *Mughnī al-muḥtāj* of al-Khaṭīb al-Shirbīnī (d. 994/1586). Even after consulting this additional source, Shaykh ʿAlī hesitates to declare one interpretation to be the correct one. His final word on the matter is that the most important lesson is the process (*manhaj*) itself. If a question is unclear, the jurist must go back and look at the *fiqh* commentaries to gain extra insight into the matter.[55]

This insistence on the importance of *manhaj* is very much in keeping with the attitude of all three Azharī scholars whose commentaries on al-Suyūṭī

[54] Shaykh ʿAlī Gumʿa, commentary on *al-Ashbāh wa-l-naẓāʾir*, Part 4, accessed June 16, 2015, https://www.youtube.com/watch?v=ECxFOhbB6NY.

[55] Shaykh ʿAlī Gumʿa, commentary on *al-Ashbāh wa-l-naẓāʾir*, Part 5, accessed June 16, 2015, https://www.youtube.com/watch?v=KJ_483wMdIk.

are under examination here. Shaykh ʿAlī's approach and the approach of his two younger protégés do raise some troubling questions. An outside observer might well ask why the shaykh chooses to spend precious airtime dwelling on the rules of Arabic grammar and seemingly obscure points of substantive law (like the *juʿāla* example) when the institution of al-Azhar is going through an existential crisis, not to mention the nation of Egypt as a whole. Is it to avoid talking about issues that are more explicitly political, such as the role of Islamic law in the constitution or the need for reform in the religious establishment? Also, a *salafī* traditionalist listening to such a discussion might conclude that such an approach actually confirms the irrelevance of late *fiqh* commentaries like al-Shirbīnī's *Mughnī* (or al-Suyūṭī's *Ashbāh*, for that matter) rather than proving their critical importance to the *wasaṭī manhaj* as seems to be the intention.

SHAYKH ʿAMR AL-WARDĀNĪ

Like Muḥammad Wisām, Shaykh ʿAmr is from a younger generation of scholars who count Shaykh ʿAlī Gumʿa among their mentors. The two younger scholars are both seen in the videos of Shaykh ʿAlī's lessons, suggesting that they thought it necessary to show support for their mentor at a very sensitive time just before the election of Mursī and Shaykh ʿAlī's retirement as state mufti. Shaykh ʿAmr recently received his doctorate through the Azhar system and serves as a mufti and senior administrator at Dār al-Iftāʾ. Shaykh ʿAmr's series on al-Suyūṭī's *Ashbāh* is the longest of the three commentaries, so it will be necessary to select just a few points for examination here. Like the other two scholars, his focus is on methodology and pedagogy. He sees al-Suyūṭī's *Ashbāh* less as a book of *fiqh* and more as a guide to the exercise of *doing fiqh* in the sense of understanding a problem and using sources to derive a solution through abstraction (*tajrīd*) and deduction (*takhrīj*). The ultimate goal of this process on the part of the jurist is *ijtihād*, much as it was for al-Suyūṭī himself.

Shaykh ʿAmr uses as the starting point for his discussion the five point process of giving a fatwa already mentioned in Shaykh ʿAlī's commentary: picturing the issue in one's mind, identifying which legal category is the most relevant to the issue, presenting a ruling, and providing a textual basis and reasoning for the ruling. He abstracts the process even further to give a breakdown of the steps that one must take to acquire a new skill and to gain a thorough understanding of a given issue or problem. He compares this set of skills to methods of transportation that one uses to arrive at a desired destination.[56] Also, like Shaykh Muḥammad and Shaykh ʿAlī, he suggests that this process of knowledge acquisition (*al-talaqqī*) should rightly be conducted under the guidance of an experienced teacher.

Al-Suyūṭī's *Ashbāh* illustrates for the student how complex issues in jurisprudence can be boiled down to their essence, the separate components separated and abstracted into universals, and then reapplied to a new context. As al-Suyūṭī argues, the study of likenesses and similarities (*al-ashbāh wa-l-naẓāʾir*) provides the jurist with the tools not only to comprehend the issue but then to translate that comprehension into action, meaning the ability to derive rulings in cases in which there is no clear textual precedent.[57] Therefore, the statement, "Jurisprudence is the knowledge of likenesses," suggests that the larger purposes and rationales underlying the principles of *fiqh* are more important than the literal meaning of specific regulations.

As mentioned previously, al-Suyūṭī is careful to provide textual justification for each of the abstract precepts discussed in his *Ashbāh*. All three contemporary commentators respect al-Suyūṭī's ability to present and evaluate evidence from the *ḥadīth* of the Prophet and *āthār* of his Companions. Al-Suyūṭī even provides textual justification for the process of reasoning by analogy. The textual indicant in this case is a report (*athar*) attributed to the Companion ʿUmar b. al-Khaṭṭāb that contains part of a letter that he is supposed to have sent to the chief judge in Baṣra, Abū Mūsā al-Ashʿarī (d. 42/662) on the subject of judgeship (*al-qaḍāʾ*). A condensed excerpt from the letter appears in al-Suyūṭī's text (with a full chain of transmission) as the following:

> The judgeship is a prescribed duty and an established custom. Understand that when a case is brought to you, it is of no use to pronounce judgment if that

[56] Shaykh ʿAmr al-Wardānī, commentary on *al-Ashbāh wa-l-naẓāʾir*, Introduction (Part 1), accessed June 17, 2015, https://www.youtube.com/watch?v=fYpi7MhCzF4&list=PLAC3E8379673AE758.

[57] Al-Suyūṭī, *al-Ashbāh*, 25.

> judgment cannot be enforced. Nothing prevents you from retracting a judgment you have made after re-examining it and being guided to righteousness in it, because the true ruling is eternal (*fa-inna al-ḥaqq qadīm*), and re-examining a judgment is better than persisting in error. Trust that understanding comes from within your own heart. So, when you are asked to judge on a matter that is not in the Book [Qurʾān] or the Sunna, know the likenesses and analogous cases so that you can rule on the basis of analogy. Resolve the matter according to what you think is most preferable to God and closest to the truth as far as you can discern it (*fī-mā tarā*).[58]

While Orientalists have long been skeptical in regards to the historicity of ʿUmar's letter,[59] it is cited by both pre-modern and modern Muslim jurists as providing justification for the use of reasoning by analogy as a tool for *ijtihād*. One noteworthy modern example is a treatise by the Syrian reformer Jamāl al-Dīn al-Qāsimī (d. 1914) in which he affirms the importance of *ijtihād* and the ability of Islamic legal principles to adapt to new technology like the telegraph. Al-Qāsimī cites al-Suyūṭī many times in the treatise, including al-Suyūṭī's claim that *mujtahids* still exist in his era, as well as the passage from the *Ashbāh* discussed above in which al-Suyūṭī argues that a knowledge of similarities and likenesses is the essence of jurisprudence. Al-Qāsimī also quotes extensively from Ibn Qayyim al-Jawziyya (d. 751/1350) who cites the letter to prove that the Companions used analogy for cases not covered in the Qurʾān or the Sunna. Ibn al-Qayyim goes on to say that the rational ability to distinguish likenesses and differences is a God-given "property of the mind" and a necessary component of *ijtihād*.[60]

Shaykh ʿAmr, similar to the other two commentators, emphasizes the hard work and effort that goes into finding such indicants. When al-Suyūṭī says, for example, that he found a source to support the assertion that the study of similarities and likenesses is a noble pursuit and essential to the practice of jurisprudence, Shaykh ʿAmr focuses on the phrase "I have found" (*wa qad wajadtu*) to insist that such evidence does not just appear, but that

[58] Al-Suyūṭī, *al-Ashbāh*, 26.

[59] For a classic Orientalist analysis of the letter see R.B. Serjeant, "The Caliph ʿUmar's Letters to Abū Mūsā al-Ashʿarī and Muʿāwiya," *Journal of Semitic Studies* 29:1 (1984): 65–79.

[60] Jamāl al-Dīn al-Qāsimī, "Guiding Mankind to Act on the Basis of Telegraphic Messages," translated by David D. Commins, in *Modernist Islam, 1840–1940: A Sourcebook*, edited by Charles Kurzman (New York: Oxford University Press, 2002), 185.

there is an element of search and determination involved on the part of the author.[61] It is interesting to note here that the questions that Shaykh ʿAmr asks in regards to how and why this report is used in al-Suyūṭī's *Ashbāh* are very similar to the kind of questions that guide this study of al-Suyūṭī's legal persona and legacy. What does the author want to say and why does he choose to say it in the way that he does?

Shaykh ʿAmr observes that ʿUmar's letter is well known and widely accepted as authentic within the tradition,[62] so why does al-Suyūṭī go to the trouble of providing a full chain of transmission for this text? Shaykh ʿAmr draws a link between al-Suyūṭī's attention to the chain of transmission for this text and his statement earlier about how he expended great effort in providing evidence for the precepts in his book from the *ḥadīth* and *āthār*, endeavoring to authenticate the texts whenever possible.[63] These aspects of al-Suyūṭī's Introduction act as proof that the author is qualified to engage in the analysis contained in the book itself. From the introduction of works like al-Suyūṭī's *Ashbāh* or Ibn Khaldūn's famous *Muqaddima*, one can get a sense of the author's methodology as well as the importance of the work, as he perceives it, relative to the field of study as a whole. Not only does al-Suyūṭī claim in his Introduction that his book is the very best of its type, he seeks to illustrate his own competence as a jurist and *ḥadīth* scholar and prove that he deserves recognition for this superior knowledge (Shaykh ʿAmr calls this *bayān al-istiḥqāq*). Shaykh ʿAmr is quick to point out that the pride that al-Suyūṭī takes in providing exhaustive textual evidence complete with chains of transmission and evaluations of authenticity should not be construed as unjustified human arrogance. From the very beginning of *al-Ashbāh*, as in his other works,

[61] Shaykh ʿAmr al-Wardānī, commentary on *al-Ashbāh wa-l-naẓāʾir*, Introduction (Part 4), accessed June 17, 2015, https://www.youtube.com/watch?v=i2blGHWTM6Q&index=4&list=PLAC3E8379673AE758.

[62] According to Serjeant, Ibn Ḥazm (d. 456/1064) rejected the letter as "spurious" (see "The Caliph ʿUmar's Letters," 65). As a Ẓāhirī jurist who strongly favors the Qurʾān and Sunna over interpretative principles like *qiyās*, it makes sense that Ibn Ḥazm would be dubious about a source that so clearly provides legal justification for reasoning by analogy through the Prophet's Companions.

[63] Al-Suyūṭī, *al-Ashbāh*, 23. This statement will be discussed in more detail in the following section in regards to Shaykh Muḥammad Wisām's commentary.

al-Suyūṭī demonstrates that his true intention is "recounting God's blessings" (*al-taḥadduth bi-niʿmat Allāh*).[64]

Shaykh ʿAmr goes on to explain that the letter of the caliph ʿUmar to Abū Mūsā is of critical importance to the work of the judge as well as the mufti because it provides religious justification (based on the normative actions of the Companions) for the jurist's ability to use his best judgment to find a ruling that comes as close to God's eternal will as possible. In such a situation, a 'true' ruling already exists and it is thus the imperative of the jurist to "discover" the correct ruling insofar as it is within his capability to do so. Since a ruling derived through analogical reasoning can only be arrived at with probability and not certainty in most cases, it is acceptable and even encouraged to revisit or re-evaluate one's judgments with the understanding that the final word on the matter will never be pronounced by a human interpreter.

Shaykh ʿAmr seizes on this idea of re-examination (*murājaʿa*) and goes into a long impassioned speech urging his audience as legal scholars in training never to succumb to feelings of complacency or resignation.[65] He reflects that this complacency is like a fire that consumes everything one has learned about being a scholar and opens the door to greed, negligence, and caprice. He urges his listeners to make a vow between themselves and God at that very moment never to become complacent or self-satisfied.[66]

Shaykh ʿAmr's personal advice to his followers here is a reminder that the technical processes that the mufti undertakes to find a ruling based on textual evidence and analogous cases are also ethical in nature. When ʿUmar tells Abū Mūsā in the letter to "trust that understanding that is within your own heart" (or, literally, chest), the implication is that the judge's reasoning is guided by ethical principles. In other words, the heart and mind are linked. Although Shaykh ʿAmr does not identify this worldview as belonging

[64] Shaykh ʿAmr al-Wardānī, commentary on *al-Ashbāh wa-l-naẓāʾir*, Introduction (Part 4), accessed June 17, 2015, https://www.youtube.com/watch?v=i2blGHWTM6Q&index=4&list=PLAC3E8379673AE758.

[65] Shaykh ʿAmr al-Wardānī, commentary on *al-Ashbāh wa-l-naẓāʾir*, Introduction (Part 5), accessed June 19, 2015, https://www.youtube.com/watch?v=NxBRSt8NMJc.

[66] Ibid. There is some irony here since one of the most frequent criticisms leveled against Azharī scholars is that they have become complacent and corrupted due to their closeness to the regime in power.

to a Sufi model of behavior in his commentary, his portrayal of the ethics of compassion behind the dry legal precepts fits in well with the Sufi part of the Azharī *manhaj*.

Similar to Shaykh Muḥammad's appeal to his students to internalize the *qawāʿid* as a framework for living and interacting with others (*manhaj al-ḥayāt*), Shaykh ʿAmr talks about a "civilizational method" (*manhaj ʿumrānī*) that draws on Sharīʿa principles to improve the lives of human beings in society. Drawing inspiration from the great historian Ibn Khaldūn (d. 808/1406), Shaykh ʿAmr advocates a God-centered approach to the study of human history and society. He contrasts the desired *manhaj ʿumrānī* with what he sees as a materialist Western approach to social science that begins and ends with issues of power and control. Shaykh ʿAmr argues that, while the two methodologies deploy similar concepts, the fundamental assumption of the so-called Western approach is that human beings are ultimately the masters of their own environment, and that the end goal is to dominate the production of meaning in society, whereas Muslims should strive to build up and enrich civilization as servants of God.[67] Shaykh ʿAmr is not ignorant of or naïve about critical methods that have emerged out of Western scholarship in the last century. Much like al-Suyūṭī's approach to the study of Greek logic, he makes a point of familiarizing himself with the very ideas that he finds insufficient and even threatening to religious scholarship so that he can reject them.

SHAYKH MUḤAMMAD WISĀM

Of the three commentators, Shaykh Muḥammad Wisām is the most polemical in tone. He argues explicitly that there is a link between critical evaluation of textual evidence and centrist Azharī methodology in general (and an Ashʿarī sense of rationality, mediation between extremes, and distaste for *takfīr*, in particular). According to this view, the field of *qawāʿid* represents the ultimate abstraction in legal reasoning and speaks to the inherent

[67] Shaykh ʿAmr al-Wardānī, commentary on *al-Ashbāh wa-l-naẓāʾir*, Introduction (Part 2), accessed June 30, 2015, https://www.youtube.com/watch?v=krohkAP1JIM&index=2&list=PLAC3E8379673AE758.

capabilities of human beings for rational discernment.[68] At the same time, these abstract principles are grounded in scriptural evidence. The fact that al-Suyūṭī shows detailed evidence from the Sunna for the precept *al-umūr bi-maqāṣidihā* ("matters shall be judged according to their objectives"), for example, accomplishes three goals for the author (according to Shaykh Muḥammad).

First, it shows that these precepts are not ones that jurists just invented out of thin air, but are derived from authoritative sources, which in turn demonstrates the difference between a comprehensive view of the tradition and a superficial approach that takes certain texts out of context and refuses to take into account the thinking of jurists over the centuries. Secondly, al-Suyūṭī brings to the reader's attention the connection between the principles that are produced in the minds of the jurists and the textual indicants of the Sharīʿa on which these principles are based. In other words, there is a complementary relationship between the mentality of the jurists (*ʿaqliyyat al-fuqahāʾ*), the mentality of Islamic jurisprudence (*ʿaqliyyat al-fiqh al-islāmī*), and the indicants of Sharīʿa (*adillat al-Sharīʿa*). Taken together in harmony, these factors form a kind of cumulative culture of jurisprudence (*ḥaḍārat al-fiqh*) that pays respect to the text itself, to the real context in which it was produced, and to the greater understanding of it.[69]

Finally, the detailed and systematic way in which al-Suyūṭī lists the various *ḥadīth*s in support of this precept and others indicates the author's depth of learning in the *ḥadīth* sciences and in a variety of other sciences as well. Shaykh Muḥammad affirms al-Suyūṭī's own assertion that this level of proficiency was rare even in his own time (to say nothing of the present).[70] Al-Suyūṭī spells out the superiority of his methodology in regards to evaluation of evidence from the *ḥadīth* of the Prophet and his Companions as well as the importance of his book in general. He suggests that whenever a textual problem arises, he has done everything possible to resolve the issue and

[68] Shaykh Muḥammad Wisām, commentary on *al-Ashbāh wa-l-naẓāʾir*, Part 8, accessed May 20, 2015, https://www.youtube.com/watch?v=uG0tnxHL8zU.

[69] Shaykh Muḥammad Wisām, commentary on *al-Ashbāh wa-l-naẓāʾir*, Part 13, accessed May 20, 2015, https://www.youtube.com/watch?v=ajRpFo5E5PQ.

[70] Shaykh Muḥammad Wisām, commentary on *al-Ashbāh wa-l-naẓāʾir*, Part 13, accessed May 20, 2015, https://www.youtube.com/watch?v=ajRpFo5E5PQ.

that he, more than any other scholar, has the knowledge and skills necessary to engage in this type of criticism. Al-Suyūṭī writes:

> I have laid out every precept with evidence [of its origin] in either a *ḥadīth* [of the Prophet] or an *athar* [report of a Companion], and whenever there is weakness in the chain of the transmission of the *ḥadīth*, I have put all of my efforts into examining and finding proofs for authenticating it (in an abbreviated manner); this [effort] is something that one does not see jurists capable of doing nowadays (or even interested in doing so). If you consider this book of mine, you will see that it is the very best of its age.[71]

Reflecting on this passage from al-Suyūṭī, Shaykh Muḥammad suggests that this effort on the part of the fifteenth-century author reflects a depth of understanding of the textual tradition that is neglected by many so-called scholars today. Shaykh Muḥammad comments:

> Look at the difference between this Azharī *manhaj* that al-Suyūṭī (God's mercy be upon him) is propagating in his statements and phrases in his Introduction and the approaches (*manāhij*) that treat textual evidence (*al-aṣl*) as erroneous or weak and treat the weak [*ḥadīths*] as forged. [Those who use these approaches] look at the weak *ḥadīths* as though they are forged in a manner that obstructs people's [use of] the Sunna. This is not the *manhaj* of the *salaf*.[72]

Shaykh Muḥammad goes on to mock people who flip through books of Sunna blithely separating out *ḥadīths* that they consider to be true or false.[73] He reminds the listeners that this heritage is cumulative, and that it is not as

[71] Al-Suyūṭī, *al-Ashbāh*, 23. Jonathan A.C. Brown explains the tendency of *ḥadīth* scholars of the late Sunni tradition like al-Suyūṭī to take a 'big tent' approach to evaluating the authenticity of *ḥadīths*. The fact that a certain *ḥadīth* had been considered weak by earlier scholars was not reason enough to invalidate its use. Instead, scholars like al-Suyūṭī would look for ways to make even 'weak' *ḥadīths* admissible in legal reasoning (see his *Hadith: Muhammad's Legacy in the Medieval and Modern World* (Oxford, U.K.: Oneworld Publications, 2009), 106–10.

[72] Shaykh Muḥammad Wisām, commentary on *al-Ashbāh wa-l-naẓāʾir*, Part 3, accessed May 21, 2015, https://www.youtube.com/watch?v=-fBX_LQCcbY.

[73] The allusion here may be to the well-known traditionalist Salafī scholar, Muḥammad Nāṣir al-Dīn al-Albānī (d. 1999) who has written critically of the use of weak *ḥadīths* and has even published works attempting to reevaluate established *ḥadīth* collections, separating out what he considers to be sound and unreliable *ḥadīths*. One such collection subjected to al-Albānī's criticism is al-Suyūṭī's *Jāmiʿ al-ṣaghīr*. See Jonathan A.C. Brown, *Hadith*, 257. Interestingly, in spite of his focus on *ḥadīth* and skepticism toward *madhhab*-based jurisprudence, both Brown and Instisar Rabb point out that al-Albānī has been known to make use of legal precepts in his own legal writing. See Brown, *Hadith*, 261 and Rabb, "Legal Maxims," in the *Oxford Encyclopedia of Islam and Law*, Oxford Islamic Studies Online.

though scholars are just approaching it for the first time. He states that we can, however, follow the same type of thinking that earlier scholars engaged in and apply it to our own era.[74]

Shaykh Muḥammad then makes a point of mentioning that to acquire the knowledge and skills necessary to understand universal principles and to make connections between different disciplines, as al-Suyūṭī did in his time, requires the guidance of a teacher. It is the great responsibility of those associated with the ancient institution of al-Azhar to pass on this legacy to future generations of students so that these sciences will not be lost or corrupted. Successful training in a specific field of knowledge requires a knowledgeable guide (*ʿālim*), an intellectual milieu, a text, and a scholarly methodology (*manhaj ʿilmī*).[75]

Shaykh Muḥammad explains that specialization in one field should not become a reason to cut oneself off from other disciplines. One of the greatest crises facing the Muslim community today, in his view, is that this intellectual milieu is fading away. People make the mistake of thinking that they can study a few texts or memorize some pieces of information and become experts without the guidance of a teacher or the benefit of advanced training. One finds this crisis to be particularly acute in the field of the Sharīʿa sciences, in spite of the fact that this field is more important than others.[76]

Just after the passage in which al-Suyūṭī talks about his method of providing textual evidence for the precepts in his book, as well as the superiority of the book in comparison to other works of the age, he makes a distinction between three different types of scholars: those who are overcome with jealousy and think they have attained a high level of learning but who have

[74] Shaykh Muḥammad Wisām, commentary on *al-Ashbāh wa-l-naẓāʾir*, Part 3, accessed May 21, 2015, https://www.youtube.com/watch?v=-fBX_LQCcbY.

[75] He gives a similar list in Part 1 of his commentary as well as a strong statement affirming the necessity of studying *qawāʿid* in the modern age: "The reality [*al-wāqiʿ*] in which we live has become intricate and complicated and the acuteness of our need to understand the precepts of jurisprudence has become clear, as well as [our need to understand] how the *mujtahids* thought, and that the key to understanding their methodologies [*manāhijihim*] involves more than just taking a literal approach to the individual issues [that they discussed]" (accessed May 21, 2015, https://www.youtube.com/watch?v=H4aHcbIkuAI).

[76] Shaykh Muḥammad Wisām, commentary on *al-Ashbāh wa-l-naẓāʾir*, Part 4, accessed May 22, 2015, https://www.youtube.com/watch?v=o7W6HBP9frc.

not, in fact, attained that level, those who have been seized by compounded ignorance, and those for whom God has provided guidance and inspiration.[77] It is here that Shaykh Muḥammad sees a direct parallel between the struggles facing al-Suyūṭī as a rare *mujtahid* in his age surrounded by ignorance and jealousy and the crisis of authority currently besetting the Muslim community. He goes so far as to say that it is as though al-Suyūṭī is speaking in our own time, even though he did not experience the same circumstances.[78] Al-Suyūṭī's description of jurists as "the guardians and foundation of the faith" (*quwwām al-dīn wa-qiwāmuhu*) gives Shaykh Muḥammad an opening through which to refute the opinions of fellow scholars who do not live up to this role (in his view). Like al-Suyūṭī, who referred to one of his enemies simply as *al-jāhil* or "the Ignoramus," Shaykh Muḥammad does not name his rivals but makes allusion to their ideas as a "superficial" approach to legal reasoning that contrasts with the centrist, moderate *manhaj*.

Of the three commentators, Shaykh Muḥammad is by far the most explicit about defining an opposition, even without mentioning the names of specific scholars. He responds directly to a number of debates that could be termed inter-Salafī in the sense that they concern differences of opinion in both doctrine (*ʿaqīda*) and methodology (*manhaj*) amongst scholars, all of whom claim to represent the true ways of the *salaf*. The enemy, as far as Shaykh Muḥammad is concerned, is people who support burning established and respected works like Ibn Ḥajar's *al-Fatḥ al-bārī* and al-Nawawī's *Sharḥ Ṣaḥīḥ Muslim* because the authors are Ashʿarī.[79] This attitude, he says, suggests that we have arrived at a level of vileness (*danāʾa*) that bears no relation either to morals or to knowledge.[80]

In addition to the issue of *ḥadīth* criticism already mentioned, three areas of inter-Salafī debate that come up most frequently in Shaykh Muḥammad's commentary on al-Suyūṭī's *Ashbāh* are making supplication to the Prophet

[77] Al-Suyūṭī, *al-Ashbāh*, 23–4.

[78] Shaykh Muḥammad Wisām, commentary on *al-Ashbāh wa-l-naẓāʾir*, Part 4, accessed May 22, 2015, https://www.youtube.com/watch?v=o7W6HBP9frc.

[79] Shaykh Muḥammad Wisām, commentary on *al-Ashbāh wa-l-naẓāʾir*, Part 5, accessed May 26, 2015, https://www.youtube.com/watch?v=45G54m9DR94.

[80] Ibid. Traditionalist Salafīs like the late Saudi Arabian mufti Shaykh ʿAbd al-ʿAzīz b. Bāz (d. 1999) have apparently called for caution in regards to relying on Ashʿarī scholars like al-Nawawī and Ibn Ḥajar on matters of *ʿaqīda* (e.g., the names and attributes of God), but I have not seen any evidence of the actual burning of their works.

or to Sufi saints (*istighātha*), communicating with the Prophet in his grave (*tawassul* or *wasīla*), and visiting the tombs of the Prophet and of the saints (*awliyāʾ*).[81] He is highly critical of people who try to distinguish between acts of God and acts of worshippers. This kind of distinction is dangerous because it makes it much easier to accuse people of the sin of *shirk*, or worshipping someone or something other than God. According to Shaykh Muḥammad, the correct Ashʿarī ʿ*aqīda* holds that all actions are created by God and that people engage in such actions with God's permission.[82] He suggests that every action that is supposedly confined to God and that cannot be extended to anyone other than God has, in fact, been attributed to those who are not God in the Qurʾān and Sunna. Even al-Suyūṭī in his Introduction describes the importance of the jurists as those from whom one seeks enlightenment in darkness and to whom one appeals (*yustaghāthu*) for strength and comfort.[83] Does this mean that al-Suyūṭī is committing *shirk* since he mentions making supplication to someone other than God?[84] The antidote to this kind of foolish speculation is a correct knowledge of legal precepts and the principles of jurisprudence.[85]

Shaykh Muḥammad's discussion of *shirk* and *takfīr* (labeling other Muslims as apostates or unbelievers) incites more participation from the men and women in the audience than any other section of his commentary on al-Suyūṭī's *Ashbāh*. It is clear from the attention that he devotes to these issues (and from the liveliness of the response) that attacking someone's faith on matters relating to seeking intercession from the Prophet or from other saintly figures is a very divisive phenomenon in Egypt today.

It is during this part of the commentary that Shaykh Muḥammad engages in a common rhetorical practice, namely to associate his enemies with the

[81] The "saints" refers to pious men and women who have been recognized informally as possessing charismatic authority and often miraculous abilities. For background on the controversial concept of "sainthood" in Islam and its relevance to Sufi practices in contemporary Egypt, see Valerie J. Hoffman, *Sufism, Mystics and Saints in Modern Egypt* (Columbia, S.C.: University of South Carolina Press, 1995).

[82] Shaykh Muḥammad Wisām, commentary on *al-Ashbāh wa-l-naẓāʾir*, Part 5, accessed May 26, 2015, https://www.youtube.com/watch?v=45G54m9DR94.

[83] Al-Suyūṭī, *al-Ashbāh*, 21.

[84] Shaykh Muḥammad Wisām, commentary on *al-Ashbāh wa-l-naẓāʾir*, Part 5, accessed May 26, 2015, https://www.youtube.com/watch?v=45G54m9DR94.

[85] Ibid.

Kharijites (*khawārij*), a sect that rebelled against the Umayyads and ʿAbbasids before their final suppression and disappearance. Since the ʿAbbasid period (750–1258 CE), the term 'Kharijite' has been abstracted from its original context to refer to anyone who rebels against 'legitimate' authority, especially using violence and terrorism as a means with which to signal rejection of existing authority structures (like post-colonial secular governments in Egypt, Iraq, and Syria, for example).

Jeffrey Kenney points out that the use of the term 'Kharijites' to label perceived enemies of the Egyptian state goes back to the era of President Nāṣir and his attempts to bring the Muslim Brotherhood and religious establishment under state control. After a 1954 plot to assassinate Nāṣir, the Muslim Brotherhood came under greater suppression by the state and "official" religious scholars rallied to support the government. Gradually, the state-affiliated scholars stepped up their response to militant Islamism such that by the 1970s, the term 'Kharijites' had become a 'mainstay' of anti-Islamist rhetoric.[86] Using Patrick Gaffney's typology of identities and rhetorical styles adopted by modern Egyptian preachers as a frame of reference, Kenney asserts that "the voice with which the scholar speaks is always mediated—through the tradition, through the sources, through religious institutions and, more often than not in Egypt, through the political establishment which supports and controls religious institutions."[87] Attempts by religious scholars to project metaphorically the ideas of the medieval Kharijites onto modern Islamist activists and movements are made using "the traditional tools of the scholar,"[88] namely, scriptural exegesis and application of the precedents, analogies, and rational principles of the Sharīʿa as established by earlier scholars. A text like al-Suyūṭī's *Ashbāh* becomes, therefore, a tool in the hands of "official" scholars like Shaykh Muḥammad Wisām with which to contrast their own religious authority with those of competing claimants to the true heritage of the *salaf*.

[86] Jeffrey T. Kenney, *Muslim Rebels: Kharijites and the Politics of Extremism in Egypt* (Oxford: Oxford University Press, 2006), 97–8.

[87] Ibid., 97. See Patrick D. Gaffney, *The Prophet's Pulpit: Islamic Preaching in Contemporary Egypt* (Berkeley: University of California Press, 1994), 52–5.

[88] Kenney, *Muslim Rebels*, 97.

On the sensitive issues of tomb visitation (*ziyāra*) and seeking intercession from the Prophet after his death (*wasīla*), Shaykh Muḥammad states that it is the *manhaj* of the modern-day Kharijites to take verses from the Qurʾān that condemn idolaters (*mushrikīn*) and apply them to Muslims. The extremist approach turns *wasīla* into *shirk*. The difference between the two is that *wasīla* reflects a correct impulse to glorify those whom God has glorified (as the angels did when asked to bow to Adam), whereas *shirk* holds up someone or something as being equal to God or worthy of worship along with God. So, if God has favored certain people (e.g., the Prophet, his family, and the saints), states (e.g., prostration, travel), times of the year (e.g., Ramaḍān), or certain locations (e.g., Mecca), acknowledging the special status of those people, states, times, or locations does not amount to *shirk*.[89]

Modern-day Kharijites who reject the consensus of the legal schools over the centuries do so by reasoning that later jurists have strayed from the original message of the Qurʾān, but really they have only strayed from these scholars' meager understanding of the Qurʾān.[90] Those who make a distinction, for example, between the living and the dead to claim that one cannot seek intercession from someone who is no longer alive limit the power of God. Death, in this context, does not mean nonexistence but rather a transition to another state of being. Shaykh Muḥammad insists that even after death the Prophet can still communicate with people and is still involved with the *umma*. Returning to this issue in his discussion of the legal precept *al-ʿāda muḥakkama* ("custom should be made to serve as an arbiter"), Shaykh Muḥammad gives the example of the Sufi-oriented Shaykh al-Azhar, ʿAbd al-Ḥalīm Maḥmūd (d. 1978) who, just prior to the 1973 war, saw a vision

[89] Shaykh Muḥammad Wisām, commentary on *al-Ashbāh wa-l-naẓāʾir*, Part 6, accessed June 1, 2015, https://www.youtube.com/watch?v=Y-TC8gkdyPU. The tension between *wasīla* and *shirk* also relates to the issue of swearing an oath by someone other than God (by the Prophet, for example). An unsigned fatwa on Dār al-Iftāʾ's English language website discusses issues relating to seeking intercession from those who are no longer living using many of the same arguments and textual evidence that Shaykh Muḥammad does in his commentary, suggesting either that he is the author or else is in complete agreement with the author of the fatwa. See "How can we seek help from the Prophet Muḥammad if we are only allowed to seek help from God?", accessed June 3, 2015, http://eng.dar-alifta.org/foreign/ViewFatwa.aspx?ID=6881.

[90] Shaykh Muḥammad Wisām, commentary on *al-Ashbāh wa-l-naẓāʾir*, Part 6, accessed June 3, 2015, https://www.youtube.com/watch?v=Y-TC8gkdyPU.

of the Prophet crossing the Suez Canal. The shaykh reported this sight to President Sadat, and the political leadership took it as a sign of confidence and support for their policies from the Prophet himself.[91] Although intended to support the notion that the Prophet still intervenes in human affairs, it is interesting to note the connection being made in the anecdote between the head of the religious establishment and the political elites. At the very beginning of his commentary, Shaykh Muḥammad notes approvingly that al-Suyūṭī claimed to have seen the Prophet more than seventy-three times while awake and that these visions are a sign of God's blessing and favor bestowed on al-Suyūṭī.[92]

The Sufi part of the *manhaj* that Shaykh Muḥammad and his colleagues are trying to promote is described less as a matter of doctrine and more along the lines of an attitude or an ethical code of conduct. In his view, a superficial, *takfīrī* approach assumes people to be in a state of unbelief or sinfulness, whereas for the moderate, *wasaṭī* approach, the default is to treat all human beings with respect and to give people the benefit of the doubt. If someone has engaged in a sinful act but still considers him or herself to be Muslim, it is cruel and unfair to condemn that person as an apostate especially since, ultimately, only God knows the true intention in someone's heart and mind. For Shaykh Muḥammad, for example, the *qawāʿid* are rules to live by in the sense that they do not represent just abstract principles confined to the realm of legal methodology but, if internalized properly, give one a complete worldview or framework with which to live one's life (*manhaj al-ḥayāt*).

Shaykh Muḥammad relates the five universal precepts listed in al-Suyūṭī's work to the concept of *taṣawwuf* as a code of conduct. For example, the precept *al-yaqīn lā yuzāl bi-l-shakk* ("certainty is not removed by doubt") can relate directly to the problem of those who accuse other Muslims of apostasy. Since one enters into Islam with certainty, one's status as a believer cannot be overruled except by a clear renunciation of Islam that leaves no room for doubt as to one's intention to leave the faith.[93] Shaykh Muḥammad

[91] Shaykh Muḥammad Wisām, commentary on *al-Ashbāh wa-l-naẓāʾir*, Part 11, accessed June 3, 2015, https://www.youtube.com/watch?v=_rS9gU3DW7Y.

[92] Shaykh Muḥammad Wisām, commentary on *al-Ashbāh wa-l-naẓāʾir*, Part 2, accessed June 3, 2015, https://www.youtube.com/watch?v=rLSIDEjahsw.

[93] Shaykh Muḥammad Wisām, commentary on *al-Ashbāh wa-l-naẓāʾir*, Part 9, accessed June 4, 2015, https://www.youtube.com/watch?v=6AADkIm0gMU.

urges his listeners to use this precept as a guide to govern all of their interactions with events, people, and institutions in their daily lives. One should always assume that someone is innocent of wrongdoing until proven guilty because, in the end, we will all be held accountable by God on the Day of Judgment.[94]

Similarly, the precept *al-mashaqqa tajlib al-taysīr* ("hardship requires facility") speaks brilliantly to the Sufi idea that there is blessing for the believer in pain and trial (*fī miḥna minḥa*). Shaykh Muḥammad gives the example of a couple who have been married for thirty years. Their marriage contract was approved without the involvement of a legal guardian according to the Ḥanafī school, but the couple has come to doubt the validity of their marriage after hearing a shaykh condemn such contracts. Why would the shaykh want to bring unneeded hardship upon the couple? Perhaps because he has not taken this precept to heart in his dealings with people and with their concerns in daily life.[95] Shaykh ʿAlī Gumʿa cites a strikingly similar example of a couple who have lived together for fifteen years and had children but never executed a "real" marriage contract. This example comes up in the context of al-Suyūṭī's discussion of issues that fall under the precept of *al-umūr bi-maqāṣidihā* ("matters will be judged according to their objectives"). The couple's marriage should be considered valid according to their intention even if there was a technical problem with the original contract.[96] In both cases, the couple should be treated with mercy and given the benefit of the doubt rather being subjected to undue harm.

A final example of a universal precept that speaks to a larger Sufi-inspired code of conduct is *al-ḍarar yuzāl* ("harm shall be removed") based on the famous *ḥadīth* statement *lā ḍarar wa-lā ḍirār* ("no harm or reciprocal harm shall

[94] Shaykh Muḥammad Wisām, commentary on *al-Ashbāh wa-l-naẓāʾir*, Part 9, accessed June 4, 2015, https://www.youtube.com/watch?v=6AADkImOgMU.

[95] Ibid.

[96] Shaykh ʿAlī Gumʿa, commentary on *al-Ashbāh wa-l-naẓāʾir*, Part 2, accessed June 4, 2015, https://www.youtube.com/watch?v=sgfLbXtlAg0. Of course, it is not surprising that the two scholars would cite similar examples, even if the context is slightly different. Shaykh Muḥammad Wisām attended the sessions of his mentor, Shaykh ʿAlī Gumʿa. Also, Shaykh ʿAlī suggests that this example is based on a real case that was presented to him.

be imposed"). Shaykh Muḥammad comments that this precept provides guidance for many legal opinions. He cites the example of the controversial practice of female genital cutting or FGC (also known as female genital mutilation or FGM). FGC is an ancient pre-Islamic cultural practice that is still very common in Egypt and the Sudan and is not restricted to Muslims. As Shaykh Muḥammad points out, this is an issue that has divided the senior muftis of al-Azhar over the years—some have seen potential benefit in the procedure and have thus refused to condemn it outright, while others see only harm and find no convincing textual support from the Sunna to support it.[97] Shaykh Muḥammad explains the inconsistency by saying that if the earlier scholars had access to the medical studies that are available today, they would see that the evidence points to clear harm and thus the precept of *al-ḍarar yuzāl* must be applied.[98]

CONCLUSION

In December of 2011 as Egypt prepared to hold presidential elections and protests against the military-led transition government continued, the leadership of al-Azhar was shaken to the core by the loss of one of their own. Affectionately titled 'Shaykh of the Revolution,' ʿImād ʿIffat frequently risked his safety to show support for protesters in Cairo's Tahrir Square from the very beginning of the January 25 revolution up until he was fatally shot by security forces during protests outside the Cabinet building (though his killer has not been identified). Suddenly, al-Azhar had a martyr of its

[97] Former head mufti Shaykh Gād al-Ḥaqq ʿAlī Gād al-Ḥaqq (d. 1978) issued a fatwa in favor of FGC while Shaykh Muḥammad Sayyid Ṭanṭāwī (d. 2010) initially chose to defer to medical opinions on the practice but later supported the Egyptian Ministry of Health's decision to ban the practice altogether. Shaykh ʿAlī Gumʿa has spoken out against FGC and makes arguments very similar to the ones expressed here by Shaykh Muḥammad Wisām in one of his recent fatwas. See Sheikh Ali Gomaa, *Responding from the Tradition: One Hundred Contemporary Fatwas by the Grand Mufti of Egypt* (Louisville, KY: Fons Vitae, 2011), 98–104. For different opinions on FGC from Muslim legal scholars, see Kecia Ali, *Sexual Ethics and Islam: Feminist Reflections on Qur'an, Hadith, and Jurisprudence* (Oxford: Oneworld, 2006), 97–111.

[98] Shaykh Muḥammad Wisām, commentary on *al-Ashbāh wa-l-naẓāʾir*, Part 9, accessed June 8, 2015, https://www.youtube.com/watch?v=6AADkIm0gMU.

own. During the days that followed Shaykh ʿImād's death, thousands of people followed his funeral procession, many shouting anti-military slogans.[99] A few days later, Shaykh ʿAlī Gumʿa delivered an emotional eulogy at the Azhar mosque in honor of his friend and colleague. While Shaykh ʿAlī acknowledged that Shaykh ʿImād supported the revolution, he argued that the proper response to his assassination should be to engage in the (non-political) activities that Shaykh ʿImād made his life's work: the pursuit of knowledge (*ʿilm*), worship, and bearing witness to the faith (*daʿwa*). Shaykh ʿAlī challenged his colleagues to live up to the scholarly and moral standards that the great institution of al-Azhar has represented over the centuries.[100]

Five years after the January 25 revolution, Egypt's future is still very much in flux. The goals of the revolution for greater government transparency, democratic representation, and power-sharing, and an end to state-sponsored torture and repression have not yet been realized. Meanwhile, attacks by militants have increased in spite of promises of greater security and stability by the political elites. Both ideologically and politically, the battle over the identity of the religious establishment in Egypt goes on. Once again, the independence and integrity of al-Azhar is in danger of being compromised by the vocal support of its leadership for the authoritarian regime in power. At the same time, people continue to turn to the muftis of Dār al-Iftāʾ for guidance in their daily lives and to the religious scholars for instruction in the texts and principles that form the basis of Islamic jurisprudence. In their time of crisis, religious leaders who claim to represent an "orthodox" mainstream Sunnism turn to medieval scholars like al-Ghazālī and al-Suyūṭī as allies in their struggle. Once despised by many of his colleagues and condemned as arrogant and undeserving of the rank of *mujtahid* and *mujaddid*, al-Suyūṭī might gain comfort in knowing that his works are still studied and regarded as exemplary more than five hundred years after his death. Five hundred years from now, will today's scholars be considered worthy of such respect?

[99] Nada Hussein Rashwan, "Thousands bid farewell to fallen religious cleric killed in Tahrir," *Al-Ahram* Online, December 17, 2011, accessed July 1, 2015, http://english.ahram.org.eg/NewsContent/1/64/29539/Egypt/Politics-/Thousands-bid-farewell-to-fallen-religious-cleric-.aspx.

[100] "Eulogy for the martyr Shaykh ʿImād ʿIffat at the Al-Azhar Mosque," accessed July 2, 2015, https://www.youtube.com/watch?v=3NND0IEJvGs.

Conclusion

On January 1, 2015, Egypt's President ʿAbd al-Fattāḥ al-Sīsī addressed a group of religious leaders, including representatives of al-Azhar University and the Ministry of Religious Endowments (*awqāf*). On the occasion of the Prophet Muḥammad's birthday celebrations, al-Sīsī called for Muslim leaders to examine whether or not they live according to the Prophet's example today, suggesting that the *umma* has strayed from the path of the early Muslim community. He lamented the fact that religious "thinking" (*fikr*) has been a source of destruction and violence in the world and charged the *ʿulamāʾ* with the responsibility to bring about a renewal (*tajdīd*) of religious thought. Al-Sīsī went on to insist that it is the duty of the religious scholars to spread moderate (*wasaṭī*) Islam and to counter extremist ideologies that threaten not only Egypt but the entire world. While the assembled scholars and government officials sat in silence for the majority of the sixteen-minute speech, al-Sīsī received short applause when he delivered the following statement:

> I repeat, we need a religious revolution (*thawra dīniyya*). You, the imams, you are responsible before God. The whole world is awaiting [your word] ... the whole world is awaiting [your word] because this *umma* is being torn apart, this *umma* is being destroyed, and this *umma* is being lost—and it is being lost by our own hands. We are the ones that are causing it to be lost.[1]

As one might expect, al-Sīsī's speech has been received very differently depending on the political leanings of the interpreter as well as the degree to which he or she is familiar with the dynamics of Egyptian politics and

[1] "President al-Sīsī's speech at the Ministry of *Awqāf*'s celebrations of the Prophet's birthday," January 1, 2015, accessed July 7, 2015, https://www.youtube.com/watch?v=o0_Rpr4HGPM.

with discursive trends in Islamic thought. Right-wing pundits in the United States gleefully hailed al-Sīsī's heroic confirmation that Islam itself is ultimately responsible for the violent actions of Muslim terrorists and extremists, and that in order for Muslims and non-Muslims to live together peacefully, the religious tradition must undergo a radical overhaul of its core texts and traditions (and become more like the West).[2] Articles wondering simplistically whether or not al-Sīsī is "Islam's Martin Luther" were quick to follow.[3]

Other commentators, both within Egypt and outside observers, have been far more hesitant to embrace the speech as any sort of bombshell or extraordinary act of "bravery" on the part of Egypt's president. Indeed, al-Sīsī himself seemed to step back from his own words in remarks a few weeks later at the World Economic Forum in Davos in which he clarified that by "religious revolution" he means an attempt by the state-sponsored religious establishment of al-Azhar to "take a hard look at the religious discourse and weed out erratic ideas that led to violence and extremism."[4] In no way does this proposed "religious revolution" signal a reform of core religious doctrines; rather, what it seems to entail is combined nation-building efforts by Egyptian Muslims and Christians to improve Egypt's educational institutions and to police public discourse in order to bring it in line with state policies and to rid it of elements deemed extremist or dangerous to the welfare of the nation.

Certainly, al-Sīsī is not alone in pointing out the dire need to revamp Egypt's institutions of higher education in particular (and this includes al-Azhar University itself). It is, of course, no coincidence that the proposed educational reform comes at time when institutions like Cairo University and al-Azhar University have been the site of pro-Muslim Brotherhood demonstrations and internal discord among students and faculty. Therefore, it is safe to say that this "religious revolution" also serves a clear political

[2] See for example, Raymond Ibrahim, "A New Year in Egypt: The Significance of President Sisi's Speech," in *The American Spectator*, January 9, 2015, accessed July 7, 2015, http://spectator.org/articles/61428/new-year-egypt-significance-president-sisis-speech.

[3] Peter Smith, "Islam's Martin Luther?" in *Quadrant Online*, January 7, 2015, accessed July 7, 2015, http://quadrant.org.au/opinion/qed/2015/01/islams-martin-luther/.

[4] Michele Antaki, "El-Sisi Modifies Stance on Islamic Reform at Davos," in *American Thinker*, January 25, 2015, accessed July 7, 2015, http://www.americanthinker.com/articles/2015/01/elsisi_modifies_stance_on_islamic_reform_at_davos.html.

purpose as it seeks to cleanse educational institutions of dissenting voices. So far, it appears that al-Azhar's response to al-Sīsī's speech has been to expel students and professors who have exhibited "militant and provocative or fanatic thoughts," to confiscate books and purge graduate theses, and to strike from the curriculum concepts like slavery and the per capita tax on non-Muslims (*jizya*) that have been used by extremist groups.[5]

Both before and after al-Sīsī's speech, the Ministry of *Awqāf* in particular has been taking steps to bring religious leaders and institutions firmly under the supervision of the state and to suppress the activities of "rogue" preachers and unlicensed mosques.[6] The Ministry has even regulated the contents of Friday sermons and imposed restrictions on ritual practices that involve groups of people congregating in mosques, such as the communal spiritual retreats in mosques (*iʿtikāf*) that often take place during the final weeks of Ramaḍān.[7] The retreat sessions had been used by competing Salafī and Muslim Brotherhood groups as a means to gain control of mosques and to deliver political speeches.[8] The Ministry of *Awqāf* has also teamed up with the Ministry of Youth and Sports to promote a national campaign to combat "atheism" despite nods to "freedom of belief" in the Egyptian constitution.[9] Of course, all of these measures to control religious discourse in Egypt from the top down have stretched government resources to the point where the enforceability of these measures is in doubt.

[5] Walaa Hussein, "Al-Azhar Rewrites Curricula," *Al-Monitor*, June 29, 2015, accessed July 7, 2015, http://www.al-monitor.com/pulse/originals/2015/06/egypt-azhar-curriculim-revise-religious-discourse-extremism.html?utm_source=Al-Monitor+Newsletter+%5BEnglish%5D&utm_campaign=70cc4e579d-June_30_2015&utm_medium=email&utm_term=0_28264b27a0-70cc4e579d-1024621.

[6] The plan to bring more private mosques under state control hearkens back to the Mubārak era when a similar plan was proposed. In 1992, much like today, the government's plan stretched the resources of the Ministry of *Awqāf* and suffered from a shortage of Azhar-trained imams to fill the vacant positions. See Carrie Wickham's interesting discussion of the "parallel Islamic sector" in *Mobilizing Islam: Activism and Political Change in Egypt* (New York: Columbia University Press, 2002), 93–118.

[7] Rami Galal, "Egypt Clamps Down on Religious Ritual," in *Al-Monitor*, July 6, 2015, accessed July 8, 2015, http://www.al-monitor.com/pulse/originals/2015/07/egypt-religous-assembly-ramadan-regulate-conditions-mosques.html.

[8] Ahmad Rahim, "Egypt's Islamist Groups Compete for Mosques of Former Regime," in *Al-Monitor*, August 16, 2012, accessed July 8, 2015, http://www.al-monitor.com/pulse/ar/politics/2012/08/muslim-brothers-and-salafists-ar.html.

[9] Michele Dunne and Katie Bentivoglio, "Is Sisi Islam's Martin Luther?", Carnegie Endowment for International Peace, January 16, 2015, accessed July 8, 2015, http://carnegieendowment.org/syriaincrisis/?fa=57738.

In her analysis of Egypt's "religious revolution," Michele Dunne observes pessimistically that any "hopes that Sisi will push al-Azhar to put forth an enlightened religious vision are also likely to be sorely disappointed, judging by recent evidence." Dunne speaks as a former American diplomat and as a longtime expert researcher of Middle East politics who was herself recently denied entrance to the country for political reasons.[10] She argues that genuine calls for critique and self-reflection ring hollow in a political environment in which all forms of dissent are stifled in the interest of national security. Dunne concludes:

> Ceremonial visits to the Coptic pope, public statements about Muslim-Christian unity, exerting control over Muslim imams, diverting the public with salacious cases against atheists and gay people, refusing accountability for violence against Christians and other minority communities—all of these form parts of an old, sad story in Egypt and none are revolutionary.[11]

Of course, al-Sīsī's "religious revolution" speech was delivered in Arabic to an audience of Egyptian Muslim and Christian religious leaders and bureaucrats and not to the news media in the West. Therefore, one would expect the speech to contain references and allusions intended to appeal to that specific audience. Al-Sīsī is very direct in the speech in speaking to the *ʿulamāʾ* and for the benefit of the Egyptian Christian guests who are present in the room. Allusions can only be effective in terms of pragmatic communication when they are recognized by those who are the consumers of the discourse. As Amr Leheta observes, the term "revolution," for example, is "a politically charged word in Egypt today" and "Sisi's decision to use that word is designed to fit in with his narrative, which he has adopted and skillfully employed as the foundation for his legitimacy."[12] In other words, al-Sīsī and his supporters have effectively taken control of the discourse of "revolution" in Egypt such that the word no longer refers just to the January 25 uprising—the "revolution" for which Shaykh ʿImād ʿIffat gave his life—but

[10] David D. Kirkpatrick, "Egypt Says it Rejected American Over Visa," *The New York Times*, December 15, 2014, accessed July 8, 2015, http://www.nytimes.com/2014/12/16/world/middleeast/american-scholar-egypt-michele-dunne-visa.html?_r=0.

[11] Dunne and Bentivoglio, "Is Sisi Islam's Martin Luther?"

[12] Amr Leheta, "Revolutionizing Religion in Sisi's Egypt," guest blog for "From the Potomac to the Euphrates," Council on Foreign Relations, February 2, 2015, accessed July 9, 2015, http://blogs.cfr.org/cook/2015/02/02/revolutionizing-religion-in-sisis-egypt/.

to the June 30 demonstrations immediately preceding Mursī's removal from power as well. For some in Egypt, June 30 has replaced January 25 as representing the "real" revolution and al-Sīsī is the figurehead of this movement.

Another symbolic decision on al-Sīsī's part was the timing of the speech to coincide with the celebrations in honor of the Prophet's birthday. Al-Sīsī tries to suggest in his remarks that the *mawlid* is not exclusively a Muslim event, but rather a national observance, and an occasion for Muslim and Christian solidarity. Later that same week, he reinforced this sentiment by becoming the first Egyptian president to attend a Coptic Christmas mass. Though not expressed explicitly by al-Sīsī, there are other aspects to the *mawlid* in Egypt that add to its pragmatic potential as the setting for al-Sīsī's "religious revolution" speech. The first is the importance of the *mawlid* for Egypt's Sufi Muslims. Sufi brotherhood organizations in Egypt hold considerable influence, and it is significant that these groups have given their support to the religious establishment under Shaykh Aḥmad al-Ṭayyib and Shaykh ʿAlī Gumʿa as well as to the Sīsī regime.[13]

Also implicit, perhaps, in al-Sīsī's endorsement of the *mawlid* celebrations is a rebuttal of Muslims, many of whom would identify as Salafīs, who have condemned such festivities as an innovation since the practice only became common well after the Prophet's own lifetime.[14] Al-Sīsī's endorsement of the *mawlid* is therefore likely to find support from the assembled scholars who have rallied behind the government-backed imperative to promote centrist (*wasaṭī*) scholarship and to combat competing ideologies, especially those coming from Egypt's Salafī preachers. The permissibility of the *mawlid* has re-emerged in recent years as one of the divisive internal debates that preoccupy Muslim scholars today and act as a kind of ideological litmus test. Two other debates of a similar divisive nature already discussed in Chapter 5

[13] See for example, Muḥammad al-ʿAynayn, "Dozens of Sufi brotherhoods demonstrate in Alexandria against demands to expel the Shaykh al-Azhar," *al-Maṣrī al-Yawm*, May 3, 2013, accessed July 9, 2015, http://www.almasryalyoum.com/news/details/311715.

[14] N.J.G. Kaptein cites contemporary debates surrounding the permissibility of *mawlid* celebrations in Saudi Arabia, Morocco, and Indonesia. See his *Muḥammad's Birthday Festival: Early History in the Central Muslim Lands and Development in the Muslim West until the 10th/16th century* (Leiden: E.J. Brill, 1993), 45. For a detailed discussion of historical and legal discourses surrounding the celebration of the Prophet's birthday in both pre-modern and modern contexts, see Marion Holmes Katz, *The Birth of the Prophet Muḥammad: Devotional Piety in Sunni Islam* (London: Routledge, 2006).

are the visitation of saints' tombs and seeking intercession or making supplication to the Prophet or to Sufi saints after their deaths.

Members of Egypt's religious leadership, including Shaykh ʿAlī Gumʿa and Shaykh Muḥammad Wisām (whose work was considered in Chapter 5), have been challenged to issue opinions on the permissibility of *mawlid* celebrations in recent years.[15] Interestingly, one of the treatises that stands out as being indispensable to arguments in favor of celebrating the Prophet's birthday is none other than Jalāl al-Dīn al-Suyūṭī's fatwa on the subject, *Ḥusn al-maqṣid fī ʿamal al-mawlid*.[16] By al-Suyūṭī's time, the *mawlid* had become a normal part of community life in Egypt. Even so, the author still feels compelled to defend the practice and to counter arguments that would classify it as a dangerous or reprehensible innovation lacking a basis in the Sunna. Echoes of these same controversies have carried over into the present day, but with a political spin specific to contemporary Egypt. Quoting extensively from al-Suyūṭī in his own fatwa, Shaykh ʿAlī Gumʿa argues that celebrating the Prophet's birth as an expression of love for the Prophet is a praiseworthy innovation (*bidʿa ḥasana*) that does not contradict the Qurʾān, Sunna, traditions, or scholarly consensus.[17]

My interest in this book is in looking at how a fifteenth-century scholar, al-Suyūṭī, frames his own identity as a jurist in his legal writing as well as how contemporary scholars are using his legacy to define who they are in a time of crisis and upheaval. The *mawlid* debate is one in which both modern and pre-modern religious scholars take sides and demonstrate their ideological allegiances. Al-Suyūṭī represents an influential pre-modern opinion on this question as an important scholar of the Shāfiʿī legal school who also happens to be one of Egypt's own. It would seem that al-Sīsī's decision to use the Ministry of *Awqāf*' s *mawlid* celebrations as the setting for his speech serves several different pragmatic purposes for the speaker. First, it

[15] See ʿAlī Gumʿa's fatwa in *Responding from the Tradition: One Hundred Contemporary Fatwas from the Grand Mufti of Egypt*, translated by Tarek Elgawhary and Nuri Friedlander (Louisville, K.Y.: Fons Vitae, 2011), 161–7 and Muḥammad Wisām's sermon, "Legal Indicators for the Celebration of *al-mawlid al-nabawī*," January 18, 2013, accessed July 10, 2015, https://www.youtube.com/watch?v=WZ6EXmYpd5g.

[16] The fatwa can be found in al-Suyūṭī's *al-Ḥāwī li-l-fatāwī*, 2 vols. (Beirut: Dār al-Kutub al-ʿIlmiyya, 2000), 1: 181–9. A full English translation of the fatwa can be found in N.J.G Kaptein, *Muḥammad's Birthday Festival*, 48–67.

[17] Shaykh ʿAlī Gumʿa, *Responding from the Tradition*, 163.

promotes national unity and solidarity by appealing to a shared customary practice of Egyptians. Second, it affirms by implication the authority of the *ʿulamāʾ* in the room—the same *ʿulamāʾ* that al-Sīsī relies on to carry out his proposed renewal of religious discourse.[18] Finally, it provides an entry into a broader discussion of reform and religious renewal.

As Amr Leheta points out in his analysis of the "religious revolution" speech, al-Sīsī's appropriation of the concept of *tajdīd* is potentially problematic in terms of the pragmatic effect of his words in relation to the audience. The great reformers of the nineteenth and early twentieth centuries challenged the existing structures of authority in their societies, lamenting what they saw as the complacency, corruption, and weakness of their time. Today, no single faction can claim a monopoly on their legacy; their reformist thought has become "the inspiration for a multitude of Muslims today, including Middle Eastern liberals and secularists as well as all shades of political Islamists, from the moderates to the extremists."[19] If it is in fact al-Sīsī's intention to co-opt the legacy of religious renewal in Islamic thought to further his political goals, then he faces the problem that the ideologues (Ḥasan al-Banna, Sayyid Quṭb) whose thought underpins the very movements and activists that he seeks to condemn as anti-Egyptian terrorists are, in fact, organic inheritors of this same legacy.

In the Egyptian president's talk of the renewal (*tajdīd*) of religious discourse, once again echoes of al-Suyūṭī abound for the attuned listener. The language of *ijtihād* and *tajdīd* extends through many centuries of Islamic thought and has been appropriated by a diverse range of intellectuals. I argued in Chapter 4 that al-Suyūṭī initiated a new phase in Islamic *tajdīd* discourse. As a transitional figure whose work links the pre-modern and early modern, al-Suyūṭī plays a significant role in the transformation of the "*tajdīd* genre" into a set of concepts, symbols, and references that

[18] In his ethnographic study of Syria's *ʿulamāʾ*, Thomas Pierret observes that the celebration of the *mawlid* is used to unite Muslims "around the founding figure of Muhammad" but also serves as "first and foremost a ritualized spectacle staging the authority of the ulama." See Pierret, "Staging the Authority of the Ulama: The Celebration of the Mawlid in Urban Syria," in *Ethnographies of Islam: Ritual Performances and Everyday Practices*, edited by Baudouin Dupret, Thomas Pierret, Paulo G. Pinto, and Kathryn Spellman-Poots (Edinburgh: Edinburgh University Press, 2012), 105.

[19] Leheta, "Revolutionizing Religion in Sisi's Egypt."

later thinkers have molded to suit their own purposes. Al-Suyūṭī's articulation of the concepts of *ijtihād* and *tajdīd* has proven remarkably effective in liberating the *tajdīd* tradition from the realm of Sunni polemics and making it accessible to scholars as diverse as Muḥammad ʿAbduh, Rashīd Riḍā, Muḥammad al-Shawkānī, and Muḥammad b. ʿAbd al-Wahhāb. Each new articulator of the genre builds on the work of those who came before him and helps to shape the conversation for future generations.

Al-Suyūṭī struggled to be recognized as a true *mujtahid* and as the divinely appointed reviver of the religion (*mujaddid*) of his age. In order to make these bold claims, al-Suyūṭī was forced to respond to the criticisms of his enemies, even as he condemned their ignorance. It was important to him to have the last word in any argument. If one treatise was insufficient, al-Suyūṭī would produce a second and a third (as he did in both the logic and *waqf* disputes, for example).

For the *ʿulamāʾ* of today, the competition has only gotten harder and the stakes higher. Azharī scholars, for example, are challenged to prove that their methodology (*manhaj*) is intellectually or morally more robust than those of their Salafī and secularist competitors. This process demands not only a coherent articulation of their own position and authority, but also constructive engagement with alternate interpretations (even if only in the form of indirect allusion). The tumultuous years directly following the 2011 revolution in Egypt put al-Azhar and Dār al-Iftāʾ in the spotlight and applied pressure on these established institutions to embrace new forms of media outreach. Now, al-Azhar's scholars have been enlisted to fight on the ideological front lines against the type of extremist thought that leads to violence and tarnishes the image of Islam in the world.[20]

However, real reform requires more than silencing the opposition. In the end, it was the strength of al-Suyūṭī's scholarship rather than his polemics

[20] Al-Sīsī recently gave a follow-up speech to his "religious revolution" address on the occasion of the Ministry of Awqāf's celebration of *laylat al-qadr* in the last days of Ramaḍān. In the follow-up speech, al-Sīsī indicated that he is dissatisfied with the progress the religious scholars are making in their efforts to bring about a renewal of religious discourse. He hinted that the Shaykh al-Azhar, Aḥmad al-Ṭayyib, will be held accountable for seeing that this problem is addressed. A video of the speech can be found at "Full speech of al-Sīsī on the occasion of the celebration of *laylat al-qadr*," July 14, 2015, accessed July 15, 2015, https://www.youtube.com/watch?v=k2hjeohRxkA.

that has earned him a place among the great figures of Islamic legal history. His voice can still be heard long after those of his enemies have faded into the background. Even in his wrangling with the political elites, al-Suyūṭī managed to keep the moral high ground and maintain his scholarly integrity. The *ʿulamāʾ* of today are charged with the difficult task of preserving tradition and "orthodoxy" at the same time that they are challenged to respond to the contemporary needs of believers seeking to abide by the principles of Sharīʿa. Meanwhile, the geopolitical realities that the Muslim world faces today (including the fall of post-colonial autocratic regimes and the emergence of transnational terrorist groups operating in the name of Islam) present harsh circumstances that require an innovative and resolute response.

Bibliography

Arabic Language Sources

Abū Sunna, Aḥmad Fahmī. *Qāʿidatān fiqhiyyatān: al-ʿāda muḥakkama, lā ḍarar wa-lā ḍirār*. Cairo: Dār al-Baṣāʾir, 2004.

Amīn, Muḥammad Muḥammad. *Al-Awqāf wa-l-ḥayāt al-ijtimāʿiyya fī Miṣr*. Cairo: Dār al-Nahḍa al-ʿArabiyya, 1980.

Al-ʿAmrī, Ḥusayn b. ʿAbd Allāh. *Al-Manār wa-l-Yaman, dirāsa wa-nuṣūṣ*. Damascus: Dār al-Fikr, 1987.

ʿAwaḍ, al-Sayyid Ṣāliḥ. *Athar al-ʿurf fī l-tashrīʿ al-islāmī*. Cairo: Dār al-Kitāb al-Jāmiʿī, 1981.

Al-ʿAẓīmābādī, Muḥammad Shams al-Ḥaqq. *ʿAwn al-maʿbūd fī sharḥ Sunan Abī Dāwūd*. 14 vols. Medina: Al-Maktaba al-Salafiyya, 1969.

Al-Daʿās, ʿIzzat ʿUbayd. *Al-Qawāʿid al-fiqhiyya*. Beirut: Dār al-Tirmidhī, 1989.

Al-Durūbī, Samīr Maḥmūd. *Sharḥ maqāmāt Jalāl al-Dīn al-Suyūṭī*. 2 vols. Beirut: Muʾassasat al-Risāla, 1989.

Al-Ghazālī, Abū Ḥāmid. *Al-Fayṣal al-tafriqa bayna al-islām wa-l-zandaqa*. Ed. Sulaymān Dunyā. Cairo: Dār Iḥyāʾ al-Kutub al-ʿArabiyya, 1961.

Al-Ghazālī, Abū Ḥāmid. *Iḥyāʾ ʿulūm al-dīn*. 4 vols. Cairo: Al-Maṭbaʿa al-Azhariyya al-Miṣriyya, 1898.

Al-Ghazālī, Abū Ḥāmid. *Al-Qisṭās al-mustaqīm*. Ed. Maḥmūd Bījū. Damascus: 1993.

Al-Ghazālī, Abū Ḥāmid. *Maqāṣid al-falāsifa*. Ed. Maḥmūd Bījū. Damascus: 2000.

Al-Ghazālī, Abū Ḥāmid. *Miʿyār al-ʿilm*. Ed. Sulaymān Dunyā. Cairo: Dār al-Maʿārif, 1961.

Al-Ghazālī, Abū Ḥāmid. *Al-Munqidh min al-ḍalāl*. Egypt: Maktabat al-Anjlū al-Miṣriyya, 1962.

Al-Ghazālī, Abū Ḥāmid. *Al-Mustaṣfā min ʿilm al-uṣūl*. 2 vols. Cairo: Dār al-Baṣāʾir, 2007.

Al-Ghazālī, Abū Ḥāmid. *Tahāfut al-falāsifa*. Ed. Sulaymān Dunyā. Cairo: Dār al-Maʿārif, 1962.

Al-Ghazzī, Najm al-Dīn. *Al-Kawākib al-sāʾira bi-aʿyān al-miʾa al-ʿāshira*. 3 vols. Beirut: Al-Maṭbaʿa al-Amīrkāniyya, 1945.

Al-Ghubārī, ʿAwaḍ. *Maqāmāt al-Suyūṭī: dirāsa fī fann al-maqāma al-miṣriyya*. Cairo: Dār al-Thaqāfa al-ʿArabiyya, 2005.

Al-Ghumārī, ʿAbd Allāh b. al-Ṣiddīq. *Sabīl al-tawfīq fī tarjamat ʿAbd Allāh b. al-Ṣiddīq*. Cairo: Al-Dār al-Bayḍāʾ li-l-Ṭibāʿa, 1990.

Al-Haythamī, Ibn Ḥajar. *Al-Fatāwā al-kubrā al-fiqhiyya*. 4 vols. Beirut: Dār al-Kutub al-ʿIlmiyya, 2008.

Ibn ʿĀbidīn, Muḥammad Amīn. *Majmūʿat rasāʾil Ibn ʿĀbidīn*. 2 vols. Beirut: Muʾassasat Fuʾād al-Baʿīnū li-l-Tajlīd, 1978.

Ibn al-ʿImād, ʿAbd al-Ḥayy b. Aḥmad. *Shadharāt al-dhahab fī akhbār man dhahab*. 8 vols. Cairo: Maktabat al-Qudsī, 1931–1933.

Ibn Iyās, Muḥammad b. Aḥmad. *Kitāb Badāʾiʿ al-zuhūr fī waqāʾiʿ al-duhūr*. 5 vols. Cairo: Al-Hayʾa al-Miṣriyya al-ʿĀmma li-l-Kitāb, 1984.

Ibn Nujaym, Zayn al-ʿĀbidīn. *Al-Ashbāh wa-l-naẓāʾir ʿalā madhhab Abū Ḥanīfa al-Nuʿmān*. Beirut: Dār al-Kutub al-ʿIlmiyya, 1985.

Ibn al-Ṣalāḥ al-Shahrazūrī. *Fatāwā Ibn al-Ṣalāḥ fī l-tafsīr wa-l-ḥadīth wa-l-uṣul wa-l-qawāʿid*. Cairo: Maktabat Ibn Taymiyya, 1980.

Ibn al-Ṣalāḥ al-Shahrazūrī. *Fatāwā wa-masāʾil Ibn al-Ṣalāḥ*. 2 vols. Beirut: Dār al-Maʿrifa, 1986.

Ibn Shāhīn al-Ẓāhirī, Khalīl. *Kitāb Zubdat kashf al-mamālik wa-bayān al-ṭuruq wa-l-masālik*. Cairo: Dār al-ʿArab li-l-Bustānī, 1988.

Ibn Taymiyya, Aḥmad. *Majmūʿ fatāwā Shaykh al-Islām Aḥmad b. Taymiyya*. 37 vols. Beirut: Maṭābiʿ Dār al-ʿArabiyya, 1977–1978.

Ibn al-Wakīl, Muḥammad b. ʿUmar. *Al-Ashbāh wa-l-naẓāʾir*. 2 vols. Riyadh: Maktabat al-Rushd, 1993.

Al-Isnawī, Jamāl al-Dīn ʿAbd al-Raḥīm. *Al-Tamhīd fī takhrīj al-furūʿ ʿalā al-uṣūl*. Beirut: Muʾassasat al-Risāla, 1980.

Al-Maqrīzī, Aḥmad b. ʿAlī. *Kitāb al-Sulūk li-maʿrifat duwal al-mulūk*. 4 vols. Cairo: Maṭbaʿat Dār al-Kutub wa-l-Wathāʾiq al-Qawmiyya, 2006–2007.

Al-Maqrīzī, Aḥmad b. ʿAlī. *Al-Mawāʿiẓ wa-l-iʿtibār fī dhikr al-khiṭaṭ wa-l-āthār*. 2 vols. Cairo: Dār al-Ṭibāʿa al-Miṣriyya, 1953–1954.

Al-Nabhānī, Yūsuf b. Ismāʿīl. *Kitāb Jāmiʿ karāmāt al-awliyāʾ*. 2 vols. Beirut: Dār al-Kutub al-ʿIlmiyya, 1996.

Al-Nawawī, Muḥyī al-Dīn. *Fatāwā al-Imām al-Nawawī*. Beirut: Dār al-Kutub al-ʿIlmiyya, 1982.

Al-Qalqashandī, Aḥmad b. ʿAlī. *Ṣubḥ al-aʿshā fī ṣināʿat al-inshā*. 10 vols. Cairo: Al-Muʾassasa al-Miṣriyya al-ʿĀmma li-l-Taʾlīf wa-l-Tarjama wa-l-Ṭibāʿa wa-l-Nashr, 1964.

Riḍā, Muḥammad Rashīd. *Tafsīr al-Manār*. 12 vols. Beirut: Dār al-Maʿrifa, 1973.

Riḍā, Muḥammad Rashīd. *Taʾrīkh al-Ustādh al-Imām al-Shaykh Muḥammad ʿAbduh*. 3 vols. Cairo: Dār al-Faḍīla, 2003.

Al-Sakhāwī, Muḥammad b. ʿAbd al-Raḥmān. *Al-Ḍawʾ al-lāmiʿ li-ahl al-qarn al-tāsiʿ*. 12 vols. Cairo: Maktabat al-Qudsī, 1934–1936.

Al-Sanūsī, Muḥammad b. ʿAlī. *Īqāẓ al-wasnān fī l-ʿamal bi-l-ḥadīth wa-l-Qurʾān*. Beirut: Dār al-Kitāb al-Lubnānī, 1968.

Shakʿa, Muṣṭafā. *Jalāl al-Dīn al-Suyūṭī: masīratuhu al-ʿilmiyya wa-mabāḥithuhu al-lughawiyya*. Egypt: Sharikat Maktaba wa-Maṭbaʿat Muṣṭafā al-Bābī al-Ḥalabī, 1981.

Al-Shaʿrānī, ʿAbd al-Wahhāb. *Al-Ṭabaqāt al-ṣughrā*. Cairo: Maktabat al-Thaqāfa al-Dīniyya, 2005.

Sharīf, ʿAbd al-Ḥalīm Hāshim. *Al-Suyūṭī wa-juhūduhu fī ʿulūm al-Qurʾān*. Cairo: Al-Ṣadr li-Khidamāt al-Ṭibāʿa, 1991.

Al-Shawkānī, Muḥammad. *Al-Badr al-ṭāliʿ bi-maḥāsin man baʿd al-qarn al-sābiʿ*. 2 vols. Cairo: Maṭbaʿat al-Saʿāda, 1929.

Al-Subkī, Tāj al-Dīn. *Al-Ashbāh wa-l-naẓāʾir*. Beirut: Dār al-Kutub al-ʿIlmiyya, 1991.

Al-Subkī, Tāj al-Dīn. *Muʿīd al-niʿam wa-mubīd al-niqam*. Cairo: Maktabat al-Khānjī, 1993.

Al-Subkī, Tāj al-Dīn. *Al-Ṭabaqāt al-shāfiʿiyya al-kubrā*. 10 vols. Giza: Hajr, 1992.

Al-Subkī, Taqī al-Dīn. *Fatāwā al-Subkī*. 2 vols. Cairo: Maktabat al-Qudsī, 1937.

Al-Sulamī, ʿIzz al-Dīn b. ʿAbd al-Salām. *Fatāwā Shaykh al-Islām ʿIzz al-Dīn b. ʿAbd al-Salām*. Beirut: Muʾassasat al-Risāla, 1996.

Al-Suyūṭī, Jalāl al-Dīn. *Al-Ashbāh wa-l-naẓāʾir fī l-qawāʿid al-fiqhiyya.* Cairo: Al-Maktab al-Thaqāfī li-l-Nashr wa-l-Tawzīʿ, 2007.

Al-Suyūṭī, Jalāl al-Dīn. *Al-Ḥāwī li-l-fatāwī.* 2 vols. Beirut: Dār al-Kutub al-ʿIlmiyya, 2000.

Al-Suyūṭī, Jalāl al-Dīn. *Ḥusn al-muḥāḍara fī akhbār Miṣr wa-l-Qāhira.* 2 vols. Cairo: ʿĪsā al-Bābī al-Ḥalabī, 1967–1968.

Al-Suyūṭī, Jalāl al-Dīn. *Mā rawāhu al-asāṭīn fī ʿadam al-majīʾ ilā al-salāṭīn.* Beirut: Dār Ibn Ḥazm, 1992.

Al-Suyūṭī, Jalāl al-Dīn. *Al-Radd ʿalā man akhlad ilā al-arḍ wa-jahil ann al-ijtihād fī kull ʿaṣr farḍ.* Alexandria: Muʾassasat Shabāb al-Jāmiʿa, 1985.

Al-Suyūṭī, Jalāl al-Dīn. *Ṣawn al-manṭiq wa-l-kalām ʿan fann al-manṭiq wa-l-kalām.* Egypt: Maktabat al-Khānjī, 1947.

Al-Suyūṭī, Jalāl al-Dīn. *Al-Taḥadduth bi-niʿmat Allāh.* Ed. E.M. Sartain. Cambridge, U.K.: Cambridge University Press, 1975.

Al-Suyūṭī, Jalāl al-Dīn. *Taqrīr al-istinād fī tafsīr al-ijtihād.* Alexandria: Dār al-Daʿwa, 1983.

Al-Suyūṭī, Jalāl al-Dīn. *Al-Tanbiʾa bi-man yabʿathuhu Allāh ʿalā raʾs kull miʾa.* Mecca: Dār al-Thiqa li-l-Nashr wa-l-Tawzīʿ, 1990.

Al-Zarkashī, Muḥammad b. Bahādur. *Al-Manthūr fī l-qawāʿid.* 2 vols. Beirut: Dār al-Kutub al-ʿIlmiyya, 2000.

European Language Sources

Abou El Fadl, Khaled. *Speaking in God's Name: Islamic Law, Authority and Women.* Oxford, U.K.: Oneworld Publications, 2001.

Abu-Lughod, Lila. "The Romance of Resistance: Tracing Transformations of Power Through Bedouin Women." *American Ethnologist* 17:1 (1990): 41–55.

Algar, Hamid. "The Centennial Renewer: Bediüzzaman Said Nursi and the Tradition of *Tajdīd*." *Journal of Islamic Studies* 12:3 (2001): 291–311.

Ali, Kecia. *Sexual Ethics and Islam: Feminist Reflections on Qur'an, Hadith, and Jurisprudence.* Oxford, U.K.: Oneworld Publications, 2006.

Ali, Mohamed M. Yunis. *Medieval Islamic Pragmatics: Sunni Legal Theorists' Models of Textual Communication.* Richmond, Surrey: Curzon Press, 2000.

Ali, Mufti. "Jalāl al-Dīn al-Suyūṭī Against Logic and Kalām: Analysis and Significance of *Ṣawn al-manṭiq wal-kalām ʿan fannay* [sic.] *al-manṭiq wal-kalām*." *Hamdard Islamicus* 28:2 (2005): 23–44.

Ali, Mufti. *Muslim Opposition to Logic and Theology in Light of the Works of Jalāl al-Dīn al-Suyūṭī (d. 911/1505).* Ph.D. Diss. Universiteit Leiden, 2008.

Ali, Mufti. "A Statistical Portrait of the Resistance to Logic by Sunni Muslim Scholars Based on the Works of Jalāl al-Dīn al-Suyūṭī (849–909 [sic.]/1448–1505)." *Islamic Law and Society* 15 (2008): 250–67.

Alvi, Sajida S. "The *Mujaddid* and *Tajdīd* Traditions in the Indian Subcontinent: An Historical Overview." *Journal of Turkish Studies* 18 (1994): 1–15.

ʿArab Faqīh, Shihāb al-Dīn Aḥmad b. ʿAbd al-Qādir. *Futūḥ al-Ḥabaša: The Conquest of Abyssinia [16th Century].* Trans. Lester Stenhouse. Hollywood, California: Tsehai Publishers and Distributors, 2003.

Arazi, Albert. "Al-Risāla al-Baybarsiyya d'al-Suyūṭī: Un Document sur les Problèmes d'un *Waqf* Sultanien sous les Derniers Mamlūks." *Israel Oriental Studies* 9 (1979): 329–54.

Arnaldez, R. "Manṭiḳ." *The Encyclopaedia of Islam*. Second Edition. Brill Online, 2010.

Ashtor, Eliyahu. *A Social and Economic History of the Near East in the Middle Ages*. Berkeley: University of California Press, 1976.

Baker, Raymond William. *Islam Without Fear: Egypt and the New Islamists*. Cambridge: Harvard University Press, 2003.

Bakhtin, Mikhail M. *The Dialogic Imagination: Four Essays by M.M. Bakhtin*. Ed. Michael Holquist. Austin: University of Texas Press, 1981.

Bakhtin, Mikhail M. *Problems of Dostoevsky's Poetics*. Ed. and Trans. Caryl Emerson. Minneapolis: University of Minnesota Press, 1984.

Bakhtin, Mikhail M. *Speech Genres and Other Late Essays*. Trans. Vern W. McGee. Eds. Caryl Emerson and Michael Holquist. Austin: University of Texas Press, 1986.

Benford, Robert D. and David A. Snow. "Framing Processes and Social Movements: An Overview and Assessment." *Annual Review of Sociology* 26 (2000): 611–39.

Berkey, Jonathan P. *The Formation of Islam: Religion and Society in the Near East, 600–1800*. New York: Cambridge University Press, 2003.

Berkey, Jonathan P. *The Transmission of Knowledge in Medieval Cairo: A Social History of Islamic Education*. Princeton: Princeton University Press, 1992.

Brown, Jonathan A.C. *The Canonization of al-Bukhārī and Muslim: The Formation and Function of the Sunnī Ḥadīth Canon*. Leiden: Brill, 2007.

Brown, Jonathan A.C. *Hadith: Muhammad's Legacy in the Medieval and Modern World*. Oxford, U.K.: Oneworld Publications, 2009.

Brown, Jonathan A.C. *Salafis and Sufis in Egypt*. Carnegie Endowment for International Peace, 2011.

Brown, Nathan J. "Contention in Religion and State in Postrevolutionary Egypt." *Social Research* 79:2 (2012): 531–50.

Brown, Nathan J. "Egypt: Cacophony and Consensus in the Twenty-first Century." *Shariʿa Politics: Islamic Law and Society in the Modern World*. Ed. Robert W. Hefner. Bloomington: Indiana University Press, 2011.

Brustad, Kristen. "Imposing Order: Reading the Conventions of Representation in al-Suyūṭī's Autobiography." *Edebiyāt* 7:2 (1997): 327–44.

Calder, Norman. "Al-Nawawī's Typology of *Muftīs* and its Significance for a General Theory of Islamic Law." *Islamic Law and Society* 3:2 (1996): 137–64.

Cardinal, Monique. "Islamic Legal Theory Curriculum: Are the Classics Taught Today?" *Islamic Law and Society* 12:2 (2005): 224–72.

Castelli, Elizabeth A. *Imitating Paul: A Discourse of Power*. Louisville: Westminster/John Knox Press, 1991.

Chamberlain, Michael. *Knowledge and Social Practice in Medieval Damascus, 1190–1350*. Cambridge, U.K.: University of Cambridge Press, 1994.

Chaumont, E. "al-Shāfiʿī." *The Encyclopaedia of Islam*. Second Edition. Brill Online, 2010.

Christie, Niall. "Jerusalem in the *Kitab al-Jihad* of ʿAli ibn Tahir al-Sulami." *Medieval Encounters* 13 (2007): 209–21.

Christie, Niall. "Motivating Listeners in the *Kitab al-Jihad* of ʿAli ibn Tahir al-Sulami (d. 1106)." *Crusades* 6 (2007): 1–14.

Cooperson, Michael. "Aḥmad Ibn Ḥanbal and Bishr al-Ḥāfī: A Case Study in Biographical Traditions." *Studia Islamica* 86:2 (1997): 71–101.

Cooperson, Michael. *Classical Arabic Biography: The Heirs of the Prophets in the Age of al-Maʾmūn*. Cambridge, U.K.: Cambridge University Press, 2008.

Cornell, Vincent J. *Realm of the Saint: Power and Authority in Moroccan Sufism*. Austin: University of Texas Press, 1998.

Dallal, Ahmad. "Appropriating the Past: Twentieth-Century Reconstruction of Pre-Modern Islamic Thought." *Islamic Law and Society* 7:3 (2000): 325–58.

Dallal, Ahmad. "The Origins and Objectives of Islamic Revivalist Thought, 1750–1850." *Journal of the American Oriental Society* 113:3 (1993): 341–59.

De Beaurecueil, S. "al-Anṣārī al-Harawī." *The Encyclopaedia of Islam*. Second Edition. Brill Online, 2010.

Dickinson, Eerik. "Ibn al-Ṣalāḥ al-Shahrazūrī and the *Isnād*." *Journal of the American Oriental Society* 122:3 (2002): 481–505.

Al-Dihlawī, Shāh Walī Allāh. *Shāh Walī Allāh's Treatises on Juristic Disagreement and* Taqlīd: al-Inṣāf fī bayān sabab al-ikhtilāf *and* ʿIqd al-jīd fī aḥkām al-ijtihād wa-l-taqlīd. Trans. Marcia Hermansen. Louisville: Fons Vitae, 2010.

Duderija, Adis. "Constructing the Religious Self and the Other: Neo-traditional Salafi Manhaj." *Islam and Christian-Muslim Relations* 21:1 (2010): 75–93.

Duff, David (Ed.). *Modern Genre Theory*. Harlow, U.K.: Pearson Education Limited, 2000.

Dunne, Michele Durocher. *Democracy in Contemporary Egyptian Political Discourse*. Amsterdam: John Benjamins Publishing Company, 2003.

Elisséeff, Nikita. *Nūr al-Dīn: Un Grand Prince Musulman de Syrie au Temps des Croisades (511-569/1118-1174)*. 3 vols. Damascus: Institut Français de Damas, 1967.

El-Rouayheb, Khaled. "Post-Avicennan Logicians on the Subject Matter of Logic: Some Thirteenth- and Fourteenth-Century Discussions." *Arabic Sciences and Philosophy* 22 (2012): 69–90.

El-Rouayeb, Khaled. "Sunnī Muslim Scholars on the Status of Logic, 1500-1800." *Islamic Law and Society* 11:2 (2004): 213–32.

El-Rouayeb, Khaled. "Was there a Revival of Logical Studies in Eighteenth-Century Egypt?" *Die Welt des Islams* 45:1 (2005): 1–19.

Fairclough, Norman and Ruth Wodak. "Critical Discourse Analysis." *Discourse as Social Interaction*. Ed. Teun A. van Dijk. London: Sage, 1997. 258–84.

Fakhry, Majid. *A History of Islamic Philosophy*. Third Edition. New York: Columbia University Press, 2004.

Fernandes, Leonor. *The Evolution of a Sufi Institution in Mamluk Egypt: The Khanqah*. Berlin: Klaus Schwarz Verlag, 1988.

Fernandes, Leonor. "The Foundation of Baybars al-Jashankir: Its Waqf, History, and Architecture." *Muqarnas* 4 (1987): 21–42.

Foucault, Michel. *Power/Knowledge: Selected Interviews and Other Writings 1972-1977*. Ed. Colin Gordon. New York: Pantheon Books, 1980.

Foucault, Michel. "The Subject and Power." *Michel Foucault: Beyond Structuralism and Hermeneutics*. Eds. Hubert L. Dreyfus and Paul Rabinow. Chicago: University of Chicago Press, 1983. 208–26.

Frank, R.M. *Al-Ghazālī and the Ashʿarite School*. Durham: Duke University Press, 1994.

Friedmann, Yohanan. *Prophecy Continuous: Aspects of Aḥmadī Religious Thought and Its Medieval Background*. New Delhi: Oxford University Press, 2003.

Friedmann, Yohanan. *Shaykh Aḥmad Sirhindī: An Outline of his Thought and a Study of his Image in the Eyes of Posterity*. Montreal, McGill University: Institute of Islamic Studies, 1971.

Gaffney, Patrick. *The Prophet's Pulpit: Islamic Preaching in Contemporary Egypt*. Berkeley: University of California Press, 1994.

Garcin, Jean-Claude. "Histoire, Opposition Politique et Piétisme Traditionaliste dans le Ḥusn al-Muḥāḍarat de Suyūṭī." *Espaces, Pouvoirs et Idéologies de l'Egypte Médiévale*. London: Variorum Reprints, 1987. 33–89.

Garden, Kenneth. *The First Islamic Reviver: Abu Hamid al-Ghazali and his* Revival of the Religious Sciences. New York: Oxford University Press, 2014.

Gándara, Lelia. "'They That Sow the Wind...': Proverbs and Sayings in Argumentation." *Discourse and Society* 15:2–3 (2004): 345–59.

Geoffroy, Éric. *Le Soufisme en Égype et en Syrie Sous les Derniers Mamelouks et les Premiers Ottomans: Orientations Spirituelles et Enjeux Culturels*. Damascus: Institut Français de Damas, 1995.

Al-Ghazālī, Abū Ḥāmid. *Al-Ghazali's* Tahafut al-Falasifah. Trans. Sabih Ahmad Kamali. Lahore: Pakistan Philosophical Congress, 1963.

Gilbert, Joan E. "Institutionalization of Muslim Scholarship and Professionalization of the 'Ulamā' in Medieval Damascus." *Studia Islamica* 52 (1980): 105–34.

Gilliot, Cl., R.C. Repp, K.A. Nizami, M.B. Hooker, Chang-Kuan Lin, and J.O. Hunwick. "ʿUlamāʾ." *Encyclopaedia of Islam*. Second Edition. Brill Online, 2010.

Goldziher, Ignaz. "The Attitude of Orthodox Islam Toward the Ancient Sciences." *Studies on Islam*. Ed. and Trans. M.L. Swartz. New York: Oxford University Press, 1981. 185–215.

Goldziher, Ignaz. "Ignaz Goldziher on al-Suyūṭī." Ed. and Trans. J.O. Hunwick. *The Muslim World* 68:2 (1978): 79–99.

Gomaa, Sheikh Ali. *Responding from the Tradition: One Hundred Contemporary Fatwas from the Grand Mufti of Egypt*. Trans. Tarek Elgawhary and Nuri Friedlander. Louisville: Fons Vitae, 2011.

Greenblatt, Stephen. *Renaissance Self-Fashioning: From More to Shakespeare*. Chicago: University of Chicago Press, 1980.

Gutas, Dimitri. *Avicenna and the Aristotelian Tradition: Introduction to Reading Avicenna's Philosophical Works*. Second Edition. Leiden: Brill, 2014.

Haarmann, Ulrich. "Rather the Injustice of the Turks than the Righteousness of the Arabs: Changing ʿUlamāʾ Attitudes Towards Mamluk Rule in the Late Fifteenth Century." *Studia Islamica* 68 (1988): 61–77.

Hallaq, Wael B. *A History of Islamic Legal Theories: An Introduction to Sunnī* uṣūl al-fiqh. Cambridge, U.K.: Cambridge University Press, 1997.

Hallaq, Wael B. *Authority, Continuity and Change in Islamic Law*. Cambridge, U.K.: Cambridge University Press, 2001.

Hallaq, Wael B. "Can the Shariʿa Be Restored?" *Islamic Law and the Challenges of Modernity*. Eds. Yvonne Yazbek Haddad and Barbara Freyer Stowasser. Oxford, U.K.: AltaMira Press, 2004. 21–53.

Hallaq, Wael B. "From *Fatwās* to *Furūʿ*: Growth and Change in Islamic Substantive Law." *Islamic Law and Society* 1:1 (1994): 29–65.

Hallaq, Wael B. (Ed. and Trans.). *Ibn Taymiyya Against the Greek Logicians*. Oxford, U.K.: Clarendon Press, 1993.

Hallaq, Wael B. "Logic, Formal Arguments and Formalization of Arguments in Sunnī Jurisprudence." *Arabica* 37:3 (1990): 315–58.

Hallaq, Wael B. "Was the Gate of Ijtihād Closed?" *International Journal of Middle East Studies* 16 (1984): 3–41.

Halverson, Jeffrey R. *Theology and Creed in Sunni Islam: The Muslim Brotherhood, Ashʿarism, and Political Sunnism*. New York: Palgrave Macmillan, 2010.

Haykel, Bernard. *Revival and Renewal in Islam: The Legacy of Muḥammad al-Shawkānī*. Cambridge, U.K.: Cambridge University Press, 2003.

Heinrichs, Wolfhart. "*Qawāʿid* as a Genre of Legal Literature." *Studies in Islamic Legal Theory*. Ed. Bernard G. Weiss. Leiden: Brill, 2002. 365–84.

Heinrichs, Wolfhart. "Structuring the Law: Remarks on the *Furūq* Literature." *Studies in Honour of Clifford Edmund Bosworth*. Ed. Ian Richard Netton. Leiden: Brill, 2000. 332–44.

Hillenbrand, Carole. *The Crusades: Islamic Perspectives*. New York: Routledge, 2000.

Hofer, Nathan. *The Popularisation of Sufism in Ayyubid and Mamluk Egypt, 1173-1325*. Edinburgh: Edinburgh University Press, 2015.

Hoffman, Valerie J. *Sufism, Mystics and Saints in Modern Egypt*. Columbia, S.C.: University of South Carolina Press, 1995.

Homerin, T. Emil. "Sufis and their Detractors in Mamluk Egypt: A Survey of Protagonists and Institutional Settings." *Islamic Mysticism Contested*. Eds. Frederick De Jong and Bernd Radtke. Leiden: Brill, 1999. 225–46.

Hunwick, John. "Notes on a Late Fifteenth-Century Document Concerning 'al-Takrūr.'" *African Perspectives: Papers in the History, Politics and Economics of African Presented to Thomas Hodgkin*. Eds. Christopher Allen and R.W. Johnson. Cambridge, U.K.: Cambridge University Press, 1970. 7–33.

Ibn Taymiyya, Taqī al-Dīn. *Ibn Taymiyya Against the Greek Logicians*. Ed. and Trans. Wael B. Hallaq. Oxford, U.K.: Clarendon Press, 1993.

Jackson, Sherman A. *Islam and the State: The Constitutional Jurisprudence of Shihāb al-Dīn al-Qarāfī*. Leiden: Brill, 1996.

Jaques, R. Kevin. *Authority, Conflict, and the Transmission of Diversity in Medieval Islamic Law*. Leiden: Brill, 2006.

Jaques, R. Kevin. *Ibn Hajar*. New Delhi: Oxford University Press, 2009.

Kalmbach, Hilary. "Introduction: Islamic Authority and the Study of Female Religious Leaders." *Women, Leadership and Mosques: Changes in Contemporary Islamic Authority*. Eds. Masooda Bano and Hilary Kalmbach. Leiden: Brill, 2012. 1–30.

Kamali, Mohammad Hashim. "Legal Maxims and Other Genres of Literature in Islamic Jurisprudence." *Arab Law Quarterly* 20:1 (2006): 77–101.

Kamali, Mohammad Hashim. *Principles of Islamic Jurisprudence*. Third Edition. Cambridge, U.K.: Islamic Texts Society, 2003.

Kaptein, N.J.G. *Muḥammad's Birthday Festival: Early History in the Central Muslim Lands and Development in the Muslim West until the 10th/16th century*. Leiden: E.J. Brill, 1993.

Katz, Marion Holmes. *The Birth of the Prophet Muḥammad: Devotional Piety in Sunni Islam*. London: Routledge, 2006.
Kenney, Jeffrey T. *Muslim Rebels: Kharijites and the Politics of Extremism in Egypt*. New York: Oxford University Press, 2006.
Knysh, Alexander. "'Orthodoxy' and 'Heresy' in Medieval Islam: An Essay in Reassessment." *The Muslim World* 83:1 (1993): 48–67.
Krämer, Gudrun and Sabine Schmidtke. (Eds). *Speaking for Islam: Religious Authorities in Muslim Societies*. Leiden: Brill, 2006.
Kugle, Scott. *Rebel Between Spirit and Law: Ahmad Zarruq, Sainthood, and Authority in Islam*. Bloomington: Indiana University Press, 2006.
Kuypers, Jim A. *Rhetorical Criticism: Perspectives in Action*. Lanham, MD: Lexington Books, 2009.
Landau-Tasseron, Ella. "The 'Cyclical Reform': A Study of the *Mujaddid* Tradition." *Studia Islamica* 70 (1989): 79–117.
Lapidus, Ira M. *Muslim Cities in the Later Middle Ages*. Cambridge: Harvard University Press, 1967.
Lazarus-Yafeh, Hava. "*Tajdīd al-Dīn*: A Reconsideration of Its Meaning, Roots and Influence in Islam." *Studies in Islamic and Judaic Traditions*. Eds. William M. Brinner and Stephen D. Ricks. Atlanta: Scholars Press, 1986. 99–108.
Leiser, Gary La Viere. *The Restoration of Sunnism in Egypt: Madrasas and Mudarrisūn, 495-647/1101-1249*. Ph.D. Diss. University of Pennsylvania, 1976.
Levinson, Stephen C. *Pragmatics*. Cambridge, U.K.: Cambridge University Press, 1983.
Libson, Gideon. "On the Development of Custom as a Source of Law in Islamic Law: *al-rujūʿu ilā al-ʿurfi aḥadu al-qawāʿidi al-khamsi allatī yatabannā ʿalayhā al-fiqhu*." *Islamic Law and Society* 4:2 (1997): 131–55.
Lincoln, Bruce. *Authority: Construction and Corrosion*. Chicago: University of Chicago Press, 1994.
Little, Donald P. *History and Historiography of the Mamlūks*. London: Variorum Reprints, 1986.
Little, Donald P. "The Nature of *Khānqāhs*, *Ribāṭs* and *Zāwiyas* Under the Mamluks." *Islamic Studies Presented to Charles J. Adams*. Eds. Wael B. Hallaq and Donald P. Little. Leiden: Brill, 1991. 91–105.
Little, Donald P. "Notes on Mamluk Madrasahs." *Mamlūk Studies Review* 6 (2002): 9–20.
Llewellyn, Karl N. "Remarks on the Theory of Appellate Decision and the Rules or Canons about how Statutes are to be Construed." *Vanderbilt Law Review* 3 (1950): 395–406.
Mahmood, Saba. *Politics of Piety: The Islamic Revival and the Feminist Subject*. Princeton: Princeton University Press, 2005.
Makdisi, George. "Ashʿarī and the Ashʿarites in Islamic Religious History I." *Studia Islamica* 17 (1962): 37–80.
Makdisi, George. *The Rise of Colleges: Institutions of Higher Learning in Islam and the West*. Edinburgh: Edinburgh University Press, 1981.
Makdisi, George. "Ṭabaqāt-Biography: Law and Orthodoxy in Classical Islam." *Islamic Studies* 32:4 (1993): 371–96.
Al-Maqrīzī, Aḥmad b. ʿAlī. *Mamluk Economics: A Study and Translation of al-Maqrīzī's* Ighāthah. Ed. Adel Allouche. Salt Lake City: University of Utah Press, 1994.

Masud, Muhammad Khalid, Brinkley Messick, and David S. Powers. "Muftis, Fatwas, and Islamic Legal Interpretation." *Islamic Legal Interpretation: Muftis and Their Fatwas*. Eds. Muhammad Khalid Masud, Brinkley Messick, and David S. Powers. Cambridge: Harvard University Press, 1996.

Mawdūdī, Mawlānā. *A Short History of the Revivalist Movement in Islam*. Trans. Al-Ashʿarī. Second Edition. Lahore: Islamic Publications, 1972.

Melchert, Christopher. *Aḥmad Ibn Ḥanbal*. Oxford, U.K.: Oneworld, 2006.

Messick, Brinkley. *The Calligraphic State: Textual Domination and History in a Muslim Society*. Berkeley: University of California Press, 1993.

Miller, Geoffrey P. "Pragmatics and the Maxims of Interpretation." *Wisconsin Law Review* (1990): 1179–227.

Mohammed, Khaleel. "The Islamic Law Maxims." *Islamic Studies* 44:2 (2005): 191–207.

Moore, Robert Hunter. *The Role of the* Madrasah *in the Structure of Islamic Legal Education in Mamluk Egypt (1250–1517)*. Ph.D. Diss. Emory University, 2010.

Morson, Gary Saul and Caryl Emerson. *Mikhail Bakhtin: Creation of a Prosaics*. Stanford: Stanford University Press, 1990.

Mourad, Suleiman A. and James E. Lindsay. "A Muslim Response to the Second Crusade: Ibn ʿAsākir of Damascus as Propagandist of Jihad." *The Second Crusade: Holy War on the Periphery of Latin Christendom*. Eds. Jason T. Roche and Janus Møller Jensen. Turnhout, Belgium: Brepols, 2015. 91–111.

Mourad, Suleiman A. and James E. Lindsay. "Rescuing Syria from the Infidels: The Contribution of Ibn ʿAsākir to the Jihad Campaign of Sultan Nur al-Din." *Crusades* 6 (2007): 37–55.

Newman, Saul. "New Reflections on the Theory of Power: A Lacanian Perspective." *Contemporary Political Theory* 3 (2004): 148–67.

Nielsen, Jørgen S. "Sultan al-Ẓāhir Baybars and the Appointment of Four Chief Qāḍīs, 663/1265." *Studia Islamica* 60 (1984): 167–76.

Opwis, Felicitas M.M. Maṣlaḥa *and the Purpose of the Law: Islamic Discourse on Legal Change from the 4th/10th to the 8th/14th Century*. Leiden: Brill, 2010.

Opwis, Felicitas M.M. "The Role of the Biographer in Constructing Identity and Doctrine: Al-ʿAbbādī and his *Kitāb Ṭabaqāt al-Fuqahāʾ al-Shāfiʿiyya*." *Journal of Arabic and Islamic Studies* 11 (2011): 1–35.

Palmer. H.R. "An Early Fulani Conception of Islam." *Journal of the African Society* 13 (1913–1914): 407–14; 14 (1914–1915): 53–9 and 185–92.

Parolin, Gianluca P. "Shall We Ask Al-Azhar? Maybe Not: Lessons from the Ṣukūk Bill Incident." *Middle East Law and Governance* 7 (2015): 212–35.

Peters, Rudolph. "Idjtihād and Taqlīd in 18th and 19th Century Islam." *Die Welt des Islams* 20:3–4 (1980): 131–45.

Petry, Carl F. "A Paradox of Patronage During the Later Mamluk Period." *The Muslim World* 73 (1983): 182–207.

Pierret, Thomas. *Religion and the State in Syria: The Sunni Ulama from Coup to Revolution*. New York: Cambridge University Press, 2013.

Pierret, Thomas. "Staging the Authority of the Ulama: The Celebration of the Mawlid in Urban Syria." *Ethnographies of Islam: Ritual Performances and Everyday Practices*.

Eds. Baudouin Dupret, Thomas Pierret, Paulo G. Pinto, and Kathryn Spellman-Poots. Edinburgh: University of Edinburgh Press, 2012.

Polaski, Sandra Hack. *Paul and the Discourse of Power*. Sheffield, England: Sheffield Academic Press, 1999.

Polka, Sagi. "The Centrist Stream in Egypt and its Role in the Public Discourse Surrounding the Shaping of the Country's Cultural Identity." *Middle Eastern Studies* 39:3 (2003): 39–64, DOI: 10.1080/00263200412331301667.

Pound, Roscoe. "The Maxims of Equity I: Of Maxims Generally." *Harvard Law Review* 34:8 (June, 1921): 809–36.

Al-Qāsimī, Jamāl al-Dīn. "Guiding Mankind to Act on the Basis of Telegraphic Messages." Trans. David D. Commins. *Modernist Islam, 1840-1940: A Sourcebook*. Ed. Charles Kurzman. New York: Oxford University Press, 2002. 181–7.

Rabb, Intisar A. *Doubt's Benefit: Legal Maxims in Islamic Law, 7th-16th Centuries*. Ph.D. Diss. Princeton University, 2009.

Rahman, Fazlur. *Revival and Reform in Islam: A Study of Islamic Fundamentalism*. Ed. Ebrahim Moosa. Oxford, U.K.: Oneworld Publications, 2000.

Rapoport, Yossef. "Legal Diversity in the Age of *Taqlīd*: The Four Chief *Qāḍīs* Under the Mamluks." *Islamic Law and Society* 10:2 (2003): 210–28.

Reichmuth, Stefan. "Murtaḍā az-Zabīdī (d. 1791) in Biographical and Autobiographical Accounts: Glimpses of Islamic Scholarship in the 18th Century." *Die Welt des Islams* 39:1 (1999): 64–102.

Reichmuth, Stefan. *The World of Murtaḍā al-Zabīdī (1732-91): Life, Networks and Writings*. Cambridge, U.K.: Gibb Memorial Trust, 2009.

Reisman, David. "Medieval Arabic Medical Autobiography." *Journal of the American Oriental Society* 129:4 (2009): 559–69.

Rescher, Nicholas. *The Development of Arabic Logic*. Pittsburgh: University of Pittsburgh Press, 1964.

Reynolds, Dwight F. "Childhood in One Thousand Years of Arabic Autobiography." *Edebiyāt* 7:2 (1997): 379–92.

Reynolds, Dwight F. (Ed.). *Interpreting the Self: Autobiography in the Arabic Literary Tradition*. Berkeley: University of California Press, 2001.

Reynolds, Dwight F. "Shaykh ʿAbd al-Wahhāb al-Shaʿrānī's Sixteenth-Century Defense of Autobiography." *Harvard Middle Eastern and Islamic Review* 4:1–2 (1997–1998): 122–37.

Riḍā, Rashīd. "Renewal, Renewing and Renewers." Trans. Emad Eldin Shahin. *Modernist Islam, 1840-1940: A Sourcebook*. Ed. Charles Kurzman. New York: Oxford University Press, 2002. 77–85.

Rosenthal, Franz. "Die arabische Autobiographie." *Studia Arabica* 1 (1937): 1–40.

Rosenthal, Franz. *The Classical Heritage in Islam*. Berkeley: University of California Press, 1965.

Sabra, Adam. *Poverty and Charity in Medieval Islam*. Cambridge, U.K.: Cambridge University Press, 2000.

Safi, Omid. *The Politics of Knowledge in Premodern Islam: Negotiating Ideology and Religious Inquiry*. Chapel Hill: University of North Carolina Press, 2006.

Saleh, Marlis J. "Al-Suyūṭī and His Works: Their Place in Islamic Scholarship from Mamluk Times to the Present." *Mamlūk Studies Review* 5 (2001): 73–89.

Sartain, E.M. *Jalāl al-Dīn al-Suyūṭī: Biography and Background.* Vol. 1. Cambridge, U.K.: Cambridge University Press, 1975.
Sartain, E.M. "Jalāl al-Dīn al-Suyūṭī's Relations with the People of Takrūr." *Journal of Semitic Studies* 16 (1971): 193–8.
Al-Sayyed Ahmad, ʿAzmi T. *Al-Ghazālī's Views on Logic.* Ph.D. Diss. University of Edinburgh, 1981.
Scott, Rachel M. "What Might the Muslim Brotherhood do with al-Azhar? Religious Authority in Egypt." *Die Welt des Islams* 52 (2012): 131–65.
Serjeant, R.B. "The Caliph ʿUmar's Letters to Abū Mūsā al-Ashʿarī and Muʿāwiya." *Journal of Semitic Studies* 29:1 (1984): 65–79.
Shabana, Ayman. *Custom in Islamic Law and Legal Theory: The Development of the Concepts of* ʿUrf *and* ʿĀdah *in the Islamic Legal Tradition.* New York: Palgrave Macmillan, 2010.
Sinclair, M.B.W. "Law and Language: The Role of Pragmatics in Statutory Interpretation." *University of Pittsburgh Law Review* 46 (1984–1985): 373–420.
Sivan, Emmanuel. *L'Islam et la Croisade: Idéologie et Propagande dans les Réactions Musulmanes aux Croisades.* Paris: Adrien Maisonneuve, 1968.
Sperber, Dan and Deirdre Wilson. *Relevance: Communication and Cognition.* Second Edition. Oxford, U.K.: Blackwell Publishers Ltd, 1995.
Spevack, Aaron. "Apples and Oranges: The Logic of the Early and Later Arabic Logicians." *Islamic Law and Society* 17 (2010): 159–84.
Stewart, Devin J. "Capital, Accumulation, and the Islamic Academic Biography." *Edebiyāt* 7:2 (1997): 345–62.
Stewart, Devin J. "Islamic Juridical Hierarchies and the Office of *marjiʿ al-taqlīd.*" *Shīʿite Heritage: Essays on Classical and Modern Traditions.* Ed. and trans. L. Clarke. Binghamton, N.Y.: Global Publications, 2001. 137–57.
Stewart, Devin J. *Islamic Legal Orthodoxy: Twelver Shiite Responses to the Sunni Legal System.* Salt Lake City: University of Utah Press, 1998.
Stewart, Devin J. "Recounting God's Blessings: Linguistic Prophylaxis and Self-Representation in Arabic Autobiography." *Al-ʿArabiyya* 40/41 (2007–2008): 197–219.
Street, Tony. "Arabic Logic." *Handbook of the History of Logic.* Eds. Dov M. Gabbay and John Woods. Vol. 1. Amsterdam: Elsevier B.V., 2004. 523–96.
Tabbaa, Yasser. *Constructions of Power and Piety in Medieval Aleppo.* University Park, P.A.: The Pennsylvania State University Press, 1997.
Tabbaa, Yasser. *The Transformation of Islamic Art during the Sunni Revival.* Seattle, W.A.: University of Washington Press, 2001.
Tannen, Deborah. "What's in a Frame?" *Framing in Discourse.* New York: Oxford University Press, 1993.
Van Dijk, Teun A. *Discourse and Power.* New York: Palgrave Macmillan, 2008.
Vikør, Knut S. *Sufi and Scholar on the Desert Edge: Muḥammad b. ʿAlī al-Sanūsī and his Brotherhood.* London: Hurst & Company, 1995.
Voll, John O. "Renewal and Reform in Islamic History: *Tajdid* and *Islah.*" *Voices of Resurgent Islam.* Ed. John L. Esposito. New York: Oxford University Press, 1983. 32–47.
Waldman, Marilyn Robinson. *Toward a Theory of Historical Narrative: A Case Study in Perso-Islamicate Historiography.* Columbus: Ohio State University Press, 1980.

Wenger, Etienne. *Communities of Practice: Learning, Meaning, and Identity*. New York: Cambridge University Press, 1998.

Wheeler, Brannon M. *Applying the Cannon in Islam: The Authorization and Maintenance of Interpretive Reasoning in Ḥanafī Scholarship*. Albany: State University of New York Press, 1996.

Wickham, Carrie Rosefsky. *Mobilizing Islam: Religion, Activism, and Political Change in Egypt*. New York: Columbia University Press, 2002.

Wickham, Carrie Rosefsky. *The Muslim Brotherhood: Evolution of an Islamist Movement*. Princeton: Princeton University Press, 2013.

Winter, Michael. "ʿUlamāʾ Between the State and Society in Pre-modern Sunni Islam." *Guardians of the State in Modern Times: ʿUlamāʾ in the Middle East*. Ed. Meir Hatina. Leiden: Brill, 2009. 21–45.

Wuthnow. Robert. *Communities of Discourse: Ideology and Social Structure in the Reformation, the Enlightenment, and European Socialism*. Cambridge: Harvard University Press, 1989.

Zaman, Muhammad Qasim. *The Ulama in Contemporary Islam: Custodians of Change*. Princeton: Princeton University Press, 2002.

Zeghal, Malika. "The 'Recentering' of Religious Knowledge and Discourse: The Case of al-Azhar in Twentieth-Century Egypt." *Schooling Islam: The Culture and Politics of Modern Muslim Education*. Eds. Robert W. Hefner and Muhammad Qasim Zaman. Princeton: Princeton University Press, 2007. 107–30.

Index